# UNDERSTANDING
# COLUM McCANN

Understanding Contemporary American Literature
Matthew J. Bruccoli, Series Editor

**Volumes on**

Edward Albee • Sherman Alexie • Nicholson Baker • John Barth
Donald Barthelme • The Beats • Thomas Berger
The Black Mountain Poets • Robert Bly • T. C. Boyle • Raymond Carver
Fred Chappell • Chicano Literature • Contemporary American Drama
Contemporary American Horror Fiction
Contemporary American Literary Theory
Contemporary American Science Fiction, 1926–1970
Contemporary American Science Fiction, 1970–2000
Contemporary Chicana Literature • Robert Coover • Philip K. Dick
James Dickey • E. L. Doctorow • Rita Dove • John Gardner
George Garrett • Tim Gautreaux • John Hawkes • Joseph Heller
Lillian Hellman • Beth Henley • John Irving • Randall Jarrell
Charles Johnson • Adrienne Kennedy • William Kennedy • Jack Kerouac
Jamaica Kincaid • Tony Kushner • Ursula K. Le Guin • Denise Levertov
Bernard Malamud • Bobbie Ann Mason • Colum McCann
Cormac McCarthy • Jill McCorkle • Carson McCullers • W. S. Merwin
Arthur Miller • Lorrie Moore • Toni Morrison's Fiction
Vladimir Nabokov • Gloria Naylor • Joyce Carol Oates
Tim O'Brien • Flannery O'Connor • Cynthia Ozick • Walker Percy
Katherine Anne Porter • Richard Powers • Reynolds Price • Annie Proulx
Thomas Pynchon • Theodore Roethke • Philip Roth
May Sarton • Hubert Selby, Jr. • Mary Lee Settle • Neil Simon
Isaac Bashevis Singer • Jane Smiley • Gary Snyder
William Stafford • Anne Tyler • Gerald Vizenor • Kurt Vonnegut
David Foster Wallace • Robert Penn Warren • James Welch
Eudora Welty • Tennessee Williams • August Wilson • Charles Wright

# UNDERSTANDING
# COLUM McCANN

John Cusatis

The University of South Carolina Press

Published by the University of South Carolina Press
Columbia, South Carolina 29208

www.sc.edu/uscpress

Manufactured in the United States of America

20 19 18 17 16 15 14 13 12 11 10 9 8 7 6 5 4 3 2 1

Library of Congress Cataloging-in-Publication Data

Cusatis, John.
Understanding Colum McCann / John Cusatis.
p. cm. — (Understanding contemporary American literature)
Includes bibliographical references and index.
ISBN 978-1-57003-949-2 (cloth : alk. paper)
1. McCann, Colum, 1965– I. Title.
PR6063.C335Z46 2011
823'.914—dc22
[B]

2010025484

For my father and mother, Maurice and Theresa Cusatis;
my brother, Matthew; my wife, Anna; and my children,
Giovanni, Luciano, and Annabella

There was a lust of wandering in his feet that burned to set out for the ends of the earth. On! On! his heart seemed to cry.

James Joyce, *A Portrait of the Artist as a Young Man*

# Contents

# Series Editor's Preface

The volumes of *Understanding Contemporary American Literature* have been planned as guides or companions for students as well as good nonacademic readers. The editor and publisher perceive a need for these volumes because much of the influential contemporary literature makes special demands. Uninitiated readers encounter difficulty in approaching works that depart from the traditional forms and techniques of prose and poetry. Literature relies on conventions, but the conventions keep evolving; new writers form their own conventions—which in time may become familiar. Put simply, *UCAL* provides instruction in how to read certain contemporary writers—identifying and explicating their material, themes, use of language, point of view, structures, symbolism, and responses to experience.

The word *understanding* in the titles was deliberately chosen. Many willing readers lack an adequate understanding of how contemporary literature works; that is, what the author is attempting to express and the means by which it is conveyed. Although the criticism and analysis in the series have been aimed at a level of general accessibility, these introductory volumes are meant to be applied in conjunction with the works they cover. They do not provide a substitute for the works and authors they introduce, but rather prepare the reader for more profitable literary experiences.

M.J.B.

# Acknowledgments

I would like to acknowledge the inestimable influence and kindness of two educators: Dr. Matthew J. Bruccoli (1931–2008), University of South Carolina professor, scholar, and editor; and Mrs. Rose Maree Myers, founder of the School of the Arts in Charleston, South Carolina, to whom I am forever grateful. My academic career can be divided into two distinct parts: before and after meeting them.

I would also like to thank Colum McCann for his generosity toward my students and me. Finally I extend my gratitude to Judith Baughman, Dom Cassise, Anna Cusatis, Jim Denton, Lauren DiNicola, Harold and Katie Johnson, Rene Miles, Collins Rice, Karen Rood, Marjory Wentworth, and my students at the School of the Arts.

CHAPTER 1

# Understanding Colum McCann

## Career

Colum McCann has said that the book he most enjoyed as a child was *The Second-Best Children in the World* (1972) by the Irish writer Mary Lavin. "The memory of it is like bread coming out of the oven," he recalls.[1] Lavin's story involves three young children who leave home to make their parents' lives easier. After claiming to have seen "every place in the world," the children realize that "the best place of all is home," and they return to the warm embrace of their parents.[2] In his twenty-year career as a fiction writer, McCann has continued to be drawn to the idea of leaving home and finding one's way back, on both a literal and a metaphorical level. Since 1986, when he left his native Ireland at the age of twenty-one and rode a bicycle across North America, he has wandered the globe searching what he has frequently called its "anonymous corners"—Russian military hospitals, New York City subway tunnels, Slovakian Gypsy camps—for stories. In his seven books, McCann has written poetically rendered tales of loss and redemption, stories that tend to trace the often heart-wrenching plight of lonely, disillusioned characters—geographical or emotional exiles—who cling to the often-tenuous hope that they will somehow find their way home.

Colum McCann was born on 28 February 1965 in Dublin and grew up in the suburb of Deansgrange, where he attended Catholic elementary and secondary schools. Sean McCann, his father, who worked as the features editor for the *Evening Press* in Dublin and published twenty-eight books of his own, encouraged and nurtured his son's love of books. Sean McCann was an eclectic author, choosing subjects as diverse as Oscar Wilde, gardening, and a fictional child soccer star named Georgie Goode, the underdog hero of a series of children's books that had a powerful, lingering impact on Colum. His fifth-grade teacher, he recalls, used to read these books aloud to the class on Friday afternoons: "I remember that moment of intense pride when Georgie would score the final goal. He'd bury it in the back of the net. It was always inevitable, but amazing how he got to that moment of inevitability. And I was stunned by the power of story, even then."[3] Not surprisingly McCann's first effort at professional writing was an early stint as a sportswriter. At the age of eleven he began riding his bicycle through the borough of Dun Laoghaire, collecting results of the local soccer matches, and writing one-paragraph reports for the *Irish Press*. McCann's mother, Sally McGonigle McCann, a homemaker, was born in Garvagh in County Derry, Northern Ireland, where Colum spent many summers in the 1970s and early 1980s. His experiences in that politically anguished region have also had a significant impact on his fiction.

Sean McCann made periodic trips to America—where he lectured on cultivating roses—and brought back books for his teenage son, who quickly gained an affinity for writers associated with the Beat movement, especially Richard Brautigan, William Burroughs, Lawrence Ferlinghetti, Allen Ginsberg, Jack Kerouac, and Gary Snyder, in whose work McCann found a liberating alternative to the sorrow-filled traditional Irish stories he read in school. During the summer preceding his senior year in high school, his father gave him Benedict Kiely's "A Ball of Malt and Madame Butterfly," a short story that thrilled Colum with the possibilities of Irish fiction. What moved him most about this ribald account of the unlikely romance of a literary aesthete and a prostitute was Kiely's language, which he felt vied with that of his favorite poet at that time, Dylan Thomas, whose books, McCann claims, "were strewn all about our house."[4] On graduation he decided he would write, and—against his father's advice—he embarked on a career in journalism. He reflects, "I think maybe he told me not to be a journalist because he wanted me to become a fiction writer, and he was afraid that the world of journalism would swallow me asunder."[5]

McCann enrolled in the journalism program of the College of Commerce, Rathmines, in Dublin, and in 1983 he was named "Young Journalist of the Year" for his highly acclaimed reporting on the plight of battered women in Dublin. While researching the story, McCann ventured for the first time into the seediest sections of the city, an act foreshadowing the intrepid and compassionate attraction to the margins of society that continues to characterize his work. During the summer of 1983 he wrote for the *Connaught Telegraph,* Castlebar, County Mayo, in the west of Ireland, a region for which he developed a strong affinity and which appears frequently in his early fiction. McCann graduated from Rathmines in 1984 at the age of nineteen and made his first trip to America. That summer he worked for the Universal Press Syndicate in New York while renting a one-room apartment on Brighton Beach. On his return to Dublin, he began what proved to be an unfulfilling job as a freelance journalist covering the local social and cultural scene for the *Evening Press.* With his father's encouragement, he decided to move to America to become a fiction writer.

McCann was twenty-one when he left Ireland in the summer of 1986, but unlike most of the estimated 150,000 Irish who emigrated during the second half of the 1980s, he was not compelled to leave by his country's foundering economy. He was driven by curiosity and a wanderlust he attributes to his teenage obsession with the Beats. "From a young age I imagined the America of Kerouac and Cassady," he claims, and when he left for the United States, he aimed "to write the great Irish American novel."[6] Settling in Cape Cod, Massachusetts, he began working as a cab driver and on a golf course. He purchased an old Remington typewriter, in which he inserted a continuous roll of paper in imitation of the roll Kerouac used while writing *On the Road* (1957). However, when summer ended and he had completed "only a couple of feet" of writing, he realized "it was time to get some experience beyond my immediate white-bread world."[7]

McCann set off on a bicycle trip that took him down the East Coast to Florida, across the Gulf Coast to New Orleans, and into Mexico and Texas. After arriving in New Mexico he headed north through Colorado, Wyoming, and Oregon before looping back and finishing the approximately twelve-thousand-mile trek in San Francisco. During the eighteen-month journey, McCann worked as a bicycle mechanic, dishwasher, ditchdigger, fence builder, housepainter, ranch hand, and waiter. He detailed his experiences on the road by contributing a column every two weeks to the *Evening Press* in Dublin. He frequently sought out the offices of local newspapers, where he requested the use of a typewriter, often in exchange for writing an account of his journey for the local paper. San Francisco was a fitting final destination, since it is a setting for much of Jack Kerouac's fiction, which McCann pored over along the way. Kerouac served as a model during his journey, and McCann has echoed Kerouac's claims in *On the Road* of gaining his education through his wandering. "The road, for me, was a university," he says. The bicycle journey became "the greatest gift I was ever given. . . . It was quite a trip for a middle-class Dublin kid. I went through all sorts of landscapes and met convicted murderers, crawfish fishermen, movie stars, models, firefighters, bicycle mechanics, you name it. Because I was transient—passing through people's lives if you will—they tended to tell me some of their most intimate secrets. They knew there would be no repercussions in their lives, since I was moving on. It was my education, and I think that in many ways it gave birth to me as a writer." The trip, he says, "put me in touch with an unacknowledged part of myself," and he began to see himself as a storyteller, conveying the tales of people with backgrounds very different from his own. He believes the "empathy for outsiders" that informs his work "comes originally from this journey."[8]

Among the most inspirational stops along the way was Brenham, Texas, where McCann worked for six weeks at Miracle Farm, a juvenile-detention center. After a brief stay in San Francisco, he returned to Brenham in the summer of 1988 and resumed his position as a "wilderness educator," teaching outdoor-survival skills to wayward teenagers. An outdoor enthusiast since childhood, McCann felt personally liberated and artistically inspired by the "big, empty spaces" and "dramatic landscapes" of the American Southwest,[9] and he began using his experience to write. In "Uncle Saccharine" McCann fictionalized the events of his trip; he also wrote a nonfiction book, "The Wilderness Llamas," about his experience at Miracle Farm. He mailed the manuscripts overseas to Benedict Kiely, who was able to secure a British literary agent, but the agent was unable to find a publisher. "Thankfully they were never published," McCann has commented. "They were my training ground. Ben was good to me. I think he knew they needed work, but he still brought them into the world in a way."[10] These early efforts forced him to "write myself out of my work."[11] At the suggestion of his fiancée, Allison Hawke, whom he met during a trip to New York City to confer with an American literary agent, he began writing short stories that were consciously unautobiographical.

In 1990 he moved to Austin to begin work on a bachelor's degree at the University of Texas and published his first short story, "Tresses," in Dublin's *Sunday Tribune*. Although McCann has come to see in the story the typical shortcomings of a young writer, its publication signaled the start of a promising career, as it was awarded Ireland's prestigious Hennessy Award in two categories, "Best First Short Story" and "Overall Winner." After receiving the news, McCann said, he was unable to afford the trip to Dublin for the celebration, "so I climbed onto the roof of a two-story building and jumped into a swimming pool instead."[12] During his time in Austin, he wrote a story titled "Sister," and claiming to have wallpapered his bathroom with the rejection slips he received from magazine editors, he submitted the story to *Analecta,* the small-circulation literary journal of the University of Texas. "Sister" appeared in the 1992 issue, and McCann was invited by the novelist James Michener to audit classes in the M.F.A. program. The year 1992 proved to be fortunate in other ways. McCann married his fiancée, Allison, and, after just two years at the University of Texas, graduated Phi Beta Kappa with degrees in English and U.S. history. In addition "Sister" found its way into the hands of David Marcus, an influential writer and editor in Ireland, who having recalled reading "Tresses" two years earlier in the *Sunday Tribune,* asked Sean McCann if his son had published anything else. McCann's father sent a copy of *Analecta* to Marcus, who passed it on to Giles Gordon, a literary agent and editor of an annual anthology of new fiction by writers from Ireland and the United Kingdom. Gordon chose to include "Sister"—later titled "Sisters"—in *Best Short Stories 1993;* moreover, he secured a contract for McCann's first two books: a collection of short stories and a novel.

In January 1993 McCann and his wife moved to Japan, where Allison, a teacher of English as a Second Language (ESL), studied Japanese, and Colum taught English part-time while completing the collection of short stories he had begun in Texas. *Fishing the Sloe-Black River,* which introduced McCann's lyrical style and perennial subjects of emigration, loneliness, and loss, was published in England in April 1994. The book received considerable critical attention and sold well, especially considering it was a collection of short stories by an unestablished writer. A few weeks before its publication, one of its selections, "Through the Field," appeared in *The Picador Book of Contemporary Irish Fiction* (1994), edited by Dermot Bolger; the collection was republished the following year in America as *The Vintage Book of Contemporary Irish Fiction.* Recognizing the international character of McCann's fiction, Bolger placed the story, which he felt evoked "the landscape and mind of Texas," last in the collection and noted, "It seems a highly appropriate way to finish this book." Quoting the title story of McCann's collection, Bolger writes, "More than ever it is clear that future editors will not just be turning to the banks of the Liffey, the Lee and the Lagan, but to McCann's 'the Thames or the Darling or the Hudson or the Loire or even the Rhine itself' to search out the new heart of Irish writing"[13]

In June 1994 McCann won the Rooney Prize, awarded annually for the best new work of Irish literature by an author under the age of forty. While visiting Ireland to accept the award, he ventured on a ten-day, two-hundred-mile, cross-county walk, from Dublin to Killarney—a city whose name, meaning "church of the sloe berry," is echoed in McCann's title.[14] During the summer of that year, while working on his first novel *Songdogs,* he left Japan for England to promote his earlier book. A major opportunity presented itself when the Irish writer Edna O'Brien invited him to share the stage with her at a London reading.

Publication of *Fishing the Sloe-Black River* followed in Germany and Holland, and the McCanns returned to America and settled in New York City. There McCann did final editing on *Songdogs,* a novel about a young Irish emigrant who, hoping to make sense of his past, returns home from a sojourn in North America. Published in the United States in 1995, *Songdogs* earned a laudatory review from critic Hermione Lee in the *New Yorker* and was nominated for the lucrative International IMPAC Dublin Literary Award. American publication of *Fishing the Sloe-Black River* followed in 1996 and was also greeted with warm reviews. In the following year came the production of *Flaherty's Window,* a play which McCann based on "Step We Gaily, on We Go," a selection from his first book. The production ran for six weeks off Broadway. In retrospect, McCann says, "The play was dreadful, and it should have been so far off Broadway that it could swim away down the Hudson."[15] In 1997 McCann published in *Story* magazine "As Kingfishers Catch Fire," short fiction about an Irish nurse and her scandalous love affair with a Korean soldier. The story was awarded a Pushcart Prize, which honors the best work published by small presses. During this time he was completing research for a novel set entirely in New York City, work that involved McCann's spending many months among the homeless beneath the subway systems. *This Side of*

*Brightness* (1998) became his first international best seller and was named a *New York Times* "Notable Book" and a "Best Book" by both the *Los Angeles Times* and the *Boston Globe.* The novel was also one of seven finalists for the 2000 International IMPAC Dublin Literary Award. For *Everything in This Country Must* (2000), a novella and two short stories, McCann chose Northern Ireland as the setting and treated the effects of the region's political struggles on the emotional lives of three teenage protagonists. The collection earned the unqualified praise of novelist and critic Joyce Carol Oates, who stated in the *New York Review of Books,* "No more beautifully cadenced and moving collection of short fiction is likely to appear this year than Colum McCann's provocatively titled *Everything in This Country Must.*"[16] *When the Sky Falls,* a movie about the murdered Irish investigative reporter Sinead Hamilton, for which McCann cowrote the screenplay, also appeared in 2000. That McCann's short stories were by this point appearing regularly in major new anthologies attested to the growth of his reputation. The appearance of "Fishing the Sloe-Black River" and "Cathal's Lake" in *The Anchor Book of New Irish Writing* (2000) recognized his status as a major new contemporary Irish voice, while the inclusion of "Breakfast for Enrique" in Colm Tóibín's *The Penguin Book of Irish Fiction* (1999) acknowledged his work as part of the entire canon of English-language Irish fiction beginning with Jonathan Swift. In addition *The Art of the Story: An International Anthology of Contemporary Short Stories* (1999), edited by Daniel Halpern, included "Everything in This Country Must"—first published in the *Atlantic* in 1998—signaling McCann's growing reputation as an international writer.

In 2001 McCann visited Russia to teach English while conducting research for his next novel, *Dancer,* a fictional account of the life of the Russian ballet dancer and defector Rudolf Nureyev. The following year he was awarded the first Ireland Fund of Monaco Princess Grace Memorial Literary Award. *Dancer* was published in 2003 and was another international best seller, an enormous critical success, and the recipient of the Hughes & Hughes / *Sunday Independent* Award for best Irish novel of the year. In its December issue *Esquire* named McCann the "Best and Brightest" young novelist in America. In addition *Beautiful Kid,* a movie that McCann codirected and that featured the writer Frank McCourt, won numerous awards at the Method Fest independent-film festival in Burbank, California, and earned a PRISM award for its depiction of drug addiction. On 28 February 2005, McCann's fortieth birthday, he attended the Academy Awards, as *Everything in This Country Must,* directed by Gary McKendry and based on the title story of McCann's 2000 collection, was nominated for Best Live-Action Short Film. At this time McCann was working on his next novel, *Zoli,* a fictionalization of the life of the Romani poet Papusza. His research had taken him to Austria, Hungary, Italy, and Slovakia where he spent months among the Roma. After serving as Sydney Harman Writer-in-Residence at the City University of New York's Baruch College and as professor of creative writing at Brooklyn College, McCann in 2005 joined the faculty at Hunter College, where he continues to teach fiction writing in the school's M.F.A. program. In 2006 he was inducted into Ireland's Hennessy Hall of Fame, and *Zoli* was published in England. The following year, Random House, McCann's new American publisher, released the novel to an outpouring of critical and popular acclaim.

By this time the McCanns had three children—Isabella, John Michael, and Christian—between the ages of four and ten. Wishing to avoid the extended time away from his family demanded by his preceding two projects, McCann returned to New York City for the setting of his seventh book, a novel inspired by both the 11 September 2001 bombing of the World Trade Center and Philippe Petit's 7 August 1974 tightrope walk between its towers. In June 2009, weeks after McCann was inducted into the esteemed Aosdána association for his contribution to the arts in Ireland, Random House published McCann's first "American novel" since *This Side of Brightness* in 1998. *Let the Great World Spin* attracted immediate and effusive American critical and popular attention. Frank McCourt, Pulitzer Prize–winning author of *Angela's Ashes,* wrote that this new novel "climbed higher" and "dived deeper" than either McCann's earlier effort or any other novel written about New York City.[17] The fall 2008 issue of the *Paris Review* opened with a short story titled "Phreak," which combined three excerpts from the forthcoming novel. The *Wall Street Journal,* the *Los Angeles Times,* and the *San Francisco Chronicle* included the novel among their top picks for summer reading. And the 9 June 2009 issue of *O: The Oprah Magazine* listed the novel first among its "25 Books You Can't Put Down" and briefly described it as "an act of pure bravado." The book received a further boost when Oprah.com offered a free download for forty-eight hours in early August. On 16 August 2009 *Let the Great World Spin* became McCann's first *New York Times* best seller, as he prepared to embark on an exhaustive reading tour of Europe to coincide with the novel's September release in England, France, Germany, and Ireland. While in France McCann was presented both the prestigious Chevalier des arts et lettres by the French government and the Deauville Festival of Cinema Literary Prize.

On 18 November *Let the Great World Spin* was awarded the National Book Award, which established McCann, the first Irish-born author to win the award, as a major American writer.

That same month the editors of Amazon.com named the novel its number one pick among the best one hundred novels of 2009. In December director J. J. Abrams began arrangements with McCann to direct a feature-length movie based on the novel. Abrams told the *New York Times,* "It was just a book that felt as compelling and poetic and funny and messy and heartbreaking and dizzying as any I've read."[18] Random House released the paperback edition of *Let the Great World Spin* on 2 December 2009, six months earlier than originally planned, and the book spent more than six months on the *New York Times* trade paperback best-seller list. In the meantime McCann collaborated with choreographer Alonzo King on the story line for a ballet, *Handwriting,* scheduled for summer production by the Monte Carlo Ballet.

In January 2010 McCann, whose work had already been translated into thirty languages, traveled to China in conjunction with the purchase by publisher Shangai 99 of the rights to publish all seven of McCann's novels in Chinese. "It's a thrill to be translated into a language one never imagined one would," he said. "It's a reminder that the world's getting bigger all the time and also smaller all the time."[19] In March of that year, McCann signed a two-book deal with Random House; in April he was awarded a Guggenheim Fellowship; and in June he received the Ambassador Book Award.

Shortly after the publication of *Fishing the Sloe-Black River* in 1994, Colum McCann, who had walked across Ireland and grown to love the "big, empty spaces" he found bicycling in the American Southwest, expressed his simultaneous reluctance and excitement about settling down, particularly in New York City: "In a way I wish I wasn't going there, but I like to wander about in that environment, too. I think we'll try to put some roots there for maybe a year."[20] More than fifteen years later the McCanns seem to have found a permanent home in New York City. "I've spent the early stages of my career going on these great journeys," McCann stated in the January–February 2007 issue of *Poets & Writers*. "Now I still travel, but I primarily restrict my voyages to what goes on in my mind. I still roam, but from the privacy of my own home."[21] Today McCann calls himself "an Irish New Yorker" but prefers the title "international bastard," a phrase he borrows from Canadian novelist Michael Ondaatje, who was born in Sri Lanka and raised in England. McCann defines "international bastards" as "people who have no motherland of fatherland."[22] A citizen of both Ireland and the United States, McCann is part of a growing number of international writers, including fellow Irish authors Joseph O'Connor and Emma Donoghue, whose careers took root on foreign soil and whose work transcends geographical and cultural boundaries. In his 2008 essay "An Imagined Elsewhere," McCann recalls how "thrillingly new" his Dublin doorstep felt when he returned from a mere summer working in County Mayo at the age of seventeen. "We leave: it's inevitable," he writes. "We sometimes come home: that's our choice." In the essay McCann refers to travel as "a process of deep renewal" and describes how his concept of "home" has become at once more vivid and more borderless.[23] The tension between the enticing call of new lands and the nostalgic allure of one's original home colors McCann's work.

## Overview

Three major influences operate in Colum McCann's fiction: his Irish upbringing, his extensive reading, and his penchant for international travel. As with many of his Irish literary predecessors—most notably James Joyce—the first influence necessitated the other two. Before leaving his homeland at twenty, Joyce, who referred to Dublin as "the centre of paralysis," found refuge from Irish social, cultural, and political oppression in the liberating voice of the Norwegian playwright Henrik Ibsen. McCann has stated that, at sixteen, five years before his own self-imposed exile, "I was reading Kerouac, Ginsberg, Burroughs, Ferlinghetti, anybody at all who would get me away from Ireland."[24]

Yet McCann has acknowledged that, of all his influences, Ireland has left the most salient imprint: "It seems that wherever we are is wherever we were."[25] After more than two decades as an American resident, McCann, paraphrasing Joyce, claims to "hear the voice of Ireland in almost everything."[26] Like Joyce, McCann was under the false impression that his departure from Ireland would be temporary; but, unlike Joyce, who set all his fiction in Dublin, McCann has yet to locate more than one short story there. In fact, of his five novels, four are set entirely outside Ireland, and the other is set only partially in western Ireland. "From the very get go," he has remarked, "I was interested in expanding the boundaries of the Irish novel."[27] He has aimed, he says, to "write Irish novels that didn't have the word 'Ireland' in them whatsoever."[28] *Zoli,* for example, is set primarily in Slovakia and Italy and features no Irish-born character; yet McCann considers *Zoli* an Irish novel. What most closely connects *Zoli* and McCann's other work to the Irish literary tradition is its dominant subject: exile, an issue that he claims had been his "obsession for two decades" and that has preoccupied Irish writers for more than a century.[29] For McCann, the connection is more fundamental: "*Zoli* is an Irish novel because it was written by an Irish writer."[30]

In McCann's writing, exile takes two forms. The most obvious is geographical—that is, forced or voluntary emigration from one's homeland. Emigration, as an antidote for such hardships as famine, oppression, and poverty, has been a defining aspect of the Irish experience and, at best, a mixed blessing. McCann's protagonists are usually voluntary exiles; however, like the author himself, they inevitably feel a simultaneous aversion to and longing for their native land—be it Ireland, Argentina, Russia, or elsewhere. In *Dubliners* Joyce, too, focused on stifled protagonists who are unable to escape lonely, confining lives. McCann's characters escape, but they often realize they have lost paradise in their attempt to find it. McCann has commented that when he was a child, America represented Tir na nOg, which in Celtic mythology is the land of eternal youth. The female protagonist in McCann's earliest story, "Tresses," who becomes pregnant after immigrating to America with her boyfriend, introduces this disillusionment with and longing for home, characteristically drawing from both Irish folklore and American literature. Staring out at the Atlantic from her Massachusetts home, she muses: "*Look, girl, look way out there and we might see the dolphins, out there, past the yachts. They could carry us all the way across the ocean and we'd be home. Daddy used to say that if I went to America, I'd be in Tir na nOg, the Land of Eternal Youth. But he never said anything to me about getting off the white horse and growing old. . . . He said I would be the girl that Gatsby would ache for.*"[31]

McCann's characters tend to lament the loss of a purer time and place, a severing from one's origins that leads to an identity struggle, not just a simple longing for one's native soil. McCann has noted, "There's an interior exile that is perhaps even more significant than a geographical one."[32] McCann often portrays what critic Ben Forkner calls "the fractured soul lost in his own house."[33] The writer has referred to his characters as "wounded," emotionally broken by drug addiction, injustice, abandonment, war, self-denial, discrimination, poverty, the absence of loved ones, and other misfortunes. Loss and loneliness, perennial Irish subjects, define his heroes, but regardless of the degree of their despair, so does hope. McCann witnessed this inextinguishable hope among the homeless in the New York City subway tunnels while conducting research for *This Side of Brightness*. "No matter who they were," he says, "across all spectrums—race, gender, economics—every single one of them said, 'When I get out of here.' Not 'If I get out of here.' 'When I get out of here.' There is that deep place—no matter how dark the darkness, there is a part of us as humans that says, 'We will eventually get to some sort of light.' That's what keeps you going."[34] Thus, redemption balances loss in McCann's work. His emotional exiles also seek the road home, a spiritual reconciliation that brings them a renewed sense of identity and belongingness and restores their "rage to live."[35] Often the redemptive moments in McCann's work consist merely of the quiet recognition of joy or beauty that time cannot undo, and that is "enough." McCann does not see himself as an optimist or a pessimist, but as a "social realist."[36] "I don't believe the world's a particularly beautiful place," he remarked in an interview in the *Atlantic* in 1998, "but I do believe in redemption. There are those moments when the world comes together and we go home."[37]

Another effect of McCann's Irish upbringing is his frequent use of Christian references. Christian numerology and symbols, such as bread, water, fire, and light, are essential to his fiction. McCann uses bread as a life-affirming symbol representing grace or spiritual communion. "If you ever had anyone bake bread for you," he has said, "it's always a lovely thing, isn't it? To go into the oven and take out a fresh loaf of bread, it feels like you're home no matter where you happen to be."[38] Water, for McCann, in the form of a bath or a swim, tends to be baptismal. Yet calling to mind the Great Flood, water also can signify danger, as drownings also appear in his fiction. Rivers function as a crucial secular symbol signifying the movement of time, which can be rapid, drifting, or frozen, depending on the crisis at hand. Light in McCann's work represents either hope or understanding; and like rivers it alters its meaning depending on its intensity. Flickering light, for example, seems to indicate a transient joy, while sunlight tends to be more auspicious, though it generally enters the darkness through narrow cracks. A conflagration can represent destruction or purgation. The stars, which McCann often notes burned out long ago, can signify the edifying light the past continues to shine on the present. Just as Jesus's disciples are referred to as "fishers of men," fish take on religious imagery in McCann's work, and fishing symbolizes an attempt to reconnect with lost loved ones in McCann's books. References to kingfishers appear often, a dual symbol of divinely wrought creation and destruction, which has its source in Gerard Manley Hopkins's "As Kingfishers Catch Fire," a poem that praises the unity in creation and the individual's connection to that unity. The idea of connection is a major preoccupation for McCann's generally alienated characters. Furthermore, a few of his heroes are depicted with vivid Christlike imagery, namely Treefrog in *This Side of Brightness* and Corrigan—who calls to mind the Jesuit Hopkins himself in many ways—in *Let the Great World Spin.* Death and resurrection are also major subjects in all McCann's work, as pain and loss often engender joy and new life, either for the victim or for unsuspecting others. "I'm not a holy roller, that's for sure," McCann has commented. "I have a Christ-obsession, but that's me and three billion others. These references . . . come naturally from my youth. . . . If there's any person to be, then be Christ. Be poor, be decent, be haunted, be angry, be understanding. Of course we all fail at the most simple of these things."[39]

That the search for a revived sense of wholeness by McCann's characters is often couched in religious language is appropriate, considering that the words *whole* and *holy* are cognate, both stemming from the Old English *hālig*, meaning "healthy." *Wholeness* constitutes an unbroken, original condition, which explains why McCann's characters, from the antithetical O'Dwyer siblings in "Sisters" to the disparate Corrigan brothers in *Let the Great World Spin,* associate wholeness with home.

While growing up in Ireland has left its lingering influence on the themes in McCann's fiction, he has also acknowledged a debt to certain writers who had an early influence on his precise, lyrical style. "A writer has to acknowledge," he has stated, "that we get our voice from the voices of others. It is impossible to spring into the world unformed by anyone else."[40] Among McCann's strongest early influences were poets, particularly Dylan Thomas and Hopkins, both of whom stressed the dominating role of sound in their work. "A story writer must be just as rooted as a poet in the way words sound, look, and bump up against one another," McCann has said.[41] His highly rhythmic syntax, which relies heavily on sentence fragments and is often given further cohesion by rhyme and fixed meter as well as assonance and alliteration, attests to the influence of poet Seamus Heaney. The first prose writer McCann felt was able to use language with the same dexterity as Dylan Thomas was Benedict Kiely. For McCann, Kiely's prose "jumped, it skipped, it sang. It read itself aloud to me."[42] Skillful use of language as well as craft in storytelling have been sources of pride in Ireland dating back to the early bards and the Celtic myths. In Kiely, McCann found not only "a symphony of sound" but also a synthesis of reappropriated "songs, ballads, myths, colloquialisms, snippets from pop culture," a richly textured style that continues to impact him.[43] Another Irish writer whose influence on McCann was profound is Desmond Hogan. After discovering his 1979 story collection *The Diamonds at the Bottom of the Sea,* McCann was drawn not only to Hogan's poetic style and his tales of Irish emigrants but also to his "cleaving open of worlds," which would affect McCann's own choice of subject matter.[44]

In search of this subject matter and aiming "to find a voice that was other than Irish," McCann began his journey in America, where he discovered not only new landscapes but also other influential voices.[45] Eamonn Wall has written, "His is an Irish voice, though one which is intricately modulated by the physical and literary landscapes through which he has traveled."[46] Among the writers McCann found in America, he admired "the quality of the language" in Cormac McCarthy's work and his treatment of outcasts. He was also drawn toward "the muscle and the vision" in the writing of the poet and novelist Jim Harrison.[47] In Toni Morrison, Louise Erdrich, and Gabriel García Márquez he discovered the liberating power of magic realism, with which he experimented in a few of his early stories. He was attracted to Erdrich's poetic treatment of dispossessed Native Americans. In Morrison he found "access to the untold story,"[48] which became another of his own hallmarks. In García Márquez he discovered "the sheer beauty of finding out that there will always be writers who find new ways of telling stories."[49] The same could be said for his fascination with the work of Michael Ondaatje; his *Coming through Slaughter* with its varying points of view, nonlinear plotline, and mosaic-like blending of semi-historical documents left its mark, most vividly on *Dancer.*

McCann was also drawn to the idea that Ondaatje had imagined a story of an African American musician from New Orleans, a character about whom he knew nothing other than what he learned from one possibly unfactual sentence he had read in a newspaper. In this regard McCann is fond of quoting another major influence, the British writer John Berger: "Never again will a story be told as if it were the only one."[50] This idea is fundamental to *Dancer* and the two novels that followed it, as McCann aimed to loosen the constraints of accepted facts surrounding historical figures in an effort to distill more genuine "truths." McCann, who prefers the term *storyteller* to *fiction writer* or *nonfiction writer,* has enriched his writing with a plentitude of intertextual references to the work of these and other literary heroes.

Aside from his deft handling of language and his colorful synthesis of influences, it is McCann's view of writing as an imaginative journey that provides his fiction with its stamp of originality; his own physical journeying has largely informed this creative process. Life is often represented in his work as a perilous, existential journey, and his characters often deal with blistered, lacerated feet and torn shoes, something McCann has experienced on his walks across Ireland. Walking in his fiction often takes place in aerial environments—rooftops, crossbeams, tightropes—which, like McCann's use of dance, represents bold defiance against the threat of nothingness. While his first American literary hero, Jack Kerouac, chronicled his coast-to-coast wandering in a series of autobiographical novels, McCann refuses to write about his own life. Yet his extensive globetrotting has helped him garner many of the images, characters, and ideas for his fiction. He learned during his American bicycle trip that what interested him was the lives of other people, particularly ordinary people. "I believe in the value of those lives that are not talked about, those anonymous corners where others don't necessarily want to go."[51] It has always been his credo to "write about what you don't know, or, more exactly, write towards what you want to know."[52] He instills this paradoxical advice in his creative-writing students, explaining, "In the journey to getting towards what you supposedly don't know, you discover things that are inside you that are unconscious, that you haven't necessarily acknowledged before. So writing becomes this place of enormous digging," he says. "You're at the coal face of yourself, and you're digging things out from the inside."[53] Thus, McCann says, intuition more than intellect is the controlling creative force in his writing. "Nothing is mapped out," he claims, "and I try to move forward from place to place, sometimes blindly. It's almost a tactile thing, feeling for the right word." McCann often begins with an image; sometimes, he says, he knows the novel's first and last sentence, but "absolutely nothing in between."[54] His books, he claims, arrive "accidentally"; as he notes, paraphrasing Dostoyevsky, "I try not to disease myself by thinking of it too consciously."[55] He believes, he has commented, in "creative reading," in leaving the interpretation of his work to readers and critics who, he feels, complete the creative process he sets in motion. Above all, McCann says, he wants to write good stories that are "engaging. . . . And on a certain level I want them to be social."[56] In this regard he acknowledges John Steinbeck, "more . . . now than Kerouac," as a model for his work. Books, McCann feels, can and should "tilt the world in some tiny political, social or moral way."[57] Asked in September 2009 "What does it mean to be a writer," McCann emphasized this growing social concern: "I would hope that it means embracing empathy. Imagining the life of the other is the greatest privilege of all."[58]

In an October 2000 essay in the *Irish Times,* Colum McCann referred to himself as "a man of two countries." He explained, "I have a foot planted in the dark corners of each. Every year I try to spend long enough in Ireland to rediscover why I left it. I also spend long enough in the states to question why I would want to live here."[59] The Ireland of the twenty-first century is much different from the one he left in 1986, the days before the emergence of the "Celtic Tiger." As Dermot Bolger has written regarding the "New Irish": "Irish writers no longer go into exile, they simply commute."[60] McCann has commented: "I'm not so sure that an Irish writer can claim to be in 'exile' anymore. Not in the way that Beckett or Joyce needed to be in exile, anyway. Ireland has become so thoroughly part of the international community that what you run from will be almost exactly the same as what you run towards. The Catholic Church has lost its stranglehold; censorship is now basically nonexistent; we have a higher national wage than that of the British; we are on the cusp of our very first sense of ongoing peace; and emigration is for all intents and purposes a thing of the past." McCann says there are "not many reasons to be in exile from Ireland—except perhaps the stunning arrogance of the new money and a business mentality (the 'Celtic Tiger') that is rather sickening."[61] As the landscape of Ireland began taking on a more expansive character, McCann realized that its fiction needed to do the same. In February 2007 he responded to an interviewer's question regarding the way people will view his legacy: "Maybe that I was one of the first generation of writers who said that the international novel is viable and available, that a novel can cross all sorts of boundaries, that you as a writer have access to all sorts of things that you don't necessarily know about, but want, deeply, to understand."[62]

CHAPTER 2

# *Fishing the Sloe-Black River*

Reviewing *Fishing the Sloe-Black River* in the *Austin American-Statesman,* Carol Illig Lake measured Colum McCann against three of Ireland's greatest twentieth-century writers: "In the tradition of Yeats, McCann uses Irish lore; lush sensual language in the tradition of Joyce. And in the shadow of Beckett, he confronts the theme of nothingness."[1] In his *Los Angeles Times* review Christopher Tilghman, applauding the book's transcontinental eclecticism, noted that "the words 'dadgum' and 'critters' coexist with 'Cuchulainn' and 'Diarmoid' and 'Grainne.'"[2] Such is the character of McCann's first book, which traverses the Irish landscape and traces the American coastline from New York to New Orleans to San Francisco, a literary journey following the itinerary of McCann's own early travels while exploring the idea that a dogged determination to find redemption transcends borders.

*Fishing the Sloe-Black River* was published in England on 14 April 1994, more than two and a half years before its appearance in the United States on 10 November 1996.[3] McCann's name was not new to British reviewers in 1994, however, as "Sisters," the opening story of his collection, had appeared along with stories by such seasoned writers as Martin Amis, Edna O'Brien, and Alice Munro in editor Giles Gordon's *Best Short Stories 1993* the previous summer, and McCann was singled out in each of the major reviews of that anthology. Nick Hornby, for example, writing in the *Sunday Times* (London), claimed that "Sisters" provided evidence that "Irish writing is in excellent health,"[4] and James Saynor referred to McCann in the *Observer* (London) as "a mesmeric find."[5] In the *Times* (London) Matt Holland referred to "the tight fin de siècle snap crackle pop" of McCann's fiction and praised his ability to move "swiftly across continents and years." Holland noted that McCann's "penetrative nineties style" was a welcome contrast to the looser, gentler stories of the "silver sages."[6] British and Irish reviewers of *Fishing the Sloe-Black River* reiterated the idea that McCann was a striking new presence in Irish fiction but seemed to judge his work with regard to its "Irishness." While Philip MacCann acknowledged that his contemporary's "refreshing imaginative narrative voices" seemed to "promise a change" in response to what he felt was the Irish writer's preoccupation with Irishness, he claimed McCann still allowed tradition to stunt his originality.[7] Christina Konig praised this "accomplished" collection and placed it in the tradition of William Trevor, John McGahern, Desmond Hogan, and Dermot Bolger but said it might fit "too smoothly" in that tradition.[8] Irish writers Victoria White and Mary Morrissy, on the other hand, felt he handled his relationship with Ireland "in a quiet and oblique way." They referred to McCann as "a convincing ventriloquist" who demonstrated the "simple intensity of McGahern" and praised the tendency in his "fiercely imagined writing" to "strike home" from distant lands.[9]

American reviewers not only echoed these accolades but discerned, as did Robert Taylor in the *Boston Globe,* the tendency of the stories to "evoke an international rather a Celtic atmosphere."[10] A reviewer for *Publishers Weekly* wrote, "These are twelve exceptionally crafted and thought-provoking tales, in which we glimpse not only the immediate world of the characters but also a good deal of their origins and ancestry. This makes for rich, multilayered work."[11] David Madden in his review for the *San Francisco Chronicle* claimed that "the twelve stories in *Fishing the Sloe Black-River* are rich, powerful pieces that place author Colum McCann in the front ranks of contemporary Irish writers."[12] *Washington Post* reviewer Ambrose Clancy, drawing comparisons between McCann's fiction and that of John Cheever and Anton Chekhov, called McCann's stories "well made" and "written with fierce beauty."[13] Tilghman, in his review in the *Los Angeles Times,* found McCann's ability to deliver "hope against every odd" to be "a truly brilliant achievement." He added, "A spirit of sorts rises from the depths here, a spirit borne in the vigorous and inventive storytelling, in the lyrical language, in the affecting and richly drawn characters, and in the odd moments of satisfaction and succor that McCann does permit into these lives."[14]

The stories in *Fishing the Sloe-Black River* deal with wounded characters valiantly facing lives that have failed to fulfill the promise of younger days; yet while thematic unity connects the tales, stylistic and structural diversity distinguishes them. McCann most noticeably employs a wide variety of voices. He writes from the point of view of a young woman with a history of promiscuity, a gay man battling AIDS, and a delusional former boxing star, for example, and he draws on an array of narrative techniques. Some stories are steeped in complex symbolism, and some are starkly minimalist, while others rely on irony for their effect. In regard to symbolism, unity is evident throughout; certain motifs—rivers, bread, coins, litter, fishing, and drifting, for example—pervade the stories. In addition, color and its absence play a strongly suggestive role, as does religious numerology. Half the stories are set in Ireland, the other half in America.

The title of the collection was inspired by a line from an eighth-century Irish ballad, "Donal Og," that McCann knew from childhood: "My heart is as dark as a sloe berry." In each of the first eleven stories, a river flows, leading ultimately to the "deep and clear" lake of the final piece. McCann intended this connectedness and has compared the book, and story writing in general, to a "river of ink" in which the reader fishes.[15]

## "Sisters"

"Sisters" was inspired while McCann and his future wife were attending Pre-Cana classes at a convent on Long Island prior to their wedding. There he saw a young Irish nun and wondered, "Who is she?"—"the literal event that led me toward" the story."[16] This is the question that leads the narrator, Sheona O'Dwyer, deported from America a decade earlier, to sneak back into the country in pursuit of her sister, Brigid, a nun, who represents the unspoiled life Sheona left behind long ago in County Mayo. Sheona explains, "I have come to think of our lives as the colors of that place—hers a piece of bog cotton, mine as black as the water found when men slash too deep in the soil with a shovel."[17]

McCann portrays Sheona's second arrival in America in terms of an instinctive journey toward rebirth, a journey that began when she was impelled to return to her childhood home to reunite with the father she'd left behind, only to find he had died. "I have no idea what stirred me to see him," she explains (13). In the opening sequence, she is being carried across the Canadian border in the womblike trunk of a car, nestled in the fetal position: "It is dark and cramped and hollow and black in here. My knees are up against my breasts" (4). The rebirth motif is reinforced when the driver of the car, her former boyfriend Michael, who is of Navajo descent, refers to himself as "a coyote," Mexican slang for one who smuggles others into America. But for Michael the term recalls the Navajo creation myth which claims "that coyotes howled in the beginning of the universe" (4).

"Sisters" introduces McCann's concern with the necessity of balance. Back in County Mayo, while Brigid began a life of self-denial like her namesake saint, Sheona began a life of self-indulgence, her promiscuity becoming her "autograph" (2). Both are prostrated by the extremity of their convictions. Sheona is brutally raped in the frontier landscape of California where "the ghosts of Kerouac and John Muir" seemed to lurk. Brigid starves herself into a vegetative condition while performing a prayer vigil for three murdered nuns. "I just want some neutral ground," Sheona tells her incoherent sister when she finds her lying ruined in a convent hospital in Long Island (21).

"Sisters" also introduces McCann's most enduring symbol: bread. Sheona recalls the young Brigid perched on a rock and holding a sandwich; she scatters "the bread like a sacrament" (3). Now, Sheona remarks, "She was a house of bones, my sister, throwing away her bread" (3). The description conveys not only Brigid's frail, unhealthy body but a body lacking spiritual wholeness and denying what it needs to sustain it. In the hospital Brigid has been reduced to an elemental, spiritless "heap of dust" (21). She had been known to steal bread for the poor in Central America, but, literally and symbolically, she allowed no bread for herself. Attempting to help revive the ailing Brigid, Sheona tries to feed her a piece of toast. The gesture suggests the ministering of the Eucharist and the establishing of a spiritual communion with her sister, who, Sheona learns, had grown somewhat weary of her ascetic life and had engaged in harmless bits of "madness" (19), such as dancing, a joy she had formerly left to Sheona.

Like McCann's first published story, "Tresses," "Sisters" is a tale of disillusion. Like Grainne in "Tresses" Sheona believed that the land of eternal youth lay west of the Atlantic but instead found "the country that God gave to Cain" (6). And like "Tresses" "Sisters" echoes *The Great Gatsby,* particularly regarding the passage of time. "You can't change the past," Michael tells Sheona, to which she responds half-heartedly, "We can't, can we?" (12). Other comments convey her nascent understanding of the consuming nature of time and the unintended course one's life can take. "If we could travel faster than the speed of light we would get to a place we never really wanted to go before we even left," she remarks (8). Searching for spare change at a toll booth, she reinforces this idea of being left in time's wake: "none of these coins have our birthdates on them anymore" (9).

McCann conveys Sheona's resurrection in biblical terms. In a gesture suggestive of Mary Magdalene, about whom the nuns lectured her in Catholic school, she takes Brigid's feet into her hands while resisting the urge to take them into her mouth. This act of humility and compassion is cathartic: "There's an old feeling that's in me that's new," she remarks (23). Michael has told her of a frozen waterfall in Quebec that they could climb, and she decides she will go there after her sister recovers. The waterfall, in contrast to the flowing rivers in McCann's other works, suggests the ability to freeze time; Sheona realizes that she has not squandered all her time yet, and the idea of climbing the waterfall conveys the sense of purpose and control over her future she intends to forge. The first signs of this return to grace had been foreshadowed as Sheona entered the convent and recited to herself a line from Hopkins's poem "As Kingfishers Catch Fire": "What I do is me, for that I came" (16). Sheona's cleansing pilgrimage about to be completed, a nun remarks, "You look white." To which she responds, "I have been traveling a long time" (18).

## "Breakfast for Enrique"

McCann completed "Breakfast for Enrique" in 1993 while living in Japan; yet he drew his inspiration for this story from his friendship with two gay men whom he met in 1986 in New Orleans, a stop on his cross-country bicycle journey. His friendship with the couple spawned in the twenty-one-year-old McCann an awakening, which he details in "About Men, About Women," an essay published in the 30 October 1994 *Observer* (London): "As far as I was concerned, theirs wasn't an ordinary world," he writes. "I had grown up in a sheltered, middle-class Dublin suburb and homosexuality equated to strangeness."[18] McCann had been working as a waiter in a riverside restaurant where one of the men, Randy, tended bar and the other, Michael, cooked. Often Michael asked McCann to deliver folded notes to his "husband" at the bar, notes which McCann imagined were filled with sexual, poetic "whisperings." "I wasn't a homophobe—at least I don't want to think so—but their world so fascinated me that I conjured up these notes into something theatrical and dramatically lurid." When McCann finally opened one of these notes, it read, to his disappointment and disillusion: "Randy, have we any coffee for breakfast?"[19]

McCann notes that his brief friendship with Michael and Randy occurred, symbolically, "close to winter's solstice—it was only years later that I realized how close." When he returned for a visit in the early 1990s during the frenzy of Mardi Gras, he was told that both men had died of AIDS. Yet their lives inspired in him an awakening, which led him to write "Breakfast for Enrique": "I try these days to come to terms with Randy and Michael's world—in truth it was a very prosaic and loving and uneventful world where written notes consisted simply of what might be available for breakfast. It was no different from mine. I had created a stereotype of them from my own fear."[20]

It is this stereotype that McCann discredits in "Breakfast for Enrique." The narrator, referred to only by his surname, O'Meara—aside from the disparaging epithets hurled by his boss—postpones going to work one morning so he can prepare breakfast for his partner, Enrique, who suffers from AIDS. Both men are exiles—O'Meara from Ireland, Enrique from Argentina—living in the seemingly liberating environs of San Francisco yet barely able to sustain themselves. When McCann introduces Enrique, he lies "curled into himself" (26). This fetal image, conjuring the innocence of infancy, is juxtaposed with images of disintegration. Shards of a smashed jam jar that once held the couple's money litter the floor; the bedroom curtains "make the sound of crackling ice" (26); a final line of cocaine dissolves into the sweat of Enrique's belly. McCann further suggests the character's severed connection with the promise of his earlier life when small joys such as steak and vegetables, coffee, and a few cigarettes could be taken for granted. Searching for loose change, O'Meara discovers an Irish five-penny, a worthless anachronism. Scrounging in the grocery store, he recalls his late mother cooking "other breakfasts . . . sausages and rashers fried in a suburban Irish kitchen" (30). A yellowing photograph of a robust Enrique rafting on Argentina's Parana River adorns the wall near the couple's bed.

Rivers, fishing, and fish are crucial symbols for McCann, and his use of them in "Breakfast for Enrique" and the book's title story creates a complementary aesthetic and thematic link between these two very different pieces. In both stories, rivers represent the inevitable movement of time, which often separates children from parents. Fishing, for McCann, represents the persistent, usually desperate hope of "catching" a dream, or fish, that has managed to escape one's grip and is being carried to some remote shore. While "Fishing the Sloe-Black River" depicts the suffering of parents who "fish for their sons," "Breakfast for Enrique" portrays lost sons in their own struggle with the river, represented through the memories of Enrique, who not only once caught fish with his bare hands but also could swim, while remaining stationary, against the wild rapids of a river (33). O'Meara imagines Enrique's father "at the very tip of Tierra del Fuego reaching his arms out toward the condors that flap their wings against the red air" and wondering "where his son has gone" (32). While fish symbolize elusive hopes in McCann's fiction, the job that O'Meara is avoiding the morning the story takes place is as a fish gutter; he is both victim of and accomplice in the destruction of these elusive hopes. He evokes the fragility of Enrique's body in his description of fish gutting: "With one smooth sweep of the finger you can take out all the innards" (33).

As Enrique dozes during their morning breakfast, O'Meara watches the traffic below their balcony and experiences an epiphany regarding the couple's persistence in a passage that echoes the final lines of *The Great Gatsby:* "all of a sudden I understand that we are in the stream, Enrique and I, that the traffic below us is flowing quite steadily, trying to carry us along, while all the time he is beating his arms against the current, holding still, staying in one place" (37). The story, which opens with the hopeful image of sunlight entering the bedroom "like an old fisherman" heralding yet another day (25), concludes with another symbol containing Christian overtones. O'Meara recalls a story Enrique once told him about the ability of starfish to regenerate torn limbs into new bodies. He imagines the crass fishermen with whom he works deigning to share with him the discovery of "two fully grown starfish" that had grown from one torn starfish (38). The regenerated starfish not only suggests resurrection—even if it is short lived—but also calls to mind the Madonna Stella Maris, Mother Mary, the star of the sea; she is a patron saint to fishermen and an appropriate symbol, since all McCann's protagonists are fishing in their own ways.

### "A Basket Full of Wallpaper"

Like the preceding story, "A Basket Full of Wallpaper" focuses on a character whose difficult circumstances and outsider status have forced him into isolation. Osobe is a Japanese man who immigrated to western Ireland during the 1950s. The story is narrated, however, by a young Irishman, Sean Donnelly, who has since moved to London and offers a nostalgic, retrospective glimpse of Osobe based on their experience of working together one summer during Sean's childhood. Before identifying Osobe by name, the narrator offers up several of the identities ascribed to him by the villagers who have mythologized him over the years. The men in the pubs imagined him as a violent man who tortured American soldiers during the war. The women assured one another he was of prestigious descent and had been the victim of unrequited love. The children thought he must have been a hero, perhaps a kamikaze pilot who had magically drifted to their island (39–40).

Yet the same provincial tendencies that spawn the need to mythologize Osobe cause the villagers to remain suspicious and contemptuous of him. When one of Sean's peers throws a rock with the message "*Nip go home*" through Osobe's window (40), a few others beat the assailant, not out of sympathy for the man but because Osobe covers the window and precludes their spying. By the time he turns sixteen, the narrator has created more sophisticated scenarios, gleaned from the books the boy reads, for Osobe's coming to Ireland. When he answers the man's notice for a helper in the wallpaper business he operates, Sean hopes to learn the fabulous truth about Osobe's past. In addition, a new wave of emigration had scarred his village, so that the undertaking business of his father suffered, causing Mr. Donnelly to complain that even the number of deaths was dying. Thus the boy's parents urge him to take the job.

Much to Sean's disappointment, he learns that Osobe, who he dreams has witnessed horrific scenes after the Hiroshima bombing, is merely a simple, decent man. Because of his disappointed expectations, Sean grows to hate the man. When Sean asks him one day if he was in Hiroshima and if he hates Americans, Osobe responds, "You shouldn't think these things. You should think of making good job with wallpaper. That is important" (46). Work is his response to loneliness and loss, and Sean observes the fluidity and precision with which Osobe compulsively papers the walls of his own house. That he lives according to his own higher values is apparent in his tendency to leave ten- and twenty-pound notes lying around his house. On his last night with Osobe, Sean steals a twenty-pound note from him to compensate for his not having satisfied the boy's imagination: "He should have been a hero or a seer. He should have told me some incredible story that I could carry with me forever" (50). Before Sean leaves, Osobe gives him a hundred-pound note to help with school and compounds the boy's guilt.

McCann somewhat deifies Osobe, as three days, suggesting perhaps the three days between Christ's death and resurrection, pass between the man's death and the discovery of his body, whereupon the townspeople recognize he "was a decent sort" (52). In his love for wallpapering he had covered his own walls with approximately two feet of colorful paper, a symbol of his increasing isolation and an image that recalls the medieval monks cloistered in their thickly-walled "beehive huts" on western Ireland's remote island Skellig Michael. Sean becomes nostalgic for the "road long gone" on which he and Osobe bicycled while carrying "a basketful of wallpaper." Also moved by the memory of Osobe, Sean returns his twenty-pound note by dropping it into the Thames for "the dead, their death, and their dying too" (53).

## "Through the Field"

One of the collection's two stories set in Texas, "Through the Field" was inspired by McCann's experiences at Miracle Farm. The story is conveyed by an unnamed narrator who works as a groundskeeper at a Texas state prison where Stephen Youngblood, a juvenile convicted of murder, is serving the beginnings of a thirty-year sentence. "Through the Field" derives its effect chiefly through point of view, structure, and irony. The narrator's candor, coarse language, and knack for storytelling make him a suitable voice for this grotesque tale, which is constructed as a frame story in order to prepare for its ironic ending. The narrator begins by explaining that he and his coworker, Kevin, had been preparing to cut and bale hay they'd been cultivating, when they began discussing Stephen Youngblood. However, when the narrator told Kevin "what that boy had said," Kevin began shivering, "and he went on home to gather up mine and his family" (56). Here the narrator begins his inner story in order to lead the reader to "what that boy had said" and the reason Kevin acted as he did.

The narrator delivers his account of conversations he overheard between the boy and a University of Texas student named Ferlinghetti who counsels him. Stephen, fourteen at the time, had been released from a Baptist reform school, where he'd been sent for petty thievery. While his father was working out of town, his mother entertained a lover, William Harris. Disgusted with hearing the couple's "grunting and moaning and slapping and screaming" (62), Stephen attacks Harris with a baseball bat. Harris reacts by kicking Stephen in the mouth. After receiving stitches in the hospital, Stephen rides his bicycle toward Harris's house to inform his wife that he has been cheating; tiring along the way he steals a truck. When he arrives, Mrs. Harris, unmoved by the news of her husband's infidelity, seduces Stephen, thereby beginning their prolonged sexual relationship. When Harris catches the couple in bed and gives Stephen another beating, the boy returns armed. "An ace with the rifle on Nintendo" (64), Stephen stands outside the bedroom window while Harris and his wife are having sex and shoots him in the forehead. He enters the room and tells Mrs. Harris to pack so that they can head to Florida. He demands that she confess her love for him and kiss him in the dying man's presence. She complies, and Stephen places the barrel of the gun down Harris's throat, fires, and then shoots him two more times in the chest before running into the woods to hide. The police arrive and begin investigating, and after approximately two hours, Stephen walks out of the woods and turns himself in.

According to the narrator, Ferlinghetti spent weeks trying to persuade Stephen to reveal his reason for surrendering. One afternoon after Ferlinghetti leaves, Stephen is helping the narrator plant flowers when the boy suddenly says, "I was scared of the dark" (67). It is when the narrator conveys this revelation to his friend Kevin that the latter rushes home and returns with their families. Arranging the women and children in a line, Kevin parades them through the tall grass. As darkness descends he leads the group in laughing and dancing through the field.

McCann claims that he often encountered teenagers at Miracle Farm who had committed horrific crimes but who, when camping, would ask to sleep in his tent because they were afraid of the dark. Kevin's ritual in "Through the Field" is not only a comment on the destructive potential of fear. On a metaphysical level it represents a dance in the face of the unknown, an affront to nothingness—a subject confronted elsewhere in McCann's fiction and a major concern in such short fiction of Ernest Hemingway as "A Clean, Well-Lighted Place."

## "Stolen Child"

In his introduction to *The Penguin Book of Irish Fiction* (1999), Colm Tóibín writes, "There is no Irish novel which ends in a wedding, or a match being made. Irish fiction is not like that; Irish fiction is full of dislocation and displacement."[21] "Stolen Child" is certainly "full of dislocation and displacement," yet it does end in a wedding; a match is made, though in typical McCann style, it is hardly a predictable match. Dana, a sixteen-year-old African American blind girl, marries Will, a poor, legless, white Vietnam veteran more than twice her age. The wedding is not a solemn occasion. The priest is drunk; a guide dog barks loudly in the aisle; and Orla, the wife of the story's protagonist, Padraic Keegan, chides him in profane undertones. Life will not be easy for Will and Dana. Yet the optimism and love they exude on their wedding day penetrates the self-absorption and cynicism that envelops Padraic.

McCann borrows the title for this story from Yeats's poem "The Stolen Child," the refrain of which, "*For the world's more full of weeping than you can understand*" (78), Padraic often quotes to Dana, who lives in the children's home where he works as a counselor. Both Dana and Will understand sadness and disappointment, and their tragic pasts underscore the significance of the title. Both had their lives stolen from them at an early age. Dana was discovered locked in a cupboard, "rake-thin," while "her mother sat in the corner of the room and rocked on the balls of her toes, a bouquet of crack pipes around her feet" (74). Will's "country had given him a haircut, a set of camos, a survival pack, and a machine gun and sent him off to the war" from which he returned "in an airplane full of cripples and body bags" (80). Yet the most visibly unhappy character in the story is Padraic, who emigrated from Ireland to New York City with his wife. The title of the story could just as easily be applied to him, for like the child in Yeats's poem, he is transported to a new land, but that new land is not free of sorrow. At the home he works with "forgotten blind children, the snot rags of society," whom he compares to "birds with broken wings, unable to get off the ground" (72). Yet it is he who wishes to be carried away "to somewhere very different" (72).

McCann conveys the hopelessness that plagues Padraic in the opening lines of the story. The "heavy oak door of the children's home," which Padraic closes, seems to have been shut on his life. Furthermore, when he emerges from "the graveyard shift" at dawn, the morning sun is hardly propitious, "coming up like a stabwound" (71). When he arrives home, Orla is sleeping with a copy on her chest of Philip Larkin's *High Windows,* a significant allusion. The "high windows" in Larkin's nihilistic title poem look out on "the deep blue air, that shows / Nothing, and is nowhere, and is endless."[22] Yet for Dana, Padraic bridges the nothingness by replacing the father who never returned from a trip to the store to buy cigarettes. Padraic introduces Dana to the legend of her namesake, the Irish goddess, leader of the tribe of druids, Tuatha de Dannan, who "had magic that could control the sea, the mist, the sun, and the very sounds and shapes of the morning" (75). Dana's imagination is stirred with possibilities as Padraic talks "to her of somewhere different, someplace where her namesake had been long ago" (77). She grows increasingly self-reliant, learning Braille, painting portraits "of her own mythical Dana" (81), and taking walks alone. When she meets and becomes engaged to Will, she asks Padraic to give her away at the wedding.

Padraic is cynical on Dana's wedding day, but the "twisted affair" of the service, complete with its host of "freaks," inspires him against his will. His change begins gradually after his wife tells him to "have some heart," and "pushing at his ribcage," demands he follow Dana down the aisle. Padraic is taken aback when Will winks at him with pride, Dana pushing his chair, her face "creased into a tremendous smile" (84). Dana's transformation is suggested by her strutting, even skipping, along the aisle. Struck by the notion that the couple is "joined together somehow," Padraic does not comprehend when the aptly named Will says he has gotten his "legs back. . . . And a pair of eyes for her"

(85). Padraic's continued self-absorption is conveyed through his posture as "he shoves his fists deep into his pockets" (86). But suddenly he notices for the first time Dana's beauty. He becomes pensive and is embarrassed that he forgot to polish his shoes. Pulling his hands from his pockets, he moves toward his wife, who holds two glasses of champagne. Again the image of bread signifies a homecoming, a communion. Padraic nods to his wife, "slowly at first, like a bird beginning to peck at a few crumbs lying on the ground" (87).

## "Step We Gaily, on We Go"

Even more so than "Stolen Child," "Step We Gaily, on We Go" is rooted in Irish culture, although, like the former story, it is set in America, specifically New Orleans. McCann borrowed the title from the refrain of "Marie's Wedding," a Scottish folk song, originally written in Gaelic. Like two other works mentioned in this highly allusive story—Patrick Kavanagh's "On Raglan Road" and the traditional Irish ballad "Star of the County Down"—"Marie's Wedding" was recorded by Dublin-born Van Morrison, whose music, McCann has noted, he frequently listens to as he writes. The full refrain of the folk song reads: "Step we gaily, on we go / heel for heel and toe for toe / Arm and arm and on we go, / all for Marie's wedding." The title captures the protagonist's persistent optimism despite the fact that his "thick fists," which once made him a contender for the world heavyweight boxing title, now rummage through public washing machines in search of women's clothing (89). He takes the garments home to his wife—who, in fact, had left him twenty-five years earlier.

McCann based the story's protagonist, Danny Flaherty, on the legendary Irish boxer Big Jack Doyle, who was a friend of

McCann's grandfather, Jack McCann. Doyle, known as "The Gorgeous Gael," rose quickly in the boxing world during the early 1930s and frequently knocked out opponents in the first or second round. Like Flaherty he left his native Cobh, County Cork, for America, with a promise to return as the world heavyweight champion. Also like Flaherty he lost his only major American title fight. Doyle's loss to Bobby Baer occurred on 9 August 1938 in New York City's Madison Square Garden, a defeat from which he never bounced back; the fictitious Flaherty lost his major bout, presumably in the same arena, on 9 September 1938 to a man named Caffola. By the time he fought Baer, Doyle had become a notorious drunk who allegedly fought his bouts while intoxicated. McCann does not make reference to any excessiveness in Flaherty's past. The writer does, however, borrow a detail from a 28 February 1899 boxing match in which a boxer named Jack Bonner smeared mustard oil on his gloves in order to incapacitate his opponent, Tommy West. Flaherty's repeatedly mentioning mustard oil suggests his defeat may have come about illicitly—or perhaps he convinces himself that it has. Regardless, he once enjoyed international celebrity but, like his prototype, has been relegated to a friendless pauper's existence.

While the memory of his loss to Caffola haunts him more than fifty years later—the story takes place on 9 July 1992—another date plagues him more: 9 July 1967, the day his wife, Juanita, "slipped out the door" and left him alone in a foreign country, his own home "far away, far away" (110). Flaherty's marriage to Juanita is based on Doyle's marriage to Movita, an actress whose real name was Maria Louisa Castaneda, whom he brought back to Ireland from America. Like Flaherty and Juanita, the two toured England and sang in theaters, as Doyle was an excellent tenor. Movita, aristocratic and allegedly quite vain, left Doyle and later married actor Marlon Brando. McCann suggests that Juanita's liberal-mindedness and self-importance may have made her as poor a match for Flaherty as Movita was for Doyle.

Two important Irish literary influences apparent in "Step We Gaily, on We Go" are James Joyce and Benedict Kiely. Flaherty's stroll through the streets of New Orleans contains Joycean parallels, particularly in the stream-of-consciousness narrative that unravels in the minds of both Flaherty and Leopold Bloom. Like Joyce, McCann triggers memories or ideas by association. For example, when Flaherty nearly loses his footing descending a set of stairs, he recalls a line from "On Raglan Road" about "a man who tripped lightly along the ledge of a deep ravine where passions were pledged" (93). Such allusions are central to the story's meaning. In this case the passions pledged suggest Juanita's broken pledge or, more generally, the broken promise of Flaherty's youth. When he recalls Juanita's departure he remarks on "the sheer theater of it all, the wonder—gone. He had fallen to Caffola. She had fallen, not unlike a silver goddess" (110). Similarly, Kavanagh's poem concludes with the narrator seeing his own estranged lover among "old ghosts" on the street and finally acknowledging that he had wooed a mortal, "a creature made of clay."[23] Like many of Kiely's stories, "Step We Gaily, on We Go" is laced not only with Irish poetry but also with equally meaningful song lyrics, jokes, and even graffiti. In addition, the narrative voice is highly lyrical, making use of assonance, alliteration, varying metrical patterns, and internal and end rhyme in the manner of Joyce and Kiely: "A dirge of girls, one pregnant, prop up the streetcorner flower shop" (93). McCann's use of lyrical language heightens the pathos of the story, and the humor throughout offsets the tragedy of Flaherty's ruined life.

That the story will end tragically is foreshadowed in the opening line: "Give life long enough and it'll solve all of your problems, even the problem of being alive" (89). Like his father, who died when Flaherty was fifteen, he appears to have been "a hard working man, honest and doomed" (97). He misses the "garden of rock" in his homeland of Clare, which he swapped for a city "gray as granite" (110). As he delivers the clothing his now-imaginary wife tires of to the town prostitutes, he compares himself to Robin Hood, assuring himself, "There are Maid Marians everywhere, though the forest is paved over and gray" (94).

In reality Flaherty has become a parody of the man he was, an idea that McCann conveys through ironic symbolism. While his former protégé Tyrone Jacobs, whom he coached more than a decade earlier, is scheduled to fight a title match in Madison Square Garden the evening the story takes place, Flaherty "shuffles" around in the fierce July heat (92) and wears an old, heavy overcoat that is a bit too big for him, a mockery of the boxing robe he once sported. The thick brown belt that encircles his coat is a sad reminder of "a belt that he himself never won" (93). Flaherty does not get to hear the results of the Jacobs fight, for he unexpectedly fights his own last contest that afternoon. Having forgotten his hat, which Juanita bought for him in Ireland in the 1950s, at the Laundromat where he has pilfered his final dress, he returns, and his thievery is exposed by his nemesis, LeBlanc, the black rent collector at his apartment complex, whose name, meaning "the white," is a humorous assault on Flaherty's mild bigotry. Connecting with "an old man's roundhouse" (110), he finally feels vindicated for his loss to Caffola. LeBlanc recovers and chases him back to his apartment, where Flaherty turns to face him, stalwart to the end, "a huge skip of the heart" signaling his final fall (112).

"A Word in Edgewise"

"A Word in Edgewise" is a monologue in the style of Ring Lardner's "Haircut," though instead of a barber talking to a new client while cutting his hair, an unnamed beautician speaks to her deceased sister, Moira, while applying makeup to her corpse. But as in "Haircut" the reader learns more about the speaker than the speaker intends to reveal. What McCann conveys most pointedly in this piece is the good humor with which the speaker faces sadness and loss, a task made easier through memories and the power of storytelling. She literally laughs in the face of death. "Ah, it's a sad world sometimes, but it gives you such funny stories," she says (118). "A Word in Edgewise" begins with the speaker's recalling a poem "about a vase" (113), Keats's "Ode on a Grecian Urn," which focuses on just this idea: the power of story, or art in general, to preserve beautiful, if fleeting moments.

Despite its bawdiness and humor, "A Word in Edgewise" is a also a tale of disappointment; it calls to mind Yeats's idea that life is "a preparation for something that never happens."[24] Makeup has been a part of that preparation since the sisters' childhood, as they studied their mother applying lipstick and smeared it on their own lips, a gesture revealing their eagerness for womanhood and the relationships it promised. Yet the speaker makes it clear that after a few years of wanton sexual encounters, she married a man she could not love. Her response to her misfortune echoes that of many of McCann's characters: "Well, damn it all, anyway" (118). She is "happy enough" (122).

But life in her native Tipperary has become increasingly lonely and unfulfilling. Her children and grandchildren have moved "all over the globe" (114), she tells her sister and notes that it is "a terrible shame" to "grow up with an English accent" (116). The chemical factory that was supposed to bring jobs to the locals has merely polluted the river. She explains that the girls who still sunbathe by the river wear "little thongs thin as twigs" but concedes, "When you have it, flaunt it, I suppose. To hell with God and country." Then in the equivocal style of a Lardner narrator, she remarks, "Now I don't really mean that, Moira, but you know what I mean" (123).

Moira comes to represent the loss not only of a sister but also of more promising times, times the narrator seems to refuse to let go of, a fact suggested by her treatment of her sister as though she were still alive. At one point she addresses the corpse: "You have a body on you that the rest of us have always envied" (119). When she has finished applying Moira's makeup, the narrator is pleased to see she has restored a smile to her sister's face (126). Yet the word she uses to describe the dead Moira, *smashing,* which she repeats four times in the final paragraph of the story, echoes the shattering teapots and vases of the women's long-gone youth. The word highlights the collection's preoccupation with ruin and the fragility of life's beauty.

### "From Many, One"

"From Many, One," like "Through the Field," is set in Texas and features no Irish characters since it owes more to American influences than Irish. A starkly minimalist, highly symbolic, first-person narrative, "From Many, One" shows the influence of Raymond Carver. The plotline grew out of McCann's experience when he worked as a waiter at the Texas Showdown Saloon in Austin. When he inquired about the green and red quarters that often showed up in the cash register, he was informed by the bartender that strippers used the painted coins in the jukebox at a nearby club where they danced. At the end of the night, the club's jukebox was emptied, and the women could reclaim their color-coded quarters. McCann used this premise to construct a story about a naive husband who learns his wife is a stripper. Ultimately the man discovers a greater truth regarding the elusiveness of identity and his own presumptiveness (132).

The title of the story is an English translation of the Latin phrase "E Pluribus Unum," the motto embossed on an American quarter and the story's central symbol. Laura, the wife of the protagonist-narrator, spends much of her time painting quarters with various designs, often reconstructing George Washington's face. The title suggests that one face, or identity, can conceal many others. The coins convey a deeper symbolic meaning as well: they represent an extrinsically imposed standard of American value. By defacing them, Laura modifies their value, just as she redefines her definition of womanhood in reaction to a stale marriage. With her sexual liberation she gives color to what she must perceive as monochrome moral standards. After discovering her secret, the narrator is dumbfounded. After all, "she was from a good family," "good" because "her father was as an investment banker" (131). The unquestioned assumptions her husband maintains make her duplicity easy.

The fact that Laura paints her quarters in a greenhouse adds to the irony of the narrator's incredulity. Not only is the greenhouse a place for her creativity to blossom, most likely in rebellion to the expectations of her "good" upbringing, but it is also a place where she is working in plain view. Yet her husband is blinded to what she is doing and who she really is. The narrator, in his candor, lets the reader know how closed-minded and self-centered he is. He ignores his wife, and after only three years, both he and she neglect to acknowledge Valentine's Day. Like a "good" husband, he attends to fixing her car, but it is clear he is like the lifeless, if dutiful husband that the narrator of "A Word in Edgewise" has endured. He spends ten or twelve hours a day studying the DNA of sparrows, an activity that ironically suggests he knows more about the identity of common birds than of his own wife. He can only speculate on what her early life was like: "I guess she spent a lot of her teenage years doing paintings." He adds, "She'd always been pretty, right from the day I met her," unwittingly—and chauvinistically—implying that her beauty was worthless, or nonexistent, until she married him (131). He confesses inadvertently to his own artistic insipidness, and his frequent use of clichés further reveals his lack of imagination.

Like the other stories in this collection, "From Many, One" involves the protagonist's disillusion. On one of his wife's coins, he notices the motto "IN GOD WE TRUST" has been painted so that it reads "IN O WE TRUST" (130). In addition to its sexual implication—"O" being a demeaning synecdoche—the modified statement implies that nothing can be counted on. The story raises a question McCann explores more fully in later work: To what degree can we know others or know anything? He explains through his narrator near the end of the story: "I don't know much about things, but I know that it's amazing, the things we don't know" (133).

### "Fishing the Sloe-Black River"

Dermot Bolger, who included "Fishing the Sloe-Black River" in his anthology *Ireland in Exile: Irish Writers Abroad* even before its appearance in McCann's first book, aptly described the story as "Colum McCann's extraordinary marriage of magic realism and Westmeath."[25] McCann received his initial inspiration for the story when he was living in Texas and had a dream in which his mother was fishing in a river to find him. Thus the story begins with the intriguing opening statement, "The women fished for their sons in the sloe-black river that ran through the small Westmeath town" (135). Aside from the central idea of fishing for sons, the story is a realistic depiction of the effect emigration has had on rural Irish families whose grown children must seek work elsewhere. Eamonn Wall has treated its effect on both Irish children and parents: "If some sons and daughters are confused by unfamiliar terrain, their parents are devastated by the empty bedrooms in their homes, by the silence at the dinner tables, and by the photos on the mantelpieces of the grandchildren they rarely see."[26] His exploration of this theme felt "cutting edge" to McCann when it was published, but it seems "decidedly quaint" to him in the twenty-first century,[27] since—even in Westmeath—Irish emigration has become a thing of the past. Yet the story holds up as a beautiful depiction of loneliness and what one of Joyce's characters refers to as the only sure thing "in this stinking dunghill of a world": "a mother's love."[28]

The opening line can be interpreted in a number of ways, as the preposition *for* has a number of meanings: the women may be fishing *to obtain* their sons; or more literally, they may be fishing *on behalf of* their sons; or they may be fishing *because of* their sons. Most likely, all three readings apply. But the symbolic meaning is clear: the twenty-six women—one for each county in the Republic—are desperately hoping that their sons will return home. The river, dark as a sloe berry, hides the outcome of this hope and thereby allows the hope to endure. Freshly baked bread is, naturally, the salubrious bait they use.

Two contrasting motifs pervade the story: drifting and whipping. The low shouts of the women's husbands, who play soccer nearby "without their sons," drift "like lazy swallows" (135). "Drowsy clouds" also drift, as does a blue candy wrapper that gets caught in a gust of wind and floats down the river, an image suggestive of the town's boys, who two years earlier "had begun their drift" (135, 138). In opposition to this indolent drifting is the ferocious whipping of the women's fishing poles. McCann's diction conveys urgency and desperation as the women *rip* crusts, *impale* them on hooks, *whisk* and *thrash* their poles, *claw* at a reel, only to *haul* in an empty line; they are as persistent as the forlorn pair in Beckett's *Waiting for Godot.* With one image McCann symbolizes the plight of all the women: Mrs. Conheeny leans "against the river wall, tall and bosom-burdened" (136), sighing and casting. The image implies that, like her cohorts, she struggles with the weight of a maternal instinct that cannot be fulfilled because her sons are absent.

The husbands, in the meantime, lose another match, their physical aches and creaking joints analogous to their emotional pain. They have recruited whomever they can find to fill the field, even the hapless priest and local artist; but when Mrs. Conheeny's husband picks her up after the game, he admits, "We really need some new blood in midfield" (139). His wife meditates on the futility of their hopes: "One day she would tell him how useless it all was, this fishing for sons, when the river looked not a bit like the Thames or the Darling or the Hudson or the Loire or even the Rhine itself, where their own three sons were working in a car factory" (138–39). She knows, that despite his paternal stoicism, he too will go out that night, "silently slipping out, down to the river, to cast in vain" (139).

### "Around the Bend and Back Again"

"Around the Bend and Back Again" conveys McCann's concerns for the economic developments that threatened the Irish landscape and its heritage.[29] The structure and point of view of this piece help to create the drama that leads up to the unexpected climax, the dramatic suicide of the female protagonist, Ofeelia. The simple-minded narrator, Marty Lyons, unravels the tale in the form of an oral diary, providing daily accounts of the girl's behavior, which he perceives as "barmy" (142), though it is actually carefully calculated. As a result the reader is only slightly more prepared for the ending than Marty is.

Ofeelia's family were notorious misfits since moving to county Mayo from Dublin when she was a child and living in the abandoned caboose of a train. According to Marty's slightly skewed account, her parents were highly educated, her father specializing in astronomy and her mother in botany. They homeschooled the girl, awakening in her an appreciation for the wonders of the natural world, especially the cosmos, as her father created "maps" of the stars for her to navigate. When her parents were killed in a car accident and the bank claimed the caboose, her physical and emotional homelessness began. The girl made periodic returns to her home, crying and screaming and attempting to water her mother's flower garden. Marty claims to have observed her once "roaring her head off" as she stood under a bridge "freezing in the middle of the bloody river," a fitting image of her futile battle to defy the progress of time (144–45). She was eventually placed in the psychiatric ward where Marty is a janitor. After a mining company buys the land and turns the caboose into an office, the girl, whom the nurses have nicknamed "Ofeelia, on account of the flowers in her hair" (148), persuades Marty to help her sneak back for a visit. During a second visit she vandalizes some of the mining company's tractors and sets herself on fire in the caboose. The story ends with the hospitalized Marty recovering from the burns he suffered in his futile attempt to rescue her and considering his next move.

A reviewer for *Publishers Weekly* noted, "In 'Around the Bend and Back Again,' we ponder not only the tragedy of a fragile girl, but also the crucial tension between employment and environmentalism in an Irish town."[30] The story makes a point of the conflict between one's conscience and his desire for financial security. Marty displays an innate sense of compassion for Ofeelia—only partially motivated by sexual attraction—and a sense of attachment to the landscape, but these traits are superseded by his desire to gain employment with the mining company. He rationalizes the mining company's defiance of "the greenies," who insist "the hills are holy," with his clichés: "That's life, isn't it?" (152) "Jobs are jobs" (147), and "That's the way it goes" (147). But as he and Ofeelia approach the caboose for the final time, he observes a nimbuslike "rim of light around her hair from the stars" (163), and he gradually becomes inspired by her conviction, as she implements her destructive plan. After witnessing her martyrdom he feels a kinship with her and vows to return to "do a number on that caboose" so that "those mining boys never come back" (172), a possible suggestion of his own intentions of self-immolation. Colm Tóibín has stated that Irish "prose is attracted to fire . . . its sweeping destruction."[31] *Fishing the Sloe-Black River* contains several stories in which characters are set aflame to convey the book's concern with the "sweeping destruction" in these marginal lives.

### "Along the Riverwall"

"Along the Riverwall," the collection's only piece set in Dublin, uses as its central symbol the river Liffey, which represents loss that is gradual, not "sweeping," like fire. The protagonist, Fergus, observes the river "bellying down to Dublin Bay" (173) and filled with "the ruin of things" (182): "Shovels and stovepipes, coins and whistles, horseshoes and footballs. And many an old bicycle, no doubt" (173). To this collection of life's refuse the protagonist adds the parts of another bicycle, one his father bought him to replace the bike he was riding when he was struck by a truck, leaving him physically—and spiritually—paralyzed.

Bread again appears as a key symbol in this story, but McCann's use of it is ironic. Not only is the boy struck by a bread truck, but he is also "tossed in the air like a stale crust" (175), indicating a loss of vitality to which he has resigned himself. McCann's river imagery colors his inventive diction as the protagonist flashes back to his long stay in the hospital. Out of the window of his room he sees "a ripple of trees" (176) that appear to be curtsying, a sign of farewell to the simple joys he once knew when he "salmoned" through traffic on his bicycle (177). Now the "weeks rivered like months," and "the months eddied carelessly into one another" (176).

The "emphatic hope" (179) of Fergus's father leads the man to take a second job to purchase new bicycle parts for his son, but the unassembled bicycle represents Fergus's dismantled hopes. He knows the new bike is "a fossil . . . and the only thing it could be ridden with was a perfect cadence of the imagination" (180). He recalls his father's having once tumbled a refrigerator into the river when he could not make the payments and refused to surrender it to the collection man. He wonders if the door had been flung open, a thought that implies it will make a suitable coffin for him. Yet he does not plummet into the river, as the image seems to anticipate, but rather hurls himself forward into a mad wheelchair ride that suggests the liberating removal of his burdensome hope.

As in all the stories in this collection, triumph mixes with tragedy, and beauty offsets horror. McCann's language, for example, is lush, alliterative, and occasionally set in perfect iambs: "The Liffey guides a winter wind along its broad-backed banks," he writes (174). Yet in the following line, the protagonist, in his defiance, "lets a gob of phlegm volley out over the river" (174). A similar juxtaposition of the poetic and the vile characterizes the final story in the collection, which many critics also consider its finest.

### "Cathal's Lake"

Before the American publication of *Fishing the Sloe-Black River,* "Cathal's Lake" appeared in the Spring 1996 edition of *Story* magazine. McCann wrote the story while auditing a creative writing class at the University of Texas and "everybody hated it." The instructor, he said "didn't get it," asking whether the protagonist was "a magician."[32] Yet readers and critics have continued to discover the story's power, and McCann feels that—along with "Everything in This Country Must," which also deals with Northern Ireland—it is the most likely of his stories to live on. In her review of *Fishing the Sloe-Black River,* Bonnie Smothers wrote, "Like most lasting short story collections, this one gets better as each story is read, and the last story just nails the whole thing in place."[33]

In "Cathal's Lake" McCann combines history, magic realism, Irish mythology, and Jewish mystical teaching into what the *Irish Times* called a "fiercely imagined" story.[34] It opens with the memorable first line: "It's a sad Sunday when a man has to dig another swan from the soil" (185). The line introduces all four of these disparate elements. The historical event that causes the sadness is the Troubles of Northern Ireland. The magical realist element appears in Cathal's digging up of live swans. Irish mythology is responsible for those killed during the Troubles being transformed into swans. And the idea that Cathal "has to dig" has its basis in the Talmud.

The story reappropriates the Irish legend "The Children of Lir," in which the wife of Lir, king of the ocean, dies, and he marries her sister, who is jealous of the four children he deeply loves. Unable to muster the strength to kill them, she turns the children into swans. The spell, however, is only partially effective, as they maintain their human voices and are left with the ability to make sad, beautiful music. They are condemned to remain as swans nine hundred years until the bells of Christianity sound over the water. Alone on a lake on the day the spell is placed, they utter this mournful song: "Sad our hearts break for Lir, / red eyes searching the world for us, / hopeful in seeking shadows in forests, on mountains / seeking forms, in skies and on land. / Seeking his lost children torn from his bosom, / now in swam-form swimming, cold in waters of a / foamy strange shore.[35] The song of the children is a fitting lament for all the grieving parents, spouses, siblings, and children in *Fishing the Sloe-Black River* but particularly for the parents of the children whose transformed bodies Cathal must dig from the soil.

McCann has also commented on the influence of the Jewish story of the Lamed Vav Tzadikim, or thirty-six righteous ones, working men who must bear the world's sorrows. "There is one of these thirty-six hidden saints who is forgotten by God and has no communication with God," McCann has commented. For him Cathal is that forgotten saint. "Cathal was just cursed," he explains, "cursed to do this thing, cursed to bare the sorrows of what was happening in the North."[36]

Cathal's actions are an attempt to acknowledge the dignity of the lost lives out of which, the story implies, new life may spring. He contemplates the death of each, mourning a young boy burned to death, his life as unfinished as the sheet of homework left lying in his mother's kitchen. As in the previous story the boy's tragedy is accompanied by an ominous image of displaced hopes: "A pigeon flapping over the rooftops of Derry with a crust of white bread in his mouth" (186). As Cathal watches the newly dug up and released swan, McCann's poetic diction recalls another probable influence, Yeats's "The Wild Swans at Coole" in which the poet, his heart aching, ritualistically observes fifty-nine "mysterious, beautiful" swans.[37] McCann notes how Cathal "watches the wondrous way that the swan bursts over the lake, soil sifting off its wings, curious and lovely, looking for a place to land" (195). Amazed at the "miraculous hatred" in the world, Cathal muses, "Christ, the things a man could be doing now if he wasn't cursed to dig" (190). But "every man," he concludes "has his own peculiar curse" (196).

In "Cathal's 'Peculiar Curse': Politics and the Contemporary Writer," their introduction to *The Anchor Book of New Irish Writing,* John Somer and John J. Daly view Cathal's curse as analogous to that of the artist: "Colum McCann depicts the artist as one cursed to ignore his practical duties in order to respond with beauty to the world's ugliness. . . . To fulfill his aesthetic obligation of liberating beauty, then, the artist must embrace the human condition with all its confusion and corruption, both personal and political. In one sense, Cathal's 'peculiar curse' is the job description of all writers, but additionally, it is the destiny of Irish writers."[38] And writing in the *Boston Globe* on 4 December 1996, Robert Taylor remarked on the unusual afterlife McCann grants his dead in "Cathal's Lake" and also found a connection between his magical storytelling and the resurrection of the swans: "McCann's liberated swans, like his writing at its best, rise out of the earthbound and soar."[39]

CHAPTER 3

# *Songdogs*

McCann's first novel, *Songdogs,* was published in England on 12 June 1995 and in the United States on 30 September. McCann had begun *Songdogs* in Texas during the fall of 1991, while he was still working on the stories for his first book, and he wrote the majority of the novel in Kitakyushu, Japan. In 1993 the Irish Arts Council provided him a grant, and he continued work on the novel at the Tyrone Guthrie Center in County Monaghan, Northern Ireland, before completing final editing in New York City, where he and his wife settled in the fall of 1994. In many ways *Songdogs* is the offspring of *Fishing the Sloe-Black River:* idiosyncratic motifs recur, and colorful diction, vivid imagery, intriguing anecdotes, elliptical syntax, and rich figurative language become even more refined in this second book, which again nods intertextually to many of McCann's European and North American influences. McCann also develops central themes he explored in his first story collection. Eamonn Wall notes that "Sisters," specifically, "serves as the root from which *Songdogs* emerges."[1] Not only do both stories begin in County Mayo, but both involve a trip to America in search of a lost family member and in search of identity. Both stories are concerned with the need for a balanced life, that is, a life that is vibrant without becoming destructive, disciplined without becoming stagnant. Like "Sisters" *Songdogs,* as its title suggests, is primarily concerned with spiritual renewal. Conor Lyons's first name is derived from the Irish "Conchobhar," meaning "hound lover."

And *Songdogs* is a celebration of creation and re-creation, of life and art—a call to stand "on the rim of nothingness" and howl "the world into existence."[2]

As Mary Morrissy noted in the *Irish Times, Songdogs* is evidence that McCann had "found a distinctive voice," although she questioned whether he had "found his subject."[3] The *Observer* (London), on the other hand, called the book "hugely inventive" and "an exceptional first novel."[4] While many critics agreed with Scott Veale, who stated in the *New York Times* that "a first-novelish quality seeps in occasionally," the consensus was that, as Veale notes, "for the most part, Mr. McCann's hand is strong and sure."[5] As in reviews of McCann's first book, some critics found favor in what others disliked. While the *Independent* (London) criticized the novel as being tediously paced, lamenting the absence of "a car chase,"[6] the *Houston Chronicle* reviewer countered that McCann's attention to the poetic quality of his tale superseded his desire to write "a page-turner."[7] And *Publishers Weekly* referred to the novel as "a powerful, sometimes mesmerizing commentary on the nature of family and identity, memory and loss."[8] While the *Independent* reviewer also condemned what he considered McCann's conspicuous word choice, Veale pointed to his "keen eye and ear" and noted that his "language is full of sparkling poetry and images."[9] The British critic Hermione Lee put her finger on the nature of these conflicting opinions in her laudatory review in the *New Yorker.* She stated that the weaknesses in *Songdogs* "are tied in to the book's immensely promising virtues—its eloquent intensity, its passionate image-making, its magical feeling for space and place and time."[10]

McCann synthesizes mythological, literary, and biblical tales in *Songdogs,* while weaving together three separate plotlines, all leading to the epiphany that the protagonist, Conor Lyons, experiences on the novel's final page. This nonlinear style of storytelling helps shine light on the significance of past events when juxtaposed with the present—and vice versa. *Songdogs* resembles a slide show that has had several sections of slides shifted about. The story of Conor's return to Mayo begins and ends each chapter, while the other two plotlines—presented as flashbacks—unwind chronologically between these sections. In Joycean style McCann often moves from one story line to the next by means of association, juxtaposing related or contrasting images or ideas to assure a cohesive structure.

Also reminiscent of Joycean practice is McCann's use of a mythical foundation for his story. *Songdogs* is informed by the Irish myth of Finn, a poet who fished for seven years to catch the Salmon of Knowledge, which would transfer all the knowledge of the world to the one who ate it. Finn finally landed the salmon, but his servant Fionn accidentally obtained the first taste, and it was he, not Finn, who became endowed with knowledge. During the course of *Songdogs,* Michael Lyons, the protagonist's father, fishes for a salmon that seems to exist only in his imagination. The image recalls the title story of *Fishing the Sloe-Black River,* in which the mothers of estranged sons "fish" for them in a dark, drifting river. In *Songdogs* Conor's father is occupied with an equally futile task, as the salmon he fishes for symbolizes his estranged wife. The two other plotlines of the novel lead to Michael's current preoccupation: one traces his early life, marriage, and separation from his wife, Juanita, while the other maps Conor's quest to find his mother or at least to make sense of the events that led to his parents' separation and to his alienation from his father. Like Fionn in the Irish myth, it is Conor whose knowledge is increased as a result of his father's fishing.

As McCann has noted, Conor learns that "his father's obsessive fishing in the river was an act of love," and Conor, too, "learns how to love."[11]

Threaded throughout the mythical backdrop is a concern with the passage of time that draws on three primary literary works: Fitzgerald's *The Great Gatsby,* Keats's "Ode on a Grecian Urn," and Kerouac's *The Dharma Bums,* all of which McCann alludes to in *Fishing the Sloe-Black River.* McCann acknowledges his characters' Gatsby-like preoccupation with the past in the novel's epigraph, which appears only in the British edition: "So we beat on, boats against the current, borne back ceaselessly into the past." McCann captures this idea in Michael's lifelong penchant for swimming against a river current and in the symbolic salmon, known for swimming upstream to spawn.

At sixteen Michael discovered an antidote to time's erosive force: photography. And as Conor studies his father's old photographs, his descriptions of them read like a reworking of Keats's "Ode on a Grecian Urn," a poem that suggests art can preserve the beauty of fleeting moments. Another related theme pervading *Songdogs* is the danger of creating art at the expense of the life that art aims to capture; this becomes Michael's experience. McCann notes, "I realize now that I was unconsciously wondering whether I was going to be the sort of person who dedicates everything to his art to the detriment of my family."[12]

In this regard *Songdogs* seems to temper the theme of Keats's poem with that of Kerouac's novel. In both *The Dharma Bums* and *Songdogs,* art, in a sense, freezes time; but one's best defense against time's gnawing effects is constantly to renew his vigor and conviction for living. The most fulfilling times in Michael's and Juanita's lives are the days they spend at a fire watchtower in Wyoming. Kerouac's protagonist, Ray Smith, plays a similar role in *The Dharma Bums,* a novel that applauds not merely imaginative but physical and emotional engagement in life, or what Conor calls "a holy rage" (111). Conor learns that his feeble father still possesses this rage, even if it manifests itself only in his dressing flies to cast into a polluted river. Conor's return home results in a triumph both of the heart and of the imagination. Most important, he reconnects with his father and connects the pieces of his father's life to yield up a tragically beautiful story.

*Songdogs* begins with a vignette in which many of the apparently inconclusive strands of the story seem to find resolution.[13] That is, within this germ of the novel lies its fruition. The vignette recalls the narrator's having discovered two coyotes shot by a rancher and strung up on a fence post as a deterrent to other trespassing coyotes. The passage concludes, "*But coyotes aren't as foolish as us—they don't trespass where the dead have been. They move on and sing elsewhere*" (1). According to Navajo legend, coyotes, or "songdogs," sang the world into existence, and throughout the novel they are metaphorically represented as progenitors of both physical life and spiritual renewal. Conor discovered these coyotes, he notes, "just before I came home to Ireland," and they appeared to be "about to howl" (1), foreshadowing the rebirth he experiences when he—in both a literal and figurative sense—returns home. He becomes, McCann implies, his own songdog. The final lines in the vignette offer answers to two questions: What happened to Conor's mother, and will Conor remain with his father? First, the vignette suggests, Conor will find himself trespassing "among the dead" in Mayo, especially his mother who, the novel strongly suggests, "walked her way down to the river beyond" (208) in her despondent state twelve years earlier. Second, Conor will not remain with his father but forge his identity on more fertile soil, "move on and sing elsewhere" (3).

A seven-day time span encases the three stories that unfold, one of several biblical connections that prepares for the reconciliation and renewal involving Conor and his father. As Hermione Lee has pointed out, however, "the religion that this novel movingly extols is one of nature, art, and human energy, not of orthodox pieties."[14] Thus the days themselves have no biblical correlation; Conor arrives on a Tuesday and leaves the following Monday. On his arrival he furtively watches his father fish and recalls Michael's explaining "the law of the river" to him when he was a child: it "was bound to move things on" (5). Here Conor establishes the connection between his father's dolorous life and the sluggish, meandering river, and he begins to trace the journey that led to this state. *Songdogs* thus is itself a journey, one with archetypal, Dantesque resonance, with its pattern of descent and renewal, darkness giving way to light.

The earliest of the three journeys, Michael and Juanita's, is not intended to be as factually presented as the other two, which Conor experiences firsthand; yet this, McCann believes, is part of the beauty of storytelling. He has often posed the question, "Who *owns* a story?" The incidents that occurred before Conor's birth are based on stories told to him by his parents and Cici, a bohemian poet, and on inferences he has drawn from studying his father's photographs. Critic Mary Morrissy asked in the earliest review of the book: "Whose story is this?"[15] *Songdogs* is ultimately the story of Conor Lyons; it begins, however, with the birth of his father, a foundling left Oedipus-like on a mountain, an event that sets off the epic search for truth and identity that characterizes the novel.

Colm Tóibín has pointed to all "the dead fathers and mothers and dead children" that represent an absence of "domestic harmony" in much Irish fiction.[16] For McCann the loss of a family member shatters one's sense of home, uproots characters, and often sets them wandering. Michael Lyons could not be more rootless. He is born illegitimate; his father is killed in World War I before the boy's birth; and his mother abandons him and dies shortly thereafter. His early childhood is reminiscent of Huck Finn's; he prefers outdoor adventures to the refining influence of the old ladies who adopt him. His "unruly cowlick," which they attempt to tame, serves as a recurring symbol of his recalcitrance. Another fortuitous event colors his early life, as the two spinsters drown, leaving their fortune to the now twice-orphaned boy.

Wandering around the giant, empty house one afternoon, he discovers on old camera, the chimera that eventually dooms him. McCann describes this initial seduction with ominous, mythical imagery: "Opening the silver snaps, a pandora of dust arose around him, and he lifted the parts out onto the bed" (9). This camera "would burst him out onto the world" and offer him "the possibility of freezing time" (9). While weeds overtake his property, he treats his camera lovingly, even sleeping with it. This newfound art engenders a Faustian sense of power as he looks at the world "through a box-view" (9). Around county Mayo he becomes a sort of outlaw-celebrity who appeals to the vanity of girls wishing to be photographed in seductive poses. Hat tipped at a cocky angle, he stands in the back of the local church while the priest lectures the congregation on "graven images" (11). As for Joyce's Stephen Dedalus, art becomes Michael's religion; his studio becomes his church. But soon the torpidity of County Mayo overcomes him, and he heads to Spain, where he can photograph a war.

For Michael the issues of the Spanish civil war itself are not a concern, and he chooses to fight against the beleaguered republicans—and his friend Manley—because being with the fascist forces offers more photo opportunities. When Manley is badly wounded, Conor continues to remember him as the "sixteen-year-old with a lustful glint in his eye" that he photographed years before, "rather than a legless soldier who reeked of piss at night" (23). For Michael photography defies time and circumstances: "If a moment existed in a photograph, it was held in that particular stasis for ever," Conor says. "It was as if by taking a photo he could, at any moment, reinhabit an older life—one where a body didn't droop, or hair didn't fall out, or a future didn't have to exist. Time was held in the centre of his fist" (23). Yet while Michael achieves stasis with his photographs, he is also pulled by an insatiable need for movement.

A photographic image, not reality, beckons Michael to leave Spain and continue to indulge his rudderless journeying. While he seems to be attracted to the girl in the photograph, the sister of a soldier, it becomes clear it is the photograph itself that captivates Michael and causes him to accompany the soldier back to his native Mexico. The soldier becomes yet another ghost in Michael's life, when they are separated in Veracruz and Michael is left to wander the Chihuahuan Desert while absurdly searching for the photographic image. "Rivers of moments" carry him along, "ferrying his way ferociously to no particular place," Conor explains (31). But his art blossoms, and the characters he chooses to photograph along the way are the marginal types McCann chooses for his own fiction and whose beauty he likewise captures: "Color seemed to exist in his black and white shots," Conor notes (31); yet Michael's own life lacks the focus he manages so well with camera lenses.

In Mexico, Michael begins what later becomes a preoccupation with fishing, and the activity assumes its symbolic representation of desperate hope. Taking a job on a boat, he meets Gabriel, who in many ways foreshadows Michael's later years. Gabriel has a son named Jesus who, he hoped, "would one day walk on water" but instead "had walked elsewhere" (32). Gabriel shares memories with Michael of days when he was adventurous and vibrant. His affection for fishing resembles Michael's passionate love of photography; Gabriel even stores his bait in his mouth, believing it will garner a better catch. "If you want to be happy for a lifetime, go fishing" (32), he tells Michael, suggesting what a few reviewers have identified as a primary theme in the novel, one that calls to mind Hemingway's *The Old Man and the Sea* (1952): in the pursuit of a goal lies its fulfillment.

When Michael stumbles on the eighteen-year-old Juanita, "pursing her lips provocatively for his camera" (36), it is clear he views her as an exotic ideal, a subject to be photographed. But the couple is happy despite Michael's constant restlessness. They later tell Conor that on their wedding day they heard coyotes singing, a sign he has come to associate with the promise of new life, a promise that Michael will deflate. Juanita has a habit of assigning colors to various types of desert winds. A red wind, for example, blew desert dust. Such a wind blows on her wedding day, "stinging her bare ankles" (39), perhaps an intimation that she should stay in the open red country that will remain dear to her. Still, Conor notes, "The photograph in the church shows them smiling" (39).

The indiscretion that has characterized Michael's attempts to burst "out onto the world" with his art is evident in his photographing a child who has died in the local mines. And when a

San Francisco magazine offers him a job after seeing his mine photographs, he relishes the opportunity to move away from the land that had begun to "anchor" him. His journey begins sooner than planned, however. Michael had taken nude photographs of Juanita, and when a local man breaks into his darkroom, the pictures circulate, rumors follow, and Juanita and Michael leave Mexico in shame.

Juanita's homesickness begins nearly immediately, and she finds herself an accomplice in her own abduction. When the car breaks down, she tears a strip off her dress so that Michael can seal a hose and wonders, Conor imagines, at the first sign of what will become a life of self-sacrifice and alienation. He notes her attempt "to fix the car that was taking her from her homeland" (79). Abandoning the car in Tijuana, Michael and Juanita are offered passage on a cruise ship to California, and Michael attributes her constant vomiting to seasickness. In San Francisco Michael remains indifferent to her illness, insisting only that it is "a great day for a wander" (80). In a restroom at the magazine office she stares into a broken mirror. "She must have been amazed at what the cracks did to her face," Conor remarks, "fracturing her eyes down to her nose, sending cheekbones into a landslide" (80–81), a fitting image of her shattered and displaced identity. In the restroom Juanita meets Cici, whose immediate affection for the younger woman is rejuvenating. When Cici rebukes Michael for his lack of compassion, he responds, "We have to be somewhere" (82). He has learned that the job he had been promised is not available, but he is thrilled by the promise of another in New York.

It is 1956, and Cici personifies the nascent Beat generation, the details of her life serving as another nod to Kerouac. Like Kerouac, Cici has written a book inspired by a summer as a fire watch and, also like him, she types her work on a roll of butcher's paper, which becomes emblematic of her ceaseless energy. When Cici convinces Juanita and Michael to travel with her to Wyoming on their way to New York, they agree, and the bond between the women deepens. On the bus ride Juanita's sickness returns, and Cici, Juanita's source of spiritual renewal, feeds her bread. Cici fills the void that Michael's self-absorption has begun to create after nearly a decade of a fruitless marriage. As she and Cici hike five miles up a mountain to her lookout tower, Juanita is invigorated. Unlike in Mexico, there is no dust, just lush greenery, and the lookout tower resembles "a bird ready to explode into flight" (88), an apt symbol for the phoenixlike rejuvenation Juanita undergoes on the mountaintop with Cici.

Having been told by Juanita that they are staying in Wyoming, Michael gains a focus and a purpose for his life. Conor notes, "He began to give himself over to that summer . . . raging along with it all, catching the fires in their magnificence and brutality" (105). The fires that keep them alert and active mirror the passion for life both Michael and Juanita experience during the summer of 1956. And though time seems suspended in the mountains—the lingering days "stretched out on elastic" (106)—this joy must end. "Dawn had finished its rumour" (117), Conor notes, describing one of the final sunrises in Wyoming, as Juanita awakens feeling positive about her future with Michael; but this "rumour" is discredited as she realizes he is off somewhere. What follows, however, is another joyous morning with Cici, with whom she is clearly in love. While her friend sits on the edge of the tub scribbling lines of poetry, Juanita bathes blissfully in the trough and, immersing her head, comes up refreshed, cleansed. Later, as Juanita rises to fix sandwiches for her husband's dinner, her dress billows on a clothesline, thereby suggesting the emptiness of her life with Michael. The consummation of this vigorous summer occurs with "the hardest, purest, greyest, most beautiful rain any of them had ever felt in their lives" (122). But the rain not only extinguishes the fires, it snuffs out the passion that had characterized the summer, and Michael takes Juanita away from the liberating presence of Cici and Wyoming to the stifling confines of a Bronx neighborhood.

Much of Conor's account of his parents' life in the Bronx is based on a few photographs he found in the attic in Mayo, and for him they capture his mother's profound unhappiness. He imagines her longing for "Mexican earth, the good earth" (137), questioning why she is in New York, and wondering "if happiness is dependent on soil" (138). She wonders, he imagines, "if the weather that gives birth to the soil also gives birth to the unfathomable intricacies of the heart" (138). Wall points out that Juanita's need for the expanses of Wyoming and Mexico suggests the reaches of her imagination, which the bitter failed artist Michael forces into seclusion.[17] Their relationship suffers from continual "entropy" (138). "The world rotates on an axis of what-ifs," Conor imagines Michael musing. "What if we were somewhere else? What if we sauntered off and didn't come back?" (143). Juanita remembers Cici, and, Conor claims, memory is a reassuring reminder that she and virtually all McCann's protagonists cling to: "that there was a time of such splendid happiness, that there might be one again" (140). Conor contemplates one photograph where she is dancing, a bead of sweat running down her forehead, preserved in the way Keats's urn preserves the energy and anticipation of his wedding attendees. Conor imagines her eyeing the photograph: "I was dancing once, when I was thirty-three years old, and I didn't have a care in the world" (142).

Finally Cici visits, like an apparition, tempting Juanita to hit the road with her. She scoffs at Juanita's newly acquired kitchen appliances, which she refers to, quoting Kerouac, as "dumb white machinery" (145), symbols, for Cici, of the staid existence in which the couple has somehow become trapped. When Juanita informs Cici that she and Michael are expecting a child, Cici "tugs hard" on a joint; "suddenly a serpentine sweep of roads rises up in her mind, away from here" (146). Cici leaves while Juanita bakes bread, "waiting for the faint soothing thump of life against the wall of her womb" (146). But Juanita loses the baby and sinks deeper into despair; she writes to Cici, "Regretting is expensive, sometimes I wish I had gone with you" (147). Michael moves the couple to Mayo, ostensibly to alleviate her suffering. But she is cloistered in a farmhouse, where "spending years this way, slow as Sundays" (149), she stares at the colorless bog water. In 1970, when she is forty-two, Conor is born, and his life will represent a conflict between his father's selfish aversion to commitment and his mother's capacious imagination, which, Wall notes, manifests itself in her creative response to each of the dismal environments Michael inflicts on her.[18]

A key symbol in the Mayo sections of Conor's recollection is the stone wall Juanita builds, a fortress behind which she clings to her only hope: a return home. "It was her wall. It belonged solely to her," Conor remarks (158). It helped to "whittle away the days" until Michael (159), according to his promise, took her back to Mexico. Michael has little regard for Juanita's work, using the wall as a place to urinate, but for Juanita the wall provides a "crease in her boredom" (159). Another crease is provided by Mrs. O'Leary, the brusque pub owner who befriends Juanita and whose pub is emblematic of the listlessness Juanita battles in Mayo. The men rest on the bar all day "like dormant rags" (160), "scared of living, even more scared of dying" (161).

Despite his promise to Juanita to return with her to Mexico, Michael becomes increasingly distant from his family and preoccupied instead with his new darkroom. In one of the novel's magical moments, a sandstorm in the Sahara blows red dust all the way to Mayo, reminding Juanita of home. But her dream becomes increasingly fruitless, and one evening Michael returns from a trip to the mainland, drops a Pandora's box on the kitchen table, and cuts the string that binds it, a symbolic cut that will sever their marital bond for good, when the box's contents are revealed. Michael orders Conor to go for a swim in the chilly winter water and promises to join him. In a scene that signals Conor's ensuing alienation from his father, he no longer needs to cling to the poplar roots in the river but, "feeling that another skin had developed over my body" (169), swims deep into the cold, murky waters. He discovers a strange underworld, "immense and fascinating and slimy" (169), like the adult world he is beginning to glimpse. His father breaks his promise to swim with Conor, and when Conor surfaces for the final time, he sees his mother staring down at her crumbling wall. "I thought it would support," she muses (170). But the wall of Juanita's hopes is irreparable. Michael has spent a good portion of their savings to publish a book of nude photographs of her. Looking back, Conor imagines the book represented Michael's "epitaph for himself, a packet of light to emerge and print itself indelibly on his life, to say: *I was once great, look at these great photos I took, look how perfect they are, look how I once lived, I was alive!*" (171).

Discovering the photographs Conor feels "as if a big vacuum was sucking the air" out of him (174), his admiration for his father replaced by anger and shame. Juanita begins "buttoning everything up very high," as teenagers gawk at her through binoculars on the beach (178), and Michael stays preoccupied with flipping over dead jellyfish, suggesting his own dissolution. In a scene reminiscent of Neil Jordon's short story "Sand," a tinker offers Conor a ride on his donkey in exchange for a sexual favor from his "old dear." Conor is confused, but when he learns from classmates the next day what the tinker was referring to, he begins to loathe his father even more. Arriving home that afternoon, he finds his mother burning all the remaining books of photographs. "Out in the firepit she had burned herself, made a pyre of her past," he explains (182). One afternoon, Michael drops another box of books on the kitchen table, claiming "You won't be burning these" (186). Unaware that the books actually contain photographs taken before Michael met her, Juanita commits her final act of defiance, setting his darkroom on fire.

The rebelliousness of his mother's act seems to send Conor, now twelve, into an antiauthoritarian phase that will characterize his teenage years. Juanita, rendered nearly incoherent after her act, appears spectral as the two spend the night at Mrs. O'Leary's house. In Conor's final memory of her, she gazes in a mirror, apparently not a cracked one this time, "as if with love for what she might have come to terms with" (202). Conor, feeling "vacuumed and angry" (202), repeats prayers with Mrs. O'Leary. He describes the effort as "a litany of uselessness" and is conscious of the symbolic movement of "the exposed hands of a clock" (202). Juanita is gone the next morning and leaves behind "a small mirror catching the light" (203), a description foreshadowing the spectral "shining" salmon that flashes in Michael's imagination in the final pages of the novel (211). Rescuers halt their search for her because of a storm, which, the reader can infer, has carried her drowned body out to "some final, unalterable sea" (5). Michael immediately makes "a pariah of himself . . . his only occupation in life being the whisk of a fishing line in the air" (186). Aside from swearing at him, Conor rarely speaks to his father for the next six years, and at eighteen, he, like so many of his peers, emigrates to London. In a bookstore there, Conor flips through a travel guide to Mexico, and thus begins his own journey, in search of his mother and himself as he leaves home to find home.

Arriving in Mexico shortly before his twentieth birthday, Conor wanders around, directionless before finally asking himself, "What am I doing here?" (70). His wandering, he realizes later, was his reaction to "the lethargy of the present that terrifies us all. The slowness, the mundanity, the sheer plod of each day" (73). His search is burdensome, symbolized by his cumbersome travel bag. When Conor finds Cici in San Francisco, he asks her about the fires of 1956, and she remarks, "That's all anybody ever talks about. What it was like back twenty, thirty, a million years ago. . . . I think memory is three-quarters imagination. . . . And all the rest is pure lies" (112). Conor recalls, "Cici wasn't dying, Cici was her own songdog, Cici was still howling in the creation of other days and places" (102).

At a bus stop in Jackson Hole, Wyoming, Conor senses desperation among the crowd that seems to be "waiting for life to happen" (130), an unwitting personal indictment, and a reference to his father's early life as well. In Wyoming "birthdays pass," yet he appears to do little more than kill time (133). Here he encounters another unlikely role model, Kutch, the illegitimate son of Cici's former boyfriend, one of many abandoned children who rise above their inauspicious circumstances in McCann's fiction. Kutch and Eliza, his Native American mother, are dauntless environmental activists. In their presence Conor realizes that he is "paralysed by [his] own inaction" (134). It is Eliza who teaches him the legend of the songdogs before he returns home to find out the truth surrounding his own genesis.

The details of Conor's return, conveyed through strong religious imagery and language, make it clear that he will play the role of both redeemer and redeemed in the aftermath of Michael's fall from grace and his own rejection of his father. With his first words to Conor, Michael unwittingly initiates his son's role as savior: "Jesus Christ," he said, "if it isn't yourself" (13). Michael's final words before going to bed that night reinforce this connection and hint at Conor's own ensuing resurrection: "Conor," he states, "I thought you were dead, for Crissake" (25).

McCann describes Conor's arrival earlier that day with similarly religious overtones. His return is unannounced, and he remains hidden from his father's sight as the old man fishes beneath a poplar tree, the type of tree, according to legend, used for Christ's crucifixion. Conor notes that his father is as thin as the reeds out of which he himself twisted holy crosses in the winters of his youth. He also recalls his father teaching him to swim against the current, his mother on the shoreline waving, an ominous foreshadowing of her departure five years later. This image, however, serves a greater purpose as it provides the initial connection between Conor's mother and the elusive fish that Michael steadfastly pursues. He explains to Conor that afternoon: "I'd swear the fucken thing's taunting me. Up it rears every now and then and looks like it's waving" (14).

That night Conor bathes and feels rejuvenated by both the cleansing and the return home. He looks out into "the bible-dark of the Mayo night" (26) and recalls his bitterness toward his father on what he assured himself would be their final encounter as he boarded a train five years before. "I'm home now," he states, "and a million possibilities may still lie outside my window, curlews resurrected to the night if I want them to be" (26). His final utterance calls to mind his father's childhood tendency, mentioned a few pages earlier in flashback, to sling rocks at curlews—one of many spiritually significant birds in McCann's fiction. The passage also underscores a pervading connection with the Oedipus cycle of Sophocles as well as the book of Genesis, namely, that the sins of the father are visited on the son. However, Conor realizes, it is in his power to undo these mythical chains.

While Conor is pleased to be home, he also quickly realizes why he left. As Hermione Lee notes, while Yeats once referred to Ireland as "no country for old men," *Songdogs* reveals it has become "no country for *young* men."[19] The only change Conor notices is in the Irish coins, a symbolic representation of the change in values Ireland is slowly undergoing, one that Michael resents, just as he resents American accents. The land, however, Conor notices, does not "seep into" him like the land of the American West; "it's confined here," he muses, "doesn't feel much like mine anymore—it's like when I'm with the old man, floating around him, not really touching him" (94).

On Friday morning Conor stops by the river on his bicycle ride and experiences a Joycean epiphany. He realizes he has been living "a life of half-emergence. A consistency of acceptance" (101). He has had "enough of the old man's disease" and feels a renewed bitterness—and certainly some fear for his own future—when he returns to see him casting, "in the grip of some comfortable anaesthetic" (101–2). Conor promises himself that he will escape this life of "nothingness" (125). Visiting the seaside graves of the women who had adopted his father, he clears the weeds from their headstones, looks out to where they drowned, wades and dives in, and returns ritualistically to an earlier time. He becomes exhilarated in the darkness and "strangely light in the holiness of silence" (125). "The light hitting my eyes," he notes, "might have come from a star long imploded" (125), just as his own enlightenment has come from a deeper understanding of past events. "I felt alive at last," he claims (125); the waves seem to carry the voices of the old ladies warning him to be more sympathetic toward his father. He continues swimming and "saying hallelujah to the stars, rave on, rage on" (125–26), an allusion to Irish musician Van Morrison's life- and art-affirming song "Rave on, John Donne." Letting the waves carry him in, Conor clambers to shore, the first stage of his rebirth complete.

It is not until Saturday, however, that his understanding of Michael is genuinely altered. McCann conveys this change symbolically, as Conor, observing his father from the elevated perspective of a ladder, looks down through an opening in the barn roof. He watches the precision and artistry with which his father constructs colorful flies for fishing. Quoting an expression of his father's, the young man notes that Michael is "pissing on doom in his own peculiar way" (130). Conor seems to have his father, mother, and even himself in mind when he describes the colorful fly in all its "trapped motion" (130), suggesting the unrealized potential of the older generation, through whose example he can learn. McCann reinforces the connection between the salmon and Juanita, who loathed the monochrome life she endured in Mayo, as Michael explains to Conor, who now plays the role of apprentice, that "the salmon will rise at the sight of colours" (149). "It's all about balance" (150), Michael explains, a lesson he seems finally to have learned. As the old man works "in full and splendid concentration at the making of the fly" (150), he seems to control time, which moves "with the rhythm of an insect wing" (151). "Ya can make pretty ones until the cows come home, but if ya don't catch you're just taking a lash in the wind" (152), he says, his words conveying McCann's notion that art, like life, must be vital and purposeful. That night, Conor accompanies his father to his bedroom, and Michael puts his head against his son's shoulder before pretending to be asleep—clearly excited by the evening's camaraderie. Later, studying the "flies waiting, ready to burst into flight" (155), Conor flips a pair of tiny wings together between his fingers, signaling his own impending flight.

On Sunday morning, while Conor walks to the river to check on his sleeping father, he eats a tea-soaked biscuit, considering placing the Eucharist-like bread on his father's tongue, but he chooses, instead, what turns out to be a different rite of communion: he begins clearing the litter from the river. Significantly, his father awakens, joins in the effort, and Conor crosses the footbridge so the pair can work together. That evening Conor asks his father his burning question, "Why did ya do that to Mam?" (190). Insulted, Michael begins singing the chorus to the popular song "Hit the Road, Jack," another of the novel's allusions to Kerouac, for whom the song was titled, and a message for Conor to move on.

On Conor's final day, however, father and son attain a full reconciliation. Conor discovers on awakening that his father had furnished him with a blanket, pillow, and hot water bottle. Downstairs Michael has cooked American-style eggs, and while "rubbing his fingers over his chestbone" (193), signifying his own resuscitation, he watches the sun rise. Commenting on Conor's departure, he remarks on the tricky nature of time, to which he hopes Connor will not fall victim: "Sometimes you have too much time. Then you figure that too much time isn't any time at all" (194). Conor, still twenty-three, can not quite comprehend his father's meaning. He follows his father upstairs to chat while Michael takes a long overdue bath, and what follows is a baptism, confession, and communion. Referring to his perpetual remorse over the loss of his wife, whose dresses he keeps hanging in her closet, he claims, "We make our mistakes. . . . Then we move along. . . . You learn finally that some things aren't meant to heal" (205). As Conor helps him wash his hair, Michael plunges his head into the water, rises, turns his head, and explains that soap had gotten in his eyes. Here, Conor's father is the one who resembles the surfacing fish, suggesting that Conor himself has been fishing for his father and mother and has finally found them. Realizing Michael is crying, Conor starts to leave, but his father stops him, confessing that Juanita "could have walked her way down to the river beyond" (208). Sitting outside the room while his father completes his bath, Conor utters "The river, Dad?" (209). His father does not respond, but "the bathwater gurgling down the drain" (209) seems to answer the question for the reader.

Conor finally understands his father's connection to the river, and at dawn on his final morning in Mayo, when his father waves his arms in joy at the salmon he has imagined, Conor is no longer incredulous. "Yeah, I saw it," he admits (212). He imagines in colorful detail what his father "saw": "the flash of the belly shining" (211), his salmon caught, like the image of Juanita that remains framed on his living room mantle. The river, which in the beginning of the novel did not know "it was a river anymore" (3), suddenly knows "something about itself" (211): it is alive again. Conor has one hope that he addresses to himself and all the other symbols of ephemerality that surround him—midges, drifting clouds, swifts: “Let this joy last itself into the night” (212). This final section of *Songdogs,* a fine display of McCann’s uplifting, poetic power, ends with an image of Conor’s father “casting away as if there was no tomorrow, none at all, just casting away with all his might” (212).

CHAPTER 4

# *This Side of Brightness*

The 5 January 1998 issue of *Publishers Weekly* featured a starred review of *This Side of Brightness,* which began, "It's always a joy when a second novel lives up to the promise of a writer's debut, but this outstanding follow-up to *Songdogs* is a triumph." Commenting on McCann's ability to balance the novel's "pungent earthiness with a distinctly poetic sensibility," the reviewer concluded that "this impressive novel from young Irish expatriate McCann should solidly establish him in the international arena."[1] *This Side of Brightness* not only received critical praise on both sides of the Atlantic but also became McCann's first international best seller, with foreign rights immediately sold to publishers in Brazil, Denmark, England, France, Germany, Holland, Italy, and Spain.

Like *Songdogs* McCann's second novel focuses on a short span of days during the early 1990s—in this case not seven, but an equally biblical forty. During this time the protagonist undergoes a transformation while coming to terms with his family history. The stories of Clarence Nathan "Treefrog" Walker and his grandfather, Nathan Walker, are conveyed in alternating chapters, the narrative voice never explicitly revealing that Nathan is Treefrog's grandfather until chapter 10. Here the stories literally tunnel together, an apt metaphor, as the train and subway tunnels of New York City create a link between past and present and between the two characters: Nathan helped build these tunnels, and Treefrog now lives in them. The two stories merge at the moment when grandfather and grandson listen to a Baptist preacher tell the story of King Hezekiah, who oversaw the construction of an underground tunnel between two rivers. In the biblical story, the preacher explains, the diggers on either end of the tunnel, after taking meandering paths, finally met, and when the tunnels connected, "water began to flow between the two ancient pools."[2] An equally anticipated confluence greets the reader as the two strands of McCann's family saga converge.

McCann's interest in the men and women who live in the New York City tunnels was triggered in the fall of 1994 after he and his wife moved back to New York City from Japan. While attending a literary party in the city, McCann learned from an offhand comment that many people live beneath the streets of Manhattan. Intrigued, he ventured down to the tunnels the next day, continuing his visits four or five days a week for several months and befriending the inhabitants. He initially intended to write a story of an old Irishman who visits the homeless in the subways. However, during one of his visits to a tunnel beneath West Seventy-second Street, while "hiding from the Amtrak police" in a dark corner, he fortuitously discovered a plaque commemorating the year the tunnel was built. This was a "moment of satori," McCann says: "The very next day I went to the library on Forty-second Street and began researching how the tunnels were built. And there I found the true story of a tunnel explosion from 1905, where men were literally blown from the tunnels. I wrote a giant 'Eureka!' in my notebook and drew a crude cartoon of a man ascending towards heaven."[3] He explains, "I knew immediately that I wanted that image. In fact, I knew immediately that in some ways it would become a focal point of the novel, since I was aware that I wanted to write about resurrection in some way."[4] The discovery led him to construct a story involving one of the tunnel builders that would parallel a story involving one of the tunnel dwellers. He discarded nearly nine months of work, and after extensively researching the history of the subway system's construction, as well as interviewing both tunnel diggers and tunnel dwellers, he completed the novel toward the end of 1997. *This Side of Brightness* was published in the United Kingdom on 5 January 1998 and in the United States on 15 April.

Reviews of the novel abounded with literary comparisons reaching from the Middle Ages to modern Ireland and America. *Los Angeles Times* reviewer Richard Eder compared the "tunnel derelicts" to the damned in Dante's *Inferno*.[5] For Bonnie Smothers writing for *Booklist*, Nathan Walker called to mind "Melville's lovely Billy Budd."[6] In the *Independent* (London) Sylvia Brownrigg compared McCann's "rugged lyricism" to that of Cormac McCarthy, whose novel about outcasts, *Suttree*, McCann has credited as a major influence on *This Side of Brightness*.[7] Gail Caldwell's review in the *Boston Globe* commented on the novel's same "affectionate regard for yesteryear" as E. L. Doctorow's work and a "searing intimacy with the dispossessed" that recalls Denis Johnson's *Angels*.[8] *New York Times* reviewer David Willis McCullough praised McCann's "dazzling blend of menace and heartbreak" and fitted the novel among the recent "unnerving performances" by two other native Irishmen, Patrick McCabe's *The Butcher Boy* and Roddy Doyle's *Paddy Clarke Ha Ha Ha*.[9] John Burnside, writing for the *Herald* (Glasgow), applauded McCann's ability to find beauty amid "the drudgery and misery of hard labour" and placed the novel beside Michael Ondaatje's *In the Skin of a Lion*.[10] Ambrose Clancy in the *Washington Post* claimed that McCann warranted a favorable comparison with F. Scott Fitzgerald, as he, like Fitzgerald, "could let a story be carried by the sheer beauty of his sentences." Clancy also noted that McCann, in writing "an urban saga with a social consciousness spanning multiple generations," employed "the large canvas" that John Steinbeck once used.[11]

While McCann again pays tribute to Fitzgerald, this time with the title of his novel, which recalls *This Side of Paradise,* the influence of Steinbeck, as Clancy suggests, becomes more evident in *This Side of Brightness,* McCann's first socially conscious novel. While McCann's first two books make nearly equal use of Irish and American settings, *This Side of Brightness* is set entirely in America. Even more than its predecessors, however, McCann's third book seems to fulfill his intention of writing "about other places in an Irish context."[12] Exile, loss, and the inescapable connection to one's history—perennial Irish subjects—remain the novel's dominating concerns, and its primary focus is still the emotional struggle of the individual, and of the subculture he represents, to cope with these elements. The characters in *This Side of Brightness* are more downtrodden than those in McCann's previous work; yet they maintain a typically American frontier optimism reminiscent of that present in Steinbeck's *The Grapes of Wrath.* McCann has commented: "It seemed like such an American thing—to lay claim to a patch of land, to take on another frontier, only this one was a nightmare frontier, where people were taking their wagons (their shopping carts) across a whole different sort of landscape, they barter (for cigarettes) and they lay a piece of cardboard box (a flag) onto their own patch of land."[13]

While never an autobiographical writer, McCann chose for the first time a subject with which he had no familiarity and risked, he says, the accusation of "cultural arrogance"—a middle-class, white European assuming the voice of struggling African Americans.[14] Yet McCann considered the outsider status of his two central characters, who are both African American (Treefrog is also part Irish and part Native American), to be analogous to that of Irish immigrants. *Booklist* reviewer Bonnie Smothers was not surprised that such "a fine and bold writer" as McCann would tackle "the peculiar, unexplored, and violent nexus between the downtrodden and persecuted Irish and African Americans in a flawed promised land."[15] In fact, McCann's Irishness, he has noted, helped him maintain the trust of the tunnel dwellers: "I was never seen as part of the established order, the system. I was outside. And they were outsiders, too." McCann never pretended to be homeless, he says, insisting "homelessness is in one's eyes,"[16] nor did he place any of the homeless people he befriended directly into his novel. Treefrog, he claims, "is an amalgamation of many different characters that I met underground. He's also a sort of everyman."[17]

One fictional character who has affinities with Treefrog is Ralph Ellison's nameless protagonist in *Invisible Man*, a figure who also lives underground but ventures topside occasionally, as he, too, makes sense of the details of his past. Both protagonists set fire to once-valued items to signify the ascent they intend to undertake. Like Ellison's 1952 novel, *This Side of Brightness* is preoccupied with opposition: black and white, dark and light, ascent and descent, visible and invisible, good and evil. Both books suggest that the border between these dichotomies is absurdly thin, often no thicker than skin. "In the end, I suppose, we all share the same thumping blood, the same light, the same dark," McCann has remarked,[18] and his title captures this idea. As long as his characters maintain a germ of hope, brightness remains accessible to them. Until they move toward it, however, they remain in the margins. “Don’t crash,” Treefrog continually reminds himself, as he navigates his way through the dark with his symbolic maps and penchant for balance.

Another significant duality, which becomes a defining feature in McCann’s work, is the blend of brutal realism and poetic idealism. Even as a teenager Treefrog imagines life as “a symphony of misery and love” (216), an idea illustrated in the bathetic relationship between the homeless couple, Elijah and Angela—both ironically named—who beat each other before engaging in sex in what McCann describes as “a ritual of love and fists” (205). His realism often moves into the realm of naturalism. For example, after making love to Angela, Elijah steps out of his cubicle and urinates, “marking his territory” (69), and Angela, in her long, open fur coat, looks “like an animal that has been sliced longways, from neck to belly button” (65). Yet beneath the fur coat that she wears both to attract men and to protect herself from freezing, Treefrog locates a heartbeat, and his own heart is warmed by the contact. She epitomizes for Treefrog the nature of the world, which McCann describes as a mixture of “a palpable viciousness. . . . And yet a tenderness too” (216). At sixteen, Treefrog—still Clarence Nathan at the time—lies on his Harlem fire escape and listens to the sounds below: “Something about this part of the world seems so alive that its own heart could burst from the accumulated grief. As if it might all stumble under the gravity of living. As if the city itself has given birth to the intricacies of the human heart” (216). These “intricacies” are what interest McCann most.

*This Side of Brightness* opens with an epigraph from Louise Erdrich’s *Tracks:* “We started dying before the snow and, like the snow, we continued to fall. It was surprising there were so many of us left to die.” McCann, who considered calling his novel "We Fell like Snow," found that the epigraph fit with his novel's concern with "the anonymous, those people that are sort of forgotten about." He recalls that the line's rhythm and poetic texture "hit me in the chest."[19] The epigraph, which is the opening sentence of Erdrich's 1988 novel about the oppression and displacement of successive generations of a Native American family, refers to the multiple deaths of family members. While McCann's use of the sentence evokes the successive premature deaths of Treefrog's ancestors, beginning with his great grandfather whose body remained embedded below the East River, the term *fall* also has religious connotations, suggesting the physical descent into the tunnels, which serves as a purgatory for some and, for those in its darkest depths, a hell. Thus, a preoccupation with sin and redemption is triggered before the novel begins. McCann, like Erdrich, also uses the "tracks" his characters leave in the snow as a dual symbol. Like the train tracks in *This Side of Brightness,* the human tracks suggest an ancestral legacy that the characters inherit. In addition, the tracks that the tunnel dwellers—and Erdrich's Native Americans—leave in the snow convey the idea that these marginalized characters remain substantive; their ghostlike existence belies their indefatigable vitality.

The epigraph provides a smooth transition to the brief first chapter, "1991," which introduces the protagonist at a transitional point in his life and provides the seed out of which the major conflicts, themes, symbols and resolution develop. The chapter begins, "On the evening before the first snow fell, he saw a large bird frozen in the waters of the Hudson River" (3). Convincing himself the bird is a crane, a bird that held totemic associations for his grandfather, Treefrog preserves the image of the submerged, lifeless body in his mind. As he himself climbs into his "nest" in the succeeding pages, it becomes clear that the unfortunate bird is his analogue. He, too, is condemned to stasis, the metaphorical frustration of "attempting to fly through ice" (3). Yet Treefrog, after hurling the bricks at the ice with "ferocious intent," manages to free the dead bird, which floats "beyond the ice where the river flowed" (4), an image that prophesies the liberation Treefrog will undergo in the final chapter. The two tragic events that led to Treefrog's descent into this underworld are also subtly suggested: his grandfather's death on the tracks and his own separation from his daughter. Aware of the haunting rumbling of a train and conjuring "a vision of his daughter" (4), Treefrog plays his harmonica, "giving back to the tunnels their original music" (5), presumably the music Nathan Walker incanted in the better days, seventy-five years before, when the "equality of darkness" below the East River provided a respite from his own troubles (45).

In chapter two, "1916," the narrative travels back to those days, and in each of the even-numbered chapters in the first two-thirds of the novel, Nathan Walker is the focus. McCann's use of the present tense gives Nathan's story a sense of immediacy. When the nineteen-year-old Nathan is introduced, he is preparing to descend beneath the East River to do what he enjoys most: work. Having fled the racial oppression of southeast Georgia two years earlier, Walker relishes digging in the darkness beneath the river where "every man's blood runs the same color" (9). As Walker and the other men drop their cigarettes in preparation for entering the darkness, McCann compares the flaring "red tops of the butts" to "swarms of fireflies," a recurring symbol in the novel for the ephemeral presence of joy and hope (7). These are "hard men," who realize that death may be imminent or, as they put it, "You live as long as you do until you don't" (9). The men's faces, McCann notes, are "hollowed by the gravity of their work" (6), and his tone mirrors this gravity. He describes the economy and deliberateness of their movement with spare, precise prose in the style of Hemingway: "The men are beating the river and they are happy" (15). Walker is particularly fearless and exuberant; "he is alive, and in the yellow darkness he uses every ounce of his body to shove the river tunnel along" (13). He and his fellow diggers, known as "sandhogs," all immigrants—the Irish Con O'Leary, the Italian Rhubarb Vanucci, and the Polish Sean Power—are the unsung heroes of American progress, as they risk their lives in "darkness and damp and danger" (11), a truth that manifests itself symbolically when they are suddenly "blown upward like gods" (21). Walker, Vanucci, and Power all rise twenty-five feet on a geyser above the East River after they are sucked out through a leak in the tunnel in a surge of pressurized air. O'Leary never surfaces, and Walker begins looking after his pregnant wife, Maura.

Maura and Walker are both exiles, Maura part of the continuing Irish diaspora and Nathan part of the incipient Great Migration of black southerners to northern cities; and a longing for home, conveyed through images of flight, binds them. While Maura daydreams of "the ocher fields of Roscommon with a confetti of swans beating across the sky" (43), Walker is nostalgic for the Okefenokee Swamp with its dancing sandhill cranes. The swamp was his childhood refuge where, amid the shadows of the cypress trees, his skin color was unimportant. Walker recalls an incident in which he cut open a snake and nailed the skin to his bedroom wall, a symbolic crucifixion that suggests the sacrifices required of him by his own dark skin. His mother chastised him for killing the animal, explaining "that all creatures deserved the very same treatment, that none were mightier than others, that all were made the same" (46).

For Walker, Con O'Leary personified this maxim, and Walker tells Maura on one of his regular, furtive Sunday visits, "We miss him too, he broke the darkness for us too" (47). At a ceremony celebrating the inaugural run of the first train below the East River, bright flashbulbs annoy the sandhogs, whose humility is a stark contrast to the pride and vanity displayed by William Randall, the owner of the construction company, who exudes an "arrogant" fragrance of shaving soap and hair oil, "something the tunnel has never known before" (48). After a sandhog mischievously cuts off the power, candles are lit, and the sandhogs remember Con. Walker stares at the spot where the sandhogs were blown skyward, then "reaches his hand out and tries to catch the air in his palm, as if he could hold it, taste it, stop it, re-create the moment" (52). Suddenly he is mesmerized by the sight of children tossing candles about. He whispers to Vanucci and Power, "Them candles . . . is about the prettiest goddamn thing I seen in my entire life" (54). Like the cigarette tips and the fireflies throughout the novel, the candles symbolize the men's delicate hopes. Years later Walker explains the moment to young Eleanor, who is Maura's daughter, born eighteen days after Con's death, and whose name—cognate with Helen—means "light." "They was just like fireflies," Walker says, adding with unwitting Christian imagery, "Ya can take one and pin it on a thornbush, and it'll glow there for hours" (54). Con, whose surname means gentle, becomes a saintlike figure in the novel, martyred and suspended above the tunnel for eternity. Con once saved Walker's life after a racially motivated attack. Walker recalls Con's holding his "head against his white chest" and calling him "son," a term neither could have imagined would one day literally apply (27), when Nathan marries Eleanor.

Walker and Eleanor realize their marriage will invite persecution, but his hopefulness is conveyed in his teaching her how to crane dance on their wedding day. For Walker the dancing cranes of his youth represent a defiant celebration of life, and when the couple's son, Clarence, is born, Walker hopes to show him the dance of real cranes one day. As Walker weakens, the child grows, and Nathan watches him from a window high above the street. Envious of Clarence's youth, Nathan admires the "pure motion" of the boy doing his own dance through a series of old tires (108).

Clarence inherits not only his father's sense of moral decency and physical stamina but also the legacy of hatred, abuse, and ingratitude that Nathan endured. Having served with the newly desegregated army in the Korean War, Clarence returns home with a girlfriend and a missing eye and lives barely long enough to see the birth of his own son. One afternoon, while on her way to the Laundromat, Clarence's mother is struck by the car of a slovenly, drunken white neighbor. The neighbor, who is not arrested, examines the dents in his vehicle and swears, while Eleanor lies dead on the road, her grandson's diapers scattered around her. Clarence takes justice into his own hands, killing the driver and then a police officer, ironically with the handle of Nathan Walker's old shovel, before fleeing to the Okefenokee where he is killed by local police officers. Nathan Walker's first return home to Georgia after more than forty years is grim. When he arrives at the morgue to identify his brutally disfigured son, he is mocked by a police officer. Walker decides not to visit his treasured swampland since he prefers to preserve his childhood memories of it but instead returns to New York to bury Clarence alongside Eleanor.

Walker, too grief stricken even to consider revenge, sinks into a nihilistic depression of Hamlet-like dimension. He is unable to pray, as "prayers strike him as flaccid things now—useless supplications curling out only as far as the throats of men before falling back down into their stomachs" (175). He lies on his couch staring at the ceiling, "his body a dark room of nothingness, empty, vacant" (176). He resents the jubilant churchgoers in the street, whom he imagines lifting "their voices to some useless heaven. A unified song of self-deception. God only exists in happiness," he concludes, "or at least in the promise of happiness" (177). His grandchild, whom Clarence's girlfriend, Louisa, names Clarence Nathan Walker, lies in his crib and is to Walker "a meaningless blur of flesh" (177).

Walker's only consolation is that Louisa, who is of Chippewa descent, has vivid memories of watching cranes "going up in the air, wings fully spread" (180). Walker persuades her to imitate a crane dance and is transported into a timeless rapture. She creates "the most primitive of movements, dissolving the boundaries of her body. . . . he lets the movement surround him, breathe him, become him, ancestral and gorgeous" (181). Walker is surprised at the suppleness of his own body as he arises to embrace her. The pair moves to the crib, where Walker pronounces the phrase he used to utter to himself in the mirror during better days: "Clarence Nathan Walker, you are so goddamn handsome" (182). Here McCann inserts the anecdote of Nathan and his grandson listening to the story of King Hezekiah's tunnels; it becomes clear that the grandson is Treefrog, and the two plotlines dovetail.

As Nathan Walker's daughters marry and move away and Louisa's abuse of tequila develops into a heroin addiction, Clarence Nathan becomes the flicker of light in his grandfather's sloe-black world. Louisa's crane dances become less and less controlled, but Clarence Nathan begins to show a penchant for balance that will later torment him. His ability to scale skyscrapers looks ahead to the graceful, gravity-defying artistry at the center of both *Dancer* and *Let the Great World Spin,* courageous responses to a dangerous, seemingly meaningless world that recall the responses of Hemingway's boxers and bullfighters. One evening, as Louisa stumbles and loses consciousness while crane dancing, Nathan Walker slaps her awake, and McCann inserts a childhood reverie, recalling a lesson Walker's mother taught him regarding cranes—they always eat fish head first because, otherwise, the scales would rip their throat. "They just do it by nature. They're no fools," she explained. "They just do things the way God supposed them to do" (199). This essential lesson in moral integrity is one Walker begins to instill in Clarence Nathan, to whom he explains, "There's two types of freedom, son. The freedom to do what ya want and the freedom to do what ya should" (212). Walker means to prevent him from following in the tracks of his drug-addicted mother, a specter of "the girl she must once have been" (217).

Louisa's fatal decline is offset by Clarence Nathan's rise into the fearless, hardworking replica of his grandfather. His daring has garnered him a high-paying job building skyscrapers. Since childhood he has entertained the junkies on the roof of his apartment with his acrobatics, walking the ledge seventy feet above the ground, even leaping from rooftop to rooftop and performing handstands, "like a morphine vision, full of potential" (199). Clarence Nathan represents man at his best, all promise, unencumbered by the weight of worry, guilt, and self-consciousness that will plummet him from these heights to the tunnels. He explains his skill to his future wife, Dancesca, one afternoon: "All you have to do . . . is forget your body even exists. . . . It's all about forgetting where you are. Just pretend you're on the sidewalk" (208). Dancesca sits on the ledge watching him, "one foot dangling into nothingness, the other placed on the rooftop" (207). For McCann, like Hemingway, this is the precarious condition of mankind, a condition Clarence Nathan transforms into an aerial dance.

McCann depicts Clarence Nathan and his fellow workers, who give him the nickname Treefrog, with the same titanic imagery he used to depict Walker and his fellow sandhogs. They are paragons of masculinity, piercing "the virginity of space" with steel (229). Their "long spud wrenches knock against their thighs" (230), as they climb, in the same phallic manner as the shovels of the sandhogs. "The businessmen," McCann writes, "seem small and useless and feminine around them" (228). Treefrog, like Nathan Walker, takes immense pride in his work: "If he raises his head, a skeleton of his own creation rises toward a cloudless Manhattan sky" (229), an early prefiguring of his resurrection from the tunnels. McCann invests his prose with Nietzschean allegory. Nietzsche, who equated gravity with the devil, wrote, "I learned to stand and walk and run and jump and climb and dance."[20] Treefrog and his friend Cricket challenge each other in feats of bravery, such as walking with eyes closed at deadly heights. They swing on a steel ball from column to column, stepping into "nothingness" as if disembodied (231).

In Jean-Paul Sartre's terms, this invulnerability to "nothingness" transforms drastically into an obsession with "being" after Treefrog helplessly witnesses the death of Nathan Walker.

Treefrog goes from taunting the metaphysical abyss to being swallowed by it and cursed to verify and map its boundaries. After reluctantly accompanying his grandfather on a dangerous stroll along the tracks of the East River tunnel to say hello to the dead Con O'Leary, Treefrog reaches down to lift Nathan onto the platform, and one of his hands slips. Treefrog recalls Walker's final expression of satisfaction, looking up at him as if to say "What do we do now, son, now that we're happy" (260). Walker is killed by the oncoming train, his death occurring in the same subterranean setting into which Treefrog later retreats to forge a resurrection. "I was paralyzed," Treefrog recalls, "nothing there in my hands" (260). In the ensuing weeks Treefrog's penchant for balance turns into a tormenting obsessive-compulsive disorder. Haunted by the feeling of "nothing" in the hand that slipped from his grandfather, he begins touching everything with both hands, as if to ensure it exists. Naturally, this obsession inhibits his ability to climb, and on one of his last days of work, he sits relaxing with Cricket forty-seven stories in the air. In a vigil to Walker, Treefrog begins lighting cigarettes and tossing them to Cricket and is mesmerized by the "little red ends" (261). At one point he stamps a cigarette into the back of his hand and begins an obsession with self-mutilation that turns his skin into a mosaic of burns and scars. Mental and physical suffering become his defense against the nothingness, become his assurance that he himself exists.

Treefrog's self-torment is exacerbated the following summer when Dancesca encourages him to take their daughter, Lenora, to the playground on her eleventh birthday. While he is pushing her on the swing, his hand slips, brushing her on the side of the chest, and he is compelled to repeat the action with the other hand. Later, a similar incident occurs while she is in her nightdress, and he soon faces the accusations of a social worker.[21] His livid wife leaves with Lenora, and Treefrog takes to the streets and begins sleeping throughout the city. One day he observes a pigeon slip into the entrance of a tunnel, and following the bird, he descends into the "gracious" darkness, sensing "that he belongs here, that this is his place" (276). After repeatedly pummeling a wall until he bloodies his loathsome hands, he discovers his nest, climbs in and curls up, as if returning to the womb to prepare for his rebirth.

When Treefrog first appears in the opening chapter, he has been living in his nest for approximately four years. It is the eve of his forty-day journey toward spiritual renewal and his ultimate physical exodus from this self-imposed exile in Manhattan's underworld—fittingly, a forty-foot ascent. Chapter three opens on day one, as Treefrog is "waking" yet "thinks he might not wake forever" (28). McCann's opening line is as ambiguous as the novel's title. Is Treefrog afraid that he is dead, or does he fear he may not live eternally? Like the title, the phrase suggests he is teetering in the balance; yet the second sentence is clear and fraught with auspicious meaning. To "make sure he is still alive," he "touches his liver and remembers the crane found frozen yesterday in the Hudson" (28). Here McCann establishes Treefrog's connection with the captive Prometheus on whose liver vultures feasted in the evening; the connection implies that pain has become the defining characteristic in Treefrog's life, confirming for him each morning that "he is still alive."

In addition to mythological associations, Christian imagery pervades McCann's depiction of Treefrog's awakening. After he "lights a Sabbath candle" on his bedside table, he proceeds to warm his hands, which "seem disembodied in the candlelight" (28). The image calls to mind the portrait, popularly known as

"The Praying Hands," by the Renaissance painter Albrecht Dürer. Legend attributes the inspiration for this drawing to Dürer's brother, who allegedly spent four years underground as a miner to help finance his brother's art, thereby crippling his hands. On a secular level the disembodied hands represent Treefrog's sin, from which he wishes to separate himself, a literary device that has antecedents in other shame-ridden American literary characters: Sherwood Anderson's Wing Biddlebaum and Carson McCullers's John Singer, both of whom constantly conceal their hands, and Nathanael West's Homer Simpson, who wishes he could drown his hands. Treefrog's morning ritual above the flame suggests his desire to purge the sin of his hands, as he "enjoys" the pain of the heat. He maintains a sense of security with his morning rituals, the "most important" of these being his "ordnance survey profile," a detailed map of his nest that he has drawn and continues to modify, feeling around the cubicle with his eyes closed, engaged in what McCann's calls "the cartography of darkness" (31). Eyes still closed Treefrog navigates his way across a narrow beam, and descending a steel column to the floor, "he opens his eyes to the darkness" (31).

Sometimes the dark tunnel seems to be filled with suggestively healing waters, on which Treefrog envisions "a canoe being paddled with intent" (32), an image conjured from Nathan Walker's pastoral tales of childhood. He also imagines "his daughter swimming toward him, arms stretched wide; or his wife moving through the blackness . . . forgiving" (32). Below a ceiling grate, through which seeps "underground snow" and sunlight (35), Treefrog sees a mural by his neighbor Papa Love, a rendition of one of Salvador Dalí's melting clocks, the title of which, *The Persistence of Memory,* fittingly describes the cause of Treefrog's descent and looks ahead to his resurrection. As Treefrog tosses a rubber ball at the painting in his attempt to generate body heat, he aims to "hit the heart of the Melting Clock," a reference to his own process of thawing out and reviving his spirit; significantly, "the mural wiggles near clock hand four" (33), suggesting the end of his four-year sentence. As he stares at the clock, Treefrog's life is reduced to simple terms, both biological and psychological: staying warm and "keeping the ball in the air" (33). Warm, he "stretches out his arms like a man crucified," lifts his "filthy hands" to collect the falling snow, and proceeds to wash his body (37). His chest, "scrimshawed" with the scars of his self-abuse, calls to mind Christ's scourging (37). Finally, he emerges from the tunnel, "a solitary man," to dip "in the garbage cans of Manhattan" for cans and bottles (41); he is pleased at the prospect of "redeeming" them, though the splendor of the white snow above is still too much for his eyes.

While Treefrog's final days in the tunnel call to mind many forty-day biblical sojourns in which "solitary" men are granted an escape from worldly distractions—Noah's refuge from the great flood, Moses's stay on Mt. Sinai, and Jesus's fast in the desert—it also bears a likeness to an American literary antecedent: Thoreau's stay at Walden Pond. Thoreau aimed "to front only the essential facts of life and see if I could not learn what it had to teach."[22] Treefrog, too, is concerned with essentials, foundations, basic principles, in his need to come to terms with the world. His "nest" contains a "cave," which like Thoreau's woods provides a refuge where he can forge his future course out of the grip of the swift current of time. Furthermore, across from his nest is a stalactite-like icicle, which, unlike the rivers that course through McCann's other work, is "held in static" (64), symbolizing the barely discernable "drip" of time in the tunnel. As Treefrog contemplates the giant, primordial-looking icicle,

McCann comments, "The world, he knows, can still spring its small and wondrous surprises" (64).

One of these surprises appears in the form of Angela, who arrives like a savior "on the morning of the third snowfall" (64). This "angel," who stands "in the shaft of cold blue light beaming through from topside" (65), is an agent of grace as unlikely as those found in the fiction of Flannery O'Connor. A crack-addicted prostitute who "sniffs" the air for predators, Angela, nevertheless, hastens Treefrog's revival by reconnecting him with his past, initially through her resemblance to Dancesca. Angela, who has lived in the most dangerous subway tunnels, has come to Treefrog's tunnel in search of Elijah after she has been mercilessly beaten and raped. Thinking of her while she lies with Elijah below, Treefrog eats his Eucharistic breakfast, smiling, letting "some bread soften against his tongue" (75). When they meet, Angela continually speaks of how cold she is and questions why Treefrog "ain't cold" (83). It becomes clear that, like many of O'Connor's characters, she is an agent of grace, though not yet ready to receive grace herself. One night Treefrog has a dream that ties many of the novel's primary symbols together. Angela stands in his liver and digs out the filth. When she is finished, she and Treefrog dance around his liver and "are blown upward through his body and out his mouth" (85). Having purged every "ounce of pain" from his liver, she is the female Hercules, freeing him from the tormenting vultures. McCann writes, "Every now and then a dream can be impeccable in the tunnel" (85).

Another dreamlike vision that further accelerates Treefrog's ascent begins with a visit to the New York Public Library, where he enjoys the warmth and order that prevails. Here he becomes conscious that his body odor offends a polite young female student with whom he shares a table. His shame is heightened when he returns to the subway platform and detects the anxiety he triggers in an old woman who moves her coat sleeve to her nose. As with the encounter in the library, he wishes he could explain his situation and assure the woman that he, too, has his pride. He utters "Please," as the woman disappears among the commuters "swollen with shopping bags" (113). Shamed, he descends further, to "Burma Road," a labyrinth of pipes and steel girders, four floors below Grand Central Station, home to the "truly damned" (115). The hell-like denizens McCann describes "crouched under platforms strewn with clothes . . . high on steel girders, or in hidden cubby holes, or buried underneath broken pipes" (115) recall the reptilian creatures that surround the lair of Grendel's mother into which the epic hero Beowulf must descend to perform his purgation of evil. Bent on his own purgative act, Treefrog has come to bathe amid the steam of the dripping pipes. Soon he envisions the woman from the subway platform watching him. Her eyes, which are "carving their way through him," hearken back to the disapproving "razor blade" eyes of racists that Eleanor once described to Nathan: "you feel like they've just sliced you" (100). Like the shamed Adam, Treefrog "cups his hands over himself and hangs his head" (116), but the woman sniffs the air and nods with approval. As she vanishes in the steam, he proceeds to "wash himself clean" (117). Enroute to his nest he passes the empty playground where he used to take Lenora and asks her "ghost," seemingly in anticipation, "what is it like being alive and would I enjoy it?" (118).

When he arrives in his tunnel, Treefrog learns that another Prometheus-type tunnel dweller, nicknamed Faraday, was electrocuted while pretending to fish along the subway rails—perhaps McCann's most ironic use of his fishing motif to suggest the desparate hope of the abandoned. Faraday's death brings his aloof neighbors together, as they attend his funeral, agreeing—after accepting twenty dollars each from the trembling hand of the victim's father—to watch the ceremony from a distance. What amazes Elijah is that "Faraday had a family" (153), a truth about the homeless that McCann hopes will also strike his readers. The only character who does not attend is Papa Love, the most jaded of the tunnel dwellers and a significant foil for Treefrog. Papa Love is a disillusioned Vietnam veteran, a homosexual whose lover was murdered, and a potentially renowned artist who has turned his back on society. He has inscribed the credo of existentialism on his cubicle: "THERE IS NO SELF TO BE DISCOVERED, ONLY A SELF TO BE CREATED" (158). Unlike Treefrog, Papa Love is not prepared to return topside. Treefrog, while certainly undergoing a period of redefinition or "self-creation," is also learning the meaning of his ancestry—the "self to be discovered"—as he irons out his own identity.

A week before his ascent, Treefrog sits with Angela by the Hudson, as "the winter sun berths itself in the sky" and begins, tellingly, to melt the snow—signifying, as Tennyson would describe it, his "working out the beast."[23] "How come it's so cold and the sun still shining?" Angela asks, pointedly (186). The discussion turns to the rats in Elijah's cubicle, whom Angela has affectionately given names. McCann suggests the connection between these scavengers and the spiritually depraved homeless. "Someday," Angela remarks, one of the rats is "gonna take the bread right outa my hands" (187), an image that foreshadows Treefrog's healing communion with Angela.

That afternoon Treefrog draws the last of his maps, signaling the end of his prolonged contemplation and a step toward action. First he diagrams "the geography of Angela" (193), tenderly charting the topography of her face. Later he touches up the "landscape" of Dancesca and Lenora, charted years earlier, and wishes the maps would come to life (207). He draws his final map of his nest, perhaps unwittingly charting his exodus. Angela asks him why he draws these maps: "It's not as if you're going anywheres" (191). He later explains that he prepares his maps "in case God comes calling" (246). Angela asks, "You a Jesus jumper or something?" Treefrog responds, "No. It's just so He can find me" (246).

What emerges in the later chapters is one of McCann's key themes: the importance of balancing one's instincts with one's reason by remembering that one is indeed an animal but, potentially, much more—or less—than that. Treefrog in this respect strongly parallels Shakespeare's Hamlet, who asks, "What is a man, / If his chief good and market of his time / Be but to sleep and feed? a beast, no more."[24] Another of Hamlet's musings further captures the lesson that Treefrog is learning: "blest are those / Whose blood and judgment are so well co-medled, / That they are not a pipe for Fortune's finger / To sound what stop she please."[25] Like Hamlet—and Conor Lyons of *Songdogs*—Treefrog initially finds himself lost in reveries and "paralyzed by inaction" (221). He has a "tremendous urge" to speak to someone (220), to—in Shakespeare's terms—"unpack my heart with words."[26] Instead, he is called to act, and as he overhears Elijah beating Angela, he prepares to answer this call. "Slithering" away from Elijah's cubicle (221), he stands aloof, takes out his knife, and slices his palms, an image layered with symbolism. Treefrog is both Christlike and snakelike, piercing his palms and shedding his skin. His words recall Conor Lyons's preparing to plunge into the sea: "All this nothingness," Treefrog muses, "This cowardice" (221). As Elijah emerges through the splintering door, Treefrog floats "through the dark" and "stands in a definite circle of light" (223). Devil-like, Elijah tempts him forward with a crooked finger, and with swift strokes of his fist and spud wrench, Treefrog subdues this literal and allegorical enemy, who "lets out an animal howl" before falling (224). The protagonist has shed his old skin: "All the time, it feels to Treefrog that this is the first thing he has ever done in his life" (225).

Helping Angela up into his nest, Treefrog hopes he has freed her from Elijah's evil grip, but as they ascend, he notices "she seems to want to fall," acknowledging that she is not ready to make the transition for which he is preparing (226). As he assists her, he flashes back to his fearless days working on the skyscrapers. He is connecting with his old self, curling into a fetal position, and suddenly he pulls out his knife and begins cutting his hair and beard, commenting to himself, "I remember you" (247). Cleanly shorn, he lies down with Angela, and when she whispers, "Treefy," he corrects her: "Clarence Nathan" (250).

When Clarence Nathan arises, McCann offers one final disturbing, yet prophetic, image as Elijah tosses the body of Castor, Clarence Nathan's cat, into the nest. After burying Castor, his mythical dead twin, Clarence Nathan encourages Angela to follow him, assuring her he will find her some "candy" (275). His purpose is dual: to fulfill her father's broken promise of showing her the ocean, which in its vastness symbolizes possibilities (both for him and her), and to confess the circumstances leading up to his self-imposed exile and thus finally "unpack" his heart. On the beach at Coney Island, he completes his story, concluding, "a man needs time to bury his hands" (278). And as he burrows in the sand, he says, "See how they disappear" (278). He is referring not only to his vanished hands, however, but also to Nathan, Eleanor, Clarence, Louisa, Dancesca, Lenora—and now Angela, who has gone off to seek the candy man.

Clarence Nathan sleeps on the beach alone, his physical awakening paralleling his spiritual one. No longer in the time warp of the tunnel and with work to do, he is startled at "how quickly the sun rises" (279). His broken sunglasses further signal the renewed clarity of his vision, and he no longer needs them to block the light. He looks out to the ocean and senses an auspicious "shift in the weather" (279). His wounded hands have healed; he has "emptied himself of history" (281), and he is prepared to live in the present. He returns to the tunnel in "the sharp silence of a last snowfall," scrubs his face with the snow, "feels refreshed, vital, alert" (281). Moving toward his nest, he "walks quickly from light shaft to light shaft, enjoying the brief rage of brightness" (281). His movement recalls Nathan steering through the Georgia swamp, as "he moves quickly, with intent, solitary and sure" (282). Passing Elijah's cubicle, he hears Angela giggle, and realizes he must leave the couple "to their own brutalities and all the winters yet to come" (282). He envisions the ghost of himself, Treefrog, slamming his rubber ball against the wall for the final time, intent on keeping it aloft. His mind is filled with the visions of his history, and he nods to the ghost, who nods back in understanding. Noticing that "the stalactite has begun to drip" (284), he climbs to his nest, lights a candle, and a nimbus envelops him. Suddenly—though not "like a burning bush or a pillar of light" (285)—a lucid, unexplainable epiphany grips him, and he begins destroying the furnishings of his nest. He splinters his bedside table, hurls his maggot-infested mattress to the ground, and, finally, burns four years worth of maps, the flames a dual symbol of purgation and enlightenment. Treefrog dances cranelike across the beam in triumph.

While McCann concludes the novel with Clarence Nathan still in the tunnel, the allegorical imagery points toward his hero's redemption, whatever form it may take. He has bought his bus ticket to Chicago, and he will visit Lenora and explain the truth: "I was lifting the shoulders of Nathan Walker out from you" (288). He jumps down and climbs toward the gate, "hefting the weight of the word upon his tongue, all its possibility, all its beauty, all its hope, a single word: resurrection" (289).

CHAPTER 5

# *Everything in This Country Must*

In 1997, between the American release of *Fishing the Sloe-Black River* (1996) and the publication of *This Side of Brightness* (1998), McCann published a short story set in the Irish Republic and titled "As Kingfishers Catch Fire," and in 1999 he was awarded a Pushcart Prize for the piece. During 1998 and 1999 he published five more stories in major magazines. "Sumac" and "As If There Were Trees," also set in the Irish Republic, appeared, as had his Pushcart winner, in the highly regarded literary quarterly *Story.* The other stories were published in three of the most prestigious popular magazines in America. In July 1998 "Everything in This Country Must" appeared in the *Atlantic Monthly;* "Hunger Strike" was included in the November 1998 issue of *GQ;* and "Wood" was published in the 29 November 1999 issue of the *New Yorker.* "Everything in This Country Must," "Hunger Strike," and "Wood" share three elements: each is set in Northern Ireland; each concerns the ethno-political conflict between the predominantly Protestant unionist majority and the predominantly Catholic nationalist minority, a conflict euphemistically known as the "Troubles"; and each is told from the point of view of a child who has experienced a family tragedy that has hastened the child's transition into adulthood. Modified in varying degrees from their original magazine appearances, these three pieces make up McCann's fourth book, *Everything in This Country Must* (2000).

After setting two books partially in America and his third, entirely in New York City, McCann chose to venture back to the Emerald Isle for a variety of reasons: "I didn't want people to say McCann's gone and become a Yank," he remarked in early 2000.[1] Two days before this comment appeared in the *Irish Voice,* Charles Taylor, reviewing McCann's new book in the *New York Times Book Review* accused him of the opposite: "'The Troubles,' as they are called, are the albatross around the collective neck of Irish writers. Sooner or later, they seem expected to address it. It is almost as if an Irish writer who does not tackle the subject risks being deemed not Irish enough."[2] What Taylor failed to acknowledge is that McCann is not from Northern Ireland. The great novels that deal with the Troubles, such as Benedict Kiely's *Proxopera* and Seamus Deane's *Reading in the Dark,* are the work of writers who grew up in the North. Poets Seamus Heaney, Paul Muldoon, and John Montague, all of whom have written about the 1981 Irish hunger strike, were also raised in that region. As McCann told the *Irish Voice,* writers from the South have historically avoided the topic. "It's a risk," he commented, noting that fellow writers from the Irish Republic reacted as if Northern Ireland "was a foreign land, like Cambodia," on learning he had set his latest book there.[3]

Reviewers were quick to recognize that McCann's treatment of the Troubles is hardly typical; in fact, the political conflict is not his central concern. He explains, "It's about the glancing blows that kids get from political situations they don't entirely understand, yet the self-same situations determine the outcomes of their lives."[4] McCann assumes an unusual variety of voices in this collection: a fifteen-year-old girl, a ten-year-old boy, and a thirteen-year-old boy, each of whom reacts to his or her politically charged environment in a different way. Although he grew up in the Irish Republic, McCann remembers feeling the same confusion regarding the Troubles that his northern protagonists experience. In an 8 May 2007 editorial in the *New York Times,* he recalls visiting his mother's family farm in Derry as a child and hating the sight of "soldiers crouching in the hedges." He remarks, "I wanted desperately to know the why of Northern Ireland."[5] McCann credits his move to New York for distancing him and giving him a clearer perspective. "I just felt it was time to say something personal about the North," he claims. "It's very blinkered to believe you're separate from 700 years of history."[6]

For the first time American publication of McCann's book preceded the British release. *Everything in This Country Must,* two short stories and the novella "Hunger Strike," appeared in the United States on 7 March 2000 with British publication following on 11 May. Reviewing the collection in the *Boston Globe,* Gail Caldwell remarked that, among writers of what was being called a "new Irish renaissance in fiction," "none seems to me so finely imbued with the lyrical melancholy of the old masters—of Joyce and Yeats and, later, William Trevor—as Colum McCann." Caldwell referred to McCann's work as "equal parts death and beauty, its inescapable realism uplifted by an exquisitely soulful and visual prose."[7] Caldwell was not alone in also drawing comparisons with William Faulkner regarding the tragic voice of the young narrator in the title story. Nor was she the only one to comment on the book's brevity, which she blamed on "miserly" publishers. While acknowledging McCann's discipline and the fact that "it's more trouble to write a short book than a long one," Taylor in the *New York Times Book Review* found "the result . . . meager. . . . McCann has whittled everything—language, setting, character delineation—down to dry bone."[8] Many critics agreed in one respect: the prose is stark and restrained. But this trait was applauded in other major reviews. Joyce Carol Oates praised McCann's "understated, luminous language" in the title story; "Wood" reminded her of the "poetically rendered, elliptical fiction" of Joyce; and "Hunger Strike," she noted, is "a powerfully imagined elegy for the passing of youth's idealism" that recalled "the bittersweet, unsentimental lyricism of Edna O'Brien's early Irish stories."[9] *Irish Times* reviewer John Kenny remarked on McCann's "increasingly successful splicing of aesthetic seriousness with social concern" that gave the book "an unusual volume of density beyond its physical slightness"; he found the two short stories "flawless."[10] Maggie O'Farrell began her review in the *Independent* (London), "I knew Colum McCann was good; I just didn't know he was this good." Referring to his new work as "quieter" than *This Side of Brightness,* she continued: "That he can write so incisively, so perceptively about two such distinct environments is testament alone to his extraordinary skill." She concluded, borrowing a phrase McCann uses to describe the mountains in "Hunger Strike," by praising the "gift of simplicity" which McCann has "by the shed load."[11]

One influence, whose name eluded reviewers but whose minimalist style many of them seem to be describing, is Hemingway. Michael Pakenham commented in the *Baltimore Sun:* "McCann uses language punctiliously, fine poet that he is. His sentences are short, declarative, put together with tiny, minimalist, impressionistic descriptions." Pakenham also referred to McCann's writing as "painterly."[12] McCann has acknowledged a debt to Hemingway's slender *The Old Man and the Sea,* whose protagonist, Santiago, clearly influenced the creation of the old Lithuanian in

"Hunger Strike." Much of the Hemingway-like syntax is the result of the point of view in each story being that of a child. A look at the opening lines of the title story reveals a series of short clauses linked by *and*, creating a texture, as Pakenham notes, that is "vivid and clean"[13]: "A summer flood came and our draft horse got caught in the river. The river smashed against stones and the sound of it to me was like the turning of locks."[14]

McCann begins the book with a dedication to "Isabella and John Michael," his son and daughter, aged three and two, respectively, at the time. McCann has commented that he not only dedicated the book to them but also to some degree wrote it for them: "I think in a few years they will ask me, like I asked my old man, what the hell is going on up there?"[15] For the epigraph that follows, McCann chose the final lines of Paul Muldoon's "Dancers at the Moy": Horses buried for years / Under the foundations / Give their earthen floors / The ease of trampolines." The passage recognizes Muldoon, a friend and an early influence who himself grew up in Northern Ireland. McCann's use of these lines underscores his interest in the effect of history on the present. Knowledge of the past, his work suggests, provides buoyancy for the present. Muldoon's comparing the dead horses to trampolines is particularly significant, as it conjures a very modern image of children at play, an image far removed from but impacted by the days of men battling on horseback, whether the children recognize this fact or not. Furthermore, horses play a prominent role in Irish folklore, and they appear in all three stories in the collection.

### "Everything in This Country Must"

"Everything in This Country Must" tells the story of a farmer in County Derry whose favorite draft horse gets her hoof trapped in a river during a summer storm. With the help of his fifteen-year-old daughter, Katie, who narrates the piece, the farmer tries to save the horse from drowning. He is encouraged at the sight of an approaching vehicle which he flags down, only to sink into deep dejection on realizing that it is a British army truck. The farmer's wife and son, Katie reveals, were killed by such a truck, a tragedy that a judge dismissed as an accident and a loss with which the farmer has never been able to come to terms.

As the British soldiers take over the rescue effort, the farmer's initial anxiety over his horse becomes mingled with anger, hatred, and shame. Katie comments, "he looked . . . like he was lost, like he was punched" (6–7). His rage is heightened when a soldier places a jacket on his shivering daughter's shoulders." *Leave her alone, can't you see she's just a child?*" he hollers, shoving the soldier (9). It is clear that Katie is attracted to the men, particularly to one named Stevie, whom she watches with fascination as he enters the river after her father's failed attempt to free the horse's leg. As the first section of the story ends, Stevie is beneath the surface of the river, and Katie is "scared because Stevie and the draft horse were going to die since everything in this country must" (10).

In minimalist style McCann omits a description of the actual rescue, and the story resumes in the farmer's living room, where, to her father's chagrin, Katie serves tea and biscuits to the soldiers as the horse recovers in the barn. Tension between Katie's father and the men increases until one of the soldiers becomes indignant toward the farmer, resenting his ingratitude. Stevie, who seems to recognize the faces of the deceased family members in a photograph on the mantelpiece, calms the soldier, and the men leave. The farmer, in a fit of sobbing, goes to the barn and shoots the horse. He returns to the living room despondent, but as the story concludes, he is sitting in a chair, his face buried in his hands and no longer crying.

Aesthetically and emotionally engaging on the surface, McCann's title piece is laden with allegorical meaning that transcends its political context. On the surface it is the story of a man who shoots his favorite horse because it has been tainted by the hands of the enemy. But what he has also done is killed any trace of hope that his only living family member will remain with him. Metaphorically speaking, he realizes that, like everything in this country, the child he has loved must die. When Katie states, "I am taller than father since my last birthday" (4), McCann is implying that she has outgrown him and that she will move on. Unlike the father in "Fishing the Sloe-Black River," he resigns himself to the inevitable; and there will be no going back down "to the river, to cast in vain."[16]

McCann begins supplying clues to the analogous relationship between Katie and the draft horse in the first paragraph, and once the connection is made, the subtextual meaning of the piece reveals itself seamlessly. When Katie's father first addresses her, he has just discovered the trapped draft horse. McCann writes, "Father found her and called *Katie!*" (3). Having had no prior introduction to Katie, it appears as if the father is calling to the horse. Like the female horse, Katie is "Father's favorite" (3), his only surviving child. Unbeknownst to her father, it seems, she is quite promiscuous, having had at least a few "boys from town . . . come to the barn for love" (8). While the horse seems to have been tempted into the river by the scent of cut grass, the girl has succumbed to the temptation of her sexual curiosity. She is, however, trapped, like the draft horse, one leg trailing in childhood, the other irreversibly caught in adulthood. McCann portrays this duality in an opening image as she catches drops of water from a hole in the barn roof on her tongue, an image both juvenile and sensuous. As she attempts to help her father free the horse, she is "stretched wide like love" (4) between an overhanging tree branch and rock in the river, another image suggesting both vulnerability and maturity. As the father passes her the rope and halter to place on the mare, he shouts" *Hold it girl . . . for the love of God hold it please!*"(5), suggesting his own desperate and precarious hold on her. As the father plunges beneath the surface of the river, he clings to the root of a tree, his desire for stasis offset by Katie's clinging to the branches, a sign of growth.

When the soldiers arrive, their vigor is in direct contrast to the farmer's helplessness. The first of them jumps out to the rock Katie stands on, the phallic threat of his rifle banging "against his hip" (7), as the farmer sits staring at his horse "like a Derry windowshop dummy" (8). Unlike her father, Katie does not view the men merely as British soldiers but gives each a nickname based on his appearance; she refers only to her favorite, Stevie, by his given name. When he strips off his shirt she notices that he is "skinny and strong" (8), unlike her father, and more so than the boys who come to the barn. On her father's chiding that "*she is just a child*" (9), she covers her face and, childlike, peeps through her fingers as she feels the same embarrassment she felt in school at being more physically developed than the other girls and needing a bigger desk.

Stevie becomes a replacement for her father. He is the one who frees the horse, just as he is the one whose presence she finds to be a liberating alternative to her father's stronghold. On inviting the soldiers into the living room, she notes how they bring color to a home made drab by her father's gloominess. The green of the men's uniforms and the red of Stevie's blood suggest vitality. As Katie prepares tea for Stevie, they communicate without speaking and his finger gestures are unwittingly sexual. The farmer's anger continues to mount, particularly when Stevie smiles at Katie the third time. The number three is especially crucial in this story. Katie claims that the clock "ticked and ticked and ticked" (16), signaling that time is about to take the third family member, and Katie then hears "the sound of the bullets going into the draft horse . . . one two three" (17). While the horse had been in the river, Katie explained, her father looked at the animal struggling as if his wife and son were there. The trinity of bullets, then, signifies his having resigned himself to the loss of Mammy and Fiachra and, now, of Katie, who says with anticipation that Stevie has not come back for his jacket "yet" (15).

When the father returns to the living room, his face looks as if "it was cut from a stone" (16)—suggesting a tombstone—and he does not look at Katie because she is dead to him. Katie stands in Stevie's jacket, having shed the protective curtain in which her father had draped her. Katie had explained earlier that when the mare was trapped, "it was screaming like I never heard a horse before or after" (10). As she watches her father after the soldiers leave, she remarks that his sobs "came in big gulps like I never heard before" (15–16). The latter sentence includes a telling ellipsis: that is, she has heard and will hear these sobs "after." Her final lines tenderly capture the magnitude of her father's pathos: "and still the rain kept coming down outside one two three and I was thinking oh what a small sky for so much rain" (17).

McCann has expressed his hope that his title story would have international relevance. "From the get-go I wanted this story to be about an everywhere and yet deeply rooted in Northern Ireland. I wanted it to go across cultures," he said. "What touched and devastated me the most was when I met some U.S.

vets who were home from Iraq in early April 2009, and they read the story, then watched the film, and they said to me: 'I've been in that room, I saw that same girl, she wore a burka, but she was the same girl.' The thing for me is that I do, indeed, want that same girl to be alive in so many different places."[17]

## "Wood"

"Wood" was inspired during a visit to Northern Ireland when McCann heard someone comment, "Even a piece of wood has politics." He says, "It was a snatched piece of conversation that played and replayed itself in my imagination for years. What could it mean? In the end it meant for me everything—literally everything—in Northern Ireland has a political implication."[18] The wood mentioned in the title refers to poles that the child narrator's mother is hired to craft so they can be used to carry banners in the upcoming Orangemen marches. These marches are held annually by Protestants in Northern Ireland to celebrate the 1690 victory of the Protestant William of Orange over the Catholic king James II at the Battle of the Boyne, a battle that marked an enduring Protestant domination over the Catholic majority in Ireland. The narrator's father, who has always detested the marches, is bedridden as the result of a stroke, and the child's mother agrees to take the job without his knowing, as the family is in dire need of money. The woman and her son work in secrecy until nearly dawn for approximately seven nights until all forty poles are completed, McCann's fascination with religious numerology again revealed.

As has been his practice, McCann sought to create characters in "Wood" who defy traditional social stereotypes: "The father is a quiet peaceful man rather than some sort of rabid Orange-man; the mother is a rural woman discovering herself; the boy is the confusion between them," he claims.[19] These characters strive to maintain dignity despite the irrational political horrors to which they are inevitably, if unwillingly, tied. McCann has commented: "My mother, who is from Derry, would often look at the footage of the North on television, and she would simply shake her head and talk about the sadness of it all, how unbearable it was to watch. I think she represents a majority of Irish people—they are stunned, saddened, sickened by what is done in their name."[20] McCann has compared this victimization to "a sort of paralysis,"[21] an image that pervades this collection. Like the daughter in the title story, the child in "Wood" betrays his father's principles, although innocently. Yet the father in "Wood" is literally and figuratively paralyzed, an unwitting accomplice, whose wood mill is supplying materials for a parade that he believes "celebrates other people dying" (26). The father had once exemplified integrity, working with his hands to support his family from "last star to first" (32), but his inability to recognize his useless hands signals his loss of identity. As a result of his incapacitation, however, his wife begins to carve an identity for herself. She unmaliciously betrays him because of her family's sorrow and need, and her action serves as one of many examples in McCann's fiction of unexpected good springing from terrible afflictions.

As she and Andrew remove the chains from the logs they have hauled, it becomes clear that, rather than being further victimized by the helplessness of the patriarch, they are forging their own liberation. In the version of "Wood" published in the *New Yorker,* Andrew's mother explains to the boy: "I've never done anything before. . . . Not a single thing. This is the first."[22] McCann has acknowledged the "overt sexual implication" of the mother's cutting the poles, an act that he has said signifies "the chrysalis of a feminist agenda."[23] For the son the activity marks the assertion of his nascent masculinity and the forging of his identity as well. Ignorant of the political workings around him, he is awed by a newspaper photograph he once saw of the marchers; their white gloves seem an attractive alternative to his father's grubby work gloves, which he now wears and which, with his ill-fitting shirt, are signs of the father's displacement by the son who is not quite ready for the transition. While Andrew does a man's work, he still longs for his mother to pull him along on the logs she hauls through the snow.

Andrew's confused impressions of the adult world are the primary concern of "Wood." As he watches the concentric rings appear on a piece of timber his mother is cutting, he wonders if by cutting himself open he could "tell things" about himself (28). His conflicting motives are evident as he delicately shaves his father. His act is one of kindness and initiation, and he is careful not to cut him; but it is also a subterfuge, a distracting of his father while his mother collects the money for the poles. Regardless of the apparent necessity of the mother and child's act, "Wood" is a story of betrayal, and the image of a white eyebrow that opens the story suggests judgment. The ominous closing image of the story captures the boy's befuddlement with mankind, whose pettiness seems at odds with the well-founded integrity of the rest of creation. He stares at oak trees "going mad in the wind" of an approaching storm: "The trunks were big and solid and fat, but the branches were slapping each other around like people" (40).

### "Hunger Strike"

McCann had intended to write a story about the 1981 Irish hunger strike—a topic that, at the time, had been avoided by fiction writers—and to focus on one of the prisoners. After conducting extensive research on the strike as well as on the effects of starvation on the body, he realized the story "had to be told from outside the physical reality of the hunger strike."[24] He thus modified his original idea and concentrated on the story of Kevin, a thirteen-year-old boy from Derry, whose father had died in an automobile accident when the boy was seven. During the summer of 1981 the boy's mother takes him to County Galway, where she had vacationed as a child, to distance him from the violence in Northern Ireland. Shortly after they arrive in County Galway, they learn that the boy's paternal uncle, whom he has never met, has joined the hunger strike, a reality that the boy, gleaning bits of information from newspapers and from his mother, tries to come to terms with throughout the summer. As his uncle's body and spirit weaken, Kevin grows stronger physically and emotionally. Having arrived in Galway naive, bitter, and self-centered, he gains wisdom, understanding, and compassion by summer's end when his uncle succumbs .

"Hunger Strike," is founded on historical fact, but as in McCann's other historically founded works, the novella maintains what McCann calls "an imaginative distance."[25] The 1981 hunger strike began on 1 March when the Irish Republican Bobby Sands, an inmate at Maze Prison near Belfast, refused to eat until the British government granted political status to paramilitary prisoners. Sands, who died after sixty-six days, was the first of ten men to die before the strike ended on 30 October. McCann did not base Kevin's uncle on any particular inmate, although some of the details align him with Kieran Doherty, who like the uncle, was the fifth to join the strike and was twenty-five years old. Doherty was also a skilled chess player who allegedly carved a chessboard into the floor of his cell and played with paper chessmen. In "Hunger Strike" Kevin imagines his uncle as a great chess player. Like Doherty, Kevin's uncle takes part in both the blanket protest, in which prisoners refused to wear prison clothing, and the dirty protest, in which inmates refused to use restrooms or slop buckets. These similarities serve to ground McCann's characters in reality but are hardly meant to be read as history. And while McCann acknowledges that the protagonist, Kevin, contains "bits and pieces" of himself, "essentially," he claims, "he's made up from scratch."[26] McCann, who was sixteen at the time of the strike, felt a teenager would "be the correct vessel to carry all the grief and loss and contradiction."[27]

Susan Salter Reynolds, reviewing McCann's collection for the *Los Angeles Times,* commented on "the nexus of emotion, hormones, deprivation, and political imperative" McCann's protagonist is forced to confront, difficulties that make Holden Caulfield's crisis seem mild.[28] However, like the hero of *The Catcher in the Rye,* Kevin is an alienated, rebellious teenager struggling to assert his place in a callous world. For both Holden and Kevin, the journey reflects the inward confusion of the hero, who is torn between wanting to be a man—often associated with smoking, fighting, and sexual activity—and wanting to remain free of adult constraints. Both stories end with the characters' reluctant acceptance of a world in which their ideals are, to a large degree, ineffectual.

While Kevin's exile from Derry exacerbates his alienation, it also offers him an escape from the chaos of The Troubles and a chance to sort out his own troubles, as the division within him is clear. Kevin wears his father's shirt, a sign of his impending manhood; yet he crumples the collar in his rebelliousness, not wanting it to "look ironed" (45). McCann notes, "Inside there was still room for a whole boy more" (45), a "whole boy" that

Kevin is yet to discover. The idea of wholeness is a quality Kevin bitterly rejects; yet when he observes it in others or in the beauty of his surroundings, he is emotionally moved, despite himself. He cannot help but notice "the mountains stretching in the distance like a gift of simplicity" (45). The unspoiled landscape surrounding his mountainside abode provides a contrast to both the embattled city Kevin has left and the hubbub of the local town where Kevin seeks diversion amid the glue-sniffing teenage boys.

Kevin's nebulous sense of identity is further signified in a number of ways. Like many of McCann's rudderless characters, he has lost a parent, and his exile from Derry has augmented his confusion, making him think of himself as "a boy of two countries" (49). While he has learned to detest the British, he realizes that their language is his language and that the Irish translations of city names he reads on roadsides in county Galway are gibberish to him. Furthermore, McCann notes symbolically, as he navigates his way toward the city, "the road had no markings" (47), and he is forced imagine a white line to make his way. One of his fingers bears the beginnings of a tattooed word, unfinished because "he wasn't quite sure what the word should be" (48).

Incipient signs of Kevin's maturation appear one night when his mother suggests they play chess. At the kitchen table Kevin had been idly dipping bread into tomato sauce. As he lifts the bread with his fork, the center falls out, and he is struck by the notion "that the bread had lost its heart" (51). Once again McCann uses bread as a sacred symbol, but, for Kevin, the many sacred symbols he has been taught to honor have also become fragile and soggy. Later he observes boys inhaling glue from a bag, the movement of which resembles "the beat of a strange gray heart" (82). As Kevin's faith in divine love wanes, his reverence for both his father—who was, appropriately, a carpenter—and his uncle, a budding martyr, grows. In a moment laden with existential implication, he recalls his father's telling him "a man can make anything of anything if he wanted to" (54). He picks up the soggy bread, begins molding it into a knight, and starts to identify himself with his creation.

Kevin begins romanticizing, even deifying, the dying uncle he has never met, and he imagines a movie poster on which his uncle's face dwarfs the images of running soldiers beneath it. He carries a newspaper photograph of the man in his chest pocket. After burning the rest of the newspaper, he spits at the sky and buries his head in the grass while he envisions his uncle, whose face "looked like it belonged in a catechism" (59). He raises his eyes upward and thinks "that if there really was a God, he didn't like Him, he could never like Him" (59). Eying the horizon ominously "stained with sunset" (59), he curses God, an act rendered futile by the sea, which swallows his words. His uncle's fast is given biblical significance, as the devil-like British guards tempt him with plates of food. Kevin, in effect, assumes the role of disciple by embarking on his own hunger strike, which he endures for thirty-four hours before succumbing to a serving of chips, the vinegar of which stains his fingers, a pungent reminder of his guilt.

Kevin's anger and tension abate, however, during the patient, ordered playing of chess. A reluctant participant at first, he begins learning the rules and the patterns the pieces follow. He is particularly drawn to the "brazen and complicated" movement of the knight with its "solid breathing body of a horse, and yet something human too" (61). He recalls learning the word *centaur* in school. McCann's mythological reference underscores the boy's divided self, as his instinctive fits of temper are increasingly balanced by discipline, conveyed in one scene by his controlling a pinball machine for two hours with no more than the fifty pence his mother had given him. While running along the beach, he experiences a minor epiphany: "The sea no longer felt cold and in a moment he was running along the sand, kicking furiously and laughing, and the sea itself seemed doomed to the fact of his joy" (83).

Kevin begins to relish his own emerging manhood; he is proud of a single chest hair and compliments his physique in the mirror: "You could kick the shite out of someone. . . . You're the man for it. . . . I am indeed" (90). When his mother tells him that his grandmother wants him to remain strong during his uncle's crisis, he repeats the word *strong* impudently, noticing his changing voice crack and considering that he is "two different people within just one word, both a boy and a man" (92). The utterance suggests the difference between a strong boy, who imagines kicking "the shite out of someone," and a strong man, who is capable of looking after his mother. The precarious middle ground he occupies gives him the misguided notion that he can join the riots in his homeland; he boards a train for the North, only to be ushered back in tears to his mother by policemen who honor his childish request to activate the car's siren. Back in Galway he peeps through the window of a pub where his mother has taken a job as a singer. Previously scornful of this activity, he now resents the patrons who are not tipping her or applauding longer. As he listens she sings the popular Irish folk song "Carrickfergus," whose ominous closing lines seem to refer to his uncle: "I'm sick now, my days are numbered." When a patron blows her a kiss, the boy wishes he could kick in the man's teeth but instead snarls at a "surly and mistrustful" dog, who lopes away "to the farthest end of its chain" (102), a fitting analogue for Kevin's own constrained rebelliousness.

Ultimately it is an old Lithuanian couple whom he has watched kayaking, not the rebellious teens in town, who secure Kevin's attention. The old man, showing no tolerance for the boy's petulance or his cursing, begins teaching Kevin how to maintain balance in the boat and how to recover if he tips. The ocean, the emblem of wrath that had taunted him, is now under his control, and Kevin becomes elated, trying "to fight the happiness" the old couple's kayak affords him (107). As the boy learns to paddle with "smooth and controlled" strokes, the old man, calling to mind Hemingway's Santiago, tells him "that all good things were done with economy" (107). As Kevin masters the art of kayaking, he feels connected to his surroundings: "He felt as if the whole harbor was weighted down with implication, that each splash of the water had a meaning" (116).

However, on land Kevin's cynicism endures. At Catholic Mass he looks through the "high-windowed" interior of the church, a clear reference to Philip Larkin's nihilistic poem "High Windows." Receiving the communion host, he hears the words "body of Christ" as if for the first time and speculates about the hunger strikers possibly breaking their strike to receive the host themselves, only to die of starvation. At the end of the Mass, his mother elbows his ribs, a gesture signify the prodding of his heart. At home the boy reaches into his shirt pockets and imagines himself prodding his uncle's ribs. As he probes he imagines "he could feel the water swish in his uncle's belly" (119), as if he had pierced the flesh of the crucified Christ. As his uncle declines further, Kevin curses the man's stupidity but immediately feels guilty. He begins sculpting more chess pieces from bread, and after molding a queen in effigy of the British monarch, he bites her head off. When his mother urges him to go to bed or the bogeyman will get him, he remarks "Bogeyman. Christ!" (129), the juxtaposition of the two terms unwittingly conveying his disregard for both. As his mother relinquishes her attempts to discipline him and turns to her evening prayers, he continues cursing. However, the remarks are addressed no longer to God, but more specifically at the English queen and prime minister.

Kayaking in the harbor after enduring a three-day punishment from his mother, Kevin senses he has "achieved a rhythm with the old man" (133), as their paddling chases away thoughts of his dying uncle and the earthly troubles the man's suffering embodies. He feels as if "some invisible axle" has joined the old man and him (133). Kevin had learned earlier in the day that his uncle, going blind after fifty-one days without food, had issued a statement saying death was worth the cause he was protesting. As the kayak nears a group of seals, Kevin asks aloud how much power would be required "to club a seal to death" (134). When the man responds, "There's not much worth dying for," the boy resents the comment. "Especially if you're a seal," the old man adds, jokingly (134). It is unlikely his comment is intended as a rebuke to the boy's uncle; however, it is hardly an idle remark. The words recall the advice Holden Caulfield's former teacher, Mr. Antolini, offers to the frustrated teen: "The mark of the immature man is that he wants to die nobly for a cause, while the mark of a mature man is that he wants to live humbly for one."[29] When Kevin and the old man return, the man's wife comments on how tan Kevin's face has become, and he touches it "as if it didn't belong to him" (136), a bit of foreshadowing. On inviting him into their sparsely furnished home, the woman spots the boy's tattooed finger and utters "something quick and guttural" in Lithuanian to her husband (137). "You shouldn't do that," she chides. When the old man nods, the boy suspects "there must be a secret between them" (137). The exchange, coupled with their mysterious exile, which the old man has refused to discuss, suggests that the couple has survived the Holocaust, the woman concealing her own tattoo beneath her band of bracelets. As the boy leaves, she offers her sympathy regarding his uncle and whispers: "When you get older . . . you will learn that pain is not much of a surprise" (138).

A few days later Kevin consoles his mother, who sits with her "legs drawn up on the chair" (140), the parent and child roles seemingly reversed and the boy sounding "more and more like his father" (140). His mother begins wondering about his "poor, poor grandmother" (141), leaving the boy speechless, as he for the first time considers his grandmother's suffering and his mother's. Kevin's abandoning of his childish ways and his consideration of his mother mark a mutual rebirth in mother and son that is completed when Kevin suggests they go swimming. As she wades into the sea, the waves "break at her waist" and seem to Kevin "like the opening of hands" (142). He swims "in the salty darkness away from her" (143), and his initiation into manhood is complete. After they leave the water, Kevin helps his mother back up the hillside and thinks to himself "that his childhood had all of a sudden fallen away, that he had dropped it like a skin in the sea" (143).

On the sixty-first and final day of the hunger strike, the relationship of mother and son is free of its previous tensions. They play chess and agree to eat the opponent's pieces as they are taken, a symbolic truce that fittingly ends in a stalemate. The mother concedes the inevitability of her brother-in-law's death, and the boy consoles her, "You never know, Mammy" (144). Kevin makes another chess set, hoping to play with the old

Lithuanian man and, perhaps, solidify their relationship, but the couple is not around. So instead the boy walks around the town placing the chess pieces in a variety of seemingly random places. Yet the locations fit the pieces, some more pointedly than others. That the queen, for example, is left on "the weighing scales" outside the pharmacist's office (145) signifies a call for justice. As Kevin sits on the pier near the caravan, he begins to consider his uncle's physical suffering, the man's "body feeding on the protein of his brain now" (147). He begins to cry and then shouts "every curse he knew" out to sea (147). His mother, walking down to meet him, tells him, "Today or tomorrow" (147). As he watches the sun set, he is struck by its beauty, a "magnificent red" spilling "itself out generously into the sky" (147). Observing the seagulls and the waves in their seemingly laborious, repetitious motions, the boy thinks there is "a loneliness to everything in the world" (147). His mother tells him "to make sure he was home before night fell" (148).

The story's closing section begins, "The darkness was complete and already a couple of stars had risen in the east (148)," an image of light piercing the darkness. While the sentence indicates Kevin has not made it home before nightfall, it also suggests that the dark reality of his uncle's death has finally enveloped the boy. Yet the two stars in the east clearly point to hope, even calling to mind the Nativity. Having retrieved the kayak from behind the house of the Lithuanians, Kevin walks toward the waves, which roll "onto the sand like brothers" (149). But the boy does not feel any sense of brotherhood with the world. Instead he fastens the kayak to a life-preserver pole and begins assaulting it with rocks. Earlier in the story he assaulted the pole itself, imagining it to be a British soldier. Now however, the kayak, his source of solace, is being subjected to a scourging and crucifixion. He imagines a variety of horrific scenes in Northern Ireland as he throws a conspicuously biblical twelve rocks at the kayak before it breaks. After pummeling it with his bloody fists, he gives up, resting "his head against the coolness of the kayak" and weeping (150). When he lifts his head, he turns and sees "the light from the house of the Lithuanians," who stand with hands clasped, the woman's "large and tender" eyes recalling the eyes of his saintly looking uncle, the couple's door open (150). Like the couple, who understand his anguish, and like the other young protagonists in *Everything in This Country Must,* he will learn to live in this world.

CHAPTER 6

# *Dancer*

In an interview published in the July 1998 *Atlantic Monthly,* Colum McCann explained why he avoids incorporating stories about real people into his fiction. "I think ripping off people's lives is dangerous," he stated. "It also lacks imagination. . . . I think it's better to work in the imagination than in the real."[1] Yet the following summer he began work on *Dancer,* a novel based on the life of the Russian ballet star Rudolf Nureyev. "At the time I really believed that [the writer should avoid basing characters on real people]," McCann remarked in 2009, "which just goes to show you that you can never believe anybody at all: especially authors. Our hearts, our heads, our imaginative quests are continually changing and evolving."[2]

McCann's decision to write a fictionalized account of Nureyev is only partially inconsistent with his statement regarding "ripping off people's lives." First, he was primarily referring to the dangers of basing fiction on the lives of personal acquaintances or, as he put it, on "stories people have told me."[3] "I always felt," he remarked later, "that Rudi was more than able to look after himself."[4] Second, reviewers were quick to notice that if *Dancer* lacked anything, it was facts—certainly not imagination. One reviewer wrote: "Any notion that McCann's fictional account of Rudolf Nureyev's life is a novelistic shortcut, an easier task than creating an original character, is swiftly dispelled within the first few pages."[5] *Dancer* actually epitomizes McCann's contention that one should not write about what he knows but about what he wants to know. Before embarking on intense research and a lengthy visit to Nureyev's homeland, McCann claims, he "knew nothing about dancing, nothing about Russia."[6]

Although it at first seems markedly different from McCann's previous four books in both style and content, *Dancer* is not so much a step in a new direction as a pivotal work in his artistic development; it grows organically out of his original aesthetic and thematic predilections. The novel continues his exploration of subjects he has treated since *Fishing the Sloe-Black River:* identity, love, loss, fame, war, sexuality, betrayal, family, emigration, art, perseverance and—most notably—physical and emotional exile. "I was attracted to the century's greatest exile," McCann has commented. "Rudi was a man who could go literally everywhere, from Princess Grace's living room to Mick Jagger's dressing room, but he could not go home. And in the end we all want to be able to go home."[7] In addition to its concern with the longing for home, *Dancer* explores other themes treated in McCann's earlier books, including the life-affirming value of work, the elusive nature of identity, the pain of having passed one's prime, the power of filial and fraternal bonds, and the transience of time. Perhaps above all *Dancer* explores with conviction a theme touched on in *Songdogs* and one that becomes a major concern of McCann's work: the legitimacy of so called "facts" and the nebulous distinction between nonfiction and fiction.

*Dancer* is composed of a panorama of voices, much like the stories in McCann's first collection; in fact, the novel is as much the saga of the fictionalized Nureyev's shoemaker, his housekeeper, the husband and daughter of his first dance teacher, and an interior decorator named Victor as it is about Nureyev. The real-life Nureyev was a pioneer of the burgeoning class of international mongrels, with which McCann, an Irish New Yorker preparing to immerse himself in Russian culture, had long identified. Nureyev told a *Newsweek* reporter during a visit to the United States with London's Royal Ballet in 1965: "I have no country. For me a country is just a place to dance. Your roots are your work. Work is sacred." Describing his choreography he explained in broken English: "Here is Russian, teaching English girls how to be Spanish gypsies in the French language."[8] Yet for McCann, *Dancer,* his first book to include no major Irish characters, is nonetheless characteristically Irish. When asked by an interviewer what he found on his visit to Russia, he responded, "Vodka. Song. Sadness. Poetry. Exile. Violence. In other words, I found Ireland."[9] In fact, McCann's initial inspiration for *Dancer* has Irish origins. Around the time he was completing *Everything in This Country Must* and was "casting around for a novel that would cross all sorts of international borders and barriers," he stumbled accidentally on the idea:

> I was out in Manhattan with a friend of mine, Jimmy, who grew up in Ireland. He told me that when he was a seven-year-old boy in the early 70's, he lived in the flats of Ballymun, a really poor area of Dublin. His father used to come home almost every night and severely beat up his family. But then one night the father came home sober—and carrying a television set. The whole family gathered around the television. At first they couldn't get any reception, there was just snow, and so Jimmy was given the worst beating of his life, one he'd never forget. Later that night when he woke up he went into the living room, alone. And he plugged the tv into an extension cord and started carrying it around the room in his arms. The very first image that appeared on

> the screen was . . . Rudolf Nureyev dancing. Extraordinary! And so Rudi was all at once a father figure, a celebrity, a guide and a vision to a boy he never even met.[10]

McCann, who did not use his friend's story in *Dancer,* was fascinated by the image of this forlorn boy cradling the monochrome twentieth-century demigod. "I began to wonder what it is about our world that allows a Russian dancer to penetrate the life of a working-class Dublin boy." The image appealed not only to McCann's fascination with connectedness but also his desire to write about "the small corners that don't get talked about anywhere else."[11]

As he began to read about Nureyev, McCann "was immediately enthralled by his life, the charm of it, the recklessness, the beauty, the ruin." Yet he did not aspire to write a biographical novel. "I didn't want to catalogue his life," he has stated, "I wanted to capture the spirit of it."[12] In preparing to write *Dancer,* therefore, McCann chose not to interview Nureyev's friends, family, or acquaintances. Yet after its completion, the novel received the warm approval of many who knew Nureyev, including a former lover, the film director Wallace Potts, who told McCann that "he had captured both the angel and the devil in his dead friend."[13] Potts, who died in 2006, was a major archivist for the Rudolf Nureyev Foundation, a group whose website praises *Dancer* as a "must read," noting that it presents a "more authentic" depiction of Nureyev than many of the biographies.[14] After reading these biographies, watching documentaries, and researching subjects ranging from the construction of ballet slippers to the types of guns used by Russian infantry during World War II, McCann began constructing scenes for the novel, using the "multiple narrative viewpoints and the camera eye technique."[15] He has acknowledged a debt for this stylistic approach to John Dos Passos as well as such later "literary heroes" as John Berger, E. L. Doctorow, Toni Morrison, Peter Carey, and Michael Ondaatje, whose novel *Coming through Slaughter* has particularly strong affinities with *Dancer*—not only in its patchwork of narrative sources but also in its concern with the ultimately unknowable character of its mythical fallen protagonist, the trumpet player Buddy Bolden. Next McCann traveled to Russia, where rather than visit the places Nureyev frequented, he "hung out in stairwells . . . listening to the sights and sounds of the Russian people."[16] He notes, "I can learn as much from a smashed bottle in the stairwell as I can from a whole book about violence."[17] He also visited military hospitals and poured over the work of the Russian writers Boris Pasternak, Osip Mandelstam, and Alexander Pushkin, to get a sense of "the atmosphere of the U.S.S.R."[18]

After nearly four years of work, *Dancer* was published in America on 6 January 2003, the tenth anniversary of Rudolf Nureyev's death. After its British release three days later, it climbed to the top of the best-seller lists in England, then Ireland, and, not long after, France and Germany. For the first time, an absolute consensus bound even the most critical reviewers regarding the poetic and imaginative triumph of *Dancer.* In his interview with McCann in *Publishers Weekly,* Adam Dunn called it "a noteworthy literary achievement: a seamless narrative with a constantly roving point of view."[19] As a reviewer for the *Irish Times* put it, McCann had "matured with impressive speed over the past few years."[20] Many drew an analogy between McCann's prose and dance. Peter Kurth of the *New York Times* referred to *Dancer* in his review titled "A Story with Legs" as a "beautiful floating novel."[21] Quoting *Dancer,* the *Chicago Tribune* claimed McCann's "dazzling prose is equal to 'the quiet point the still point where there is no space, only pureness moving.'"[22] Reviews like the one in the *San Francisco Chronicle* titled "A Brilliant Leap of Imagination" continued to praise McCann's "linguistic virtuosity."[23] What most reviewers found liberating in McCann's early prose, a few had found potentially inhibiting. In a review in the *New Yorker,* for example, Laura Miller stated that some of McCann's early fiction tended "to get ensnared by a proclivity for static ornamental prose." Miller expressed her early apprehension regarding whether "Nureveyan kinesis" would succumb to "the inertia of pretty writing." But her fears were assuaged: *Dancer,* she claimed, is "the result of a novelist finally shaking off the affectations of his youth." McCann's "hankering for muchness," Miller wrote, "has been sated by the novel's many voices."[24] The reviewer for the *Irish Times* also pointed to the absence of the "verbal jewelry that threatened to overload some of his early short stories" and the enduring presence of the "inventiveness which first brought him to attention as a writer."[25]

Many reviewers praised McCann's ability to infuse his work with integrity and sensitivity despite the tabloid sensationalism surrounding his subject. The most newsworthy events in Nureyev's life—his defection, his major performances, his AIDS-related death—are attenuated or treated implicitly, if at all. Instead, McCann devoted his attention to seemingly less momentous events in which he discerned poetic implications. For example, the fact that the young Nureyev danced for wounded Russian soldiers during World War II had been relegated to little more than a sentence by Nureyev's biographers; yet McCann fashions this detail into the powerful war sequence that opens the novel and lays out many of its pervading motifs.

The liberty McCann takes with the details of Nureyev's life is consistent with the message of the epigraph that opens *Dancer.* Lifted from William Maxwell's 1980 novel, *So Long, See You Tomorrow,* the passage states in part: "Too many conflicting emotional interests are involved for a life ever to be wholly acceptable, and possibly it is the work of the storyteller to rearrange things so that they conform to this end." Facts, Maxwell notes, once fixed in the memory, are often shifted about in the imagination. In 2009 McCann explained that *Dancer* "questions the notion of what is a 'fact,'" and, he added, "the novelist composes documents that are supposedly false, but often they are more valid, more textually 'true,' and sometimes even more 'real' than what those in authority claim are 'facts.'"[26]

McCann sandwiches Nureyev's story between a partially fact-based prologue and epilogue and thereby heightens the story's dramatic effect; yet even these sections, with their fixed dates, locations, and lists, are not devoid of craft and invention. The opening section, which catalogs items bestowed on Nureyev by frenzied audience members in Paris shortly after his defection, suggests the spoils of the celebrity life into which he has been launched. Among the multitude of francs, hotel keys, and women's garments thrown on stage is a picture of the cosmonaut Yuri Gagarin, as much a Soviet hero as Nureyev is a Soviet anti-hero, yet seen by at least one fan as an analogue for the dancer, as the note attached reads, "*Soar, Rudi, Soar!*"[27] The brief closing section, which catalogs items from Nureyev's estate auctioned after his death, tacitly conveys the inevitable disintegration and descent that followed his meteoric rise. The structure, which forms an arc across the pages, mimics one of the breathtaking leaps with which Rudi awed the world.

Between these brief passages unravels a classic example of a *Künstlerroman,* a fictional account—often biographically founded—of the struggles and growth of an artist. The form is exemplified by such novels as Jack London's *Martin Eden,* Willa Cather's *The Song of the Lark,* and James Joyce's *A Portrait of the Artist as a Young Man.* In each of these works, an artistic impulse is threatened by oppressive social and economic conditions that surround the protagonist; yet a combination of the hero's unquenchable thirst for beauty and the inspiration or mentorship of others frees him from his repressive environment. At the start of *Dancer,* McCann paints a bleak and brutal picture of a frigid, starving, war-torn country, bridled by totalitarianism. Yet when he introduces his young hero, the boy sits on a cliff above it all and look out on the railroad tracks that will someday lead him away. When men return from war, many of them legless, he dances into their lives and inspires the same exhilaration and envy, pleasure and pain, that will characterize his Icarus-like flight from his homeland.

As in McCann's earlier novels, the opening pages embed in symbolic language the germ of the novel's most salient concerns. Before the reader meets Rudi, he is greeted by the world in which the boy is growing up, a bitter-cold world, filled with pain, deprivation, and horror, where men are "wasting away, dying long before they had really died" (5). The physical "dying" here parallels an inertia of the spirit that afflicts Rudi's countrymen, most of whom have resigned themselves to suffering and servility in the name of patriotism. The first paragraph closes with the image of frostbitten toes dropping from men's feet: "they could tell a man's future by the way he walked" (5). The comment prefigures a remark made later by Rudi's first dance teacher that the boy has made an art out of walking, just as he will turn living itself into his own creative adventure. The descriptions of his travels on foot in the early pages suggest daring, defiance, and the need for dominance, as he traverses snow drifts as tall as telegraph poles, ice skates "against the traffic" on the local lake (27) and wants the blades of his homemade skates to remove the marks of all who skated before him. The initial war section also anticipates the lifelong battle Rudi will fight against a world he finds petty, insipid, and foolish. He will be perceived simultaneously as hero and deserter, diplomat and traitor. And like the soldiers who "sang songs to their own absent children, but moments later they put the stub of a rifle in an enemy boy's mouth" (9), Rudi will be capable of great charity and stunning cruelty. He will engender profound spiritual rebirth in some and lead others to suicide. He will serve as the consummate vehicle to explore dichotomies that are at the heart of McCann's fiction.

While *Dancer,* like McCann's earlier novels, does not maintain a consistent linear plotline, it is told, basically, in chronological order, and, as with its predecessors, the multiple segments of the story are arranged carefully. For example, in the first chapter, the cold, detached tone of the opening war sequence shifts to a warm, intimate first-person narrative delivered by a nurse who welcomes the wounded home, washing them tenderly in warm bath water. The suffering and sadness that color the opening section are countered by the compassion and joy that characterize the second. And in this section McCann introduces the principal symbol of the novel: dance.

McCann used dance in his earlier work in much the same way as it is used in *Dancer,* as an expression of joy, an antidote to fear and suffering, an affirmation of life. As with his choice of tightrope walkers and other high-altitude daredevils, McCann's handling of dance has clear Nietzschean overtones. For Nietzsche dance defied what he called "the spirit of gravity,"[28] which seduces men into lives of servility, lives that cower to the words "thou shalt" instead of proclaiming, "I will."[29] Nietzsche thus called on "the overman" to triumph over this human tendency toward servility. It is clear from the early sections of *Dancer* that Rudolf Nureyev is born to answer Nietzsche's call.

Many of the traits that will distinguish Rudi are also delineated in the early pages. When as a six-year-old he dances for the ailing soldiers, he steps "out of the line" from the other children to perform solo (20), then walks off "rolling his shoulders from side to side" (20), an image that looks ahead to his New York City doppelgänger, or alter ego, Victor Pareci. Rudi's sense of entitlement is suggested when his mother tells him the story of a giant carpenter who pulls stars from the sky for children, one for each child, and Rudi inquires whether he will be granted two (22). His sense of invincibility is suggested when he comes home from the hospital clutching the sugar cubes he has earned for his dancing and ignores his mother's warning that the cubes will dissolve in his hands (24). His tendency to turn his back on those he perceives as weak is evident when the amputee Nurmahammed approaches him on the hospital grounds in hope of vicariously absorbing some of the joy of his dancing; instead, he causes Rudi to turn and run while imagining himself "ripping stars from the sky" (23–24).Yet McCann also suggests Rudi's capacity for empathy as "he returns home, hopping one-legged through the darkness" (24), presumably in an attempt to understand the man's plight. On going to bed, Rudi relishes the freedom of tuning in dozens of foreign cities on his radio before finding his way to Tchaikovsky.

While much of Rudi's future is prefigured in his childhood thoughts and actions, his early home life is in stark opposition to his adult life, a contrast McCann achieves through antithetical images of austerity and decadence. While the adult Rudi will fill his homes with rare, expensive paintings, his mother is forced to trade two picture frames to obtain a bar of soap. Furthermore his mother dreams of one day buying a carpet from a Turkish vendor, perhaps even hanging one on the wall to keep out the cold, whereas Rudi will fill his Parisian villa with lavish rugs costing tens of thousands of dollars and many specially made for him by a blind Moroccan. Finally, his weekly visits to the scalding steam baths that his mother assures him "will make him immune to sickness" (28) are in ironic opposition to the steam baths he will frequent in New York City as part of the lifestyle that ultimately renders his immune system defenseless.

Rudi's physical hunger is paralleled by an insatiable appetite for a life beyond Ufa. While his mother insists that hunger will make him strong, the boy associates hunger with "the high feeling of emptiness when the trains emerge from the forest and the sound bounces across the ice of the Belaya" (22). The river, once again a symbol for time in McCann's work, signifies stasis in this passage. Rudi's distaste for his homeland is augmented, ironically, when his father, Hamet, returns from nearly six years of military service. Not only is this rough man—who certainly influences Rudi's penchant for foul language—"a foreign thing" to the boy, but he also threatens to destroy Rudi's only joy, dance (26). Clutching his "warrior" to him, he crushes the cigarettes in his pocket and asks Rudi to help him repair them. "This is the dream of men," he tells Rudi, "to straighten crumpled things" (26). It becomes clear that Rudi is one of the "crumpled things" he intends to straighten.

Rudi's abandonment of his father is foreshadowed symbolically in a scene where his father, dismayed by his seemingly effete penchant for dance, takes him fishing and orders him to gut a trout. The scene gains meaning when read intertextually as part of McCann's entire canon, where fishing symbolizes the longing for reunion with a lost family member—as in "Fishing the Sloe-Black River" and *Songdogs*—and gutting fish can signify the severing of the familial bond, as in "Breakfast for Enrique." "The trout goes from living to gutted in seconds," Rudi's father assures him (32). The child is reluctant to gut the fish; yet his father—who in his unwavering patriotism comes to represent the Soviet government itself—forces him to do it, just as his unyielding disregard for the boy's passion for dance forces Rudi to sever their relationship. McCann underscores Hamet's association with the fish, noting that his face flushed and his mouth was red "as if he himself has just been hooked" (33).

The brutality and inflexibility of Rudi's father is countered by the tenderness and encouragement he receives from Anna Vasilev, a former Kirov dancer exiled in Ufa with her husband, Sergei, a political dissident. Anna, who looks "like a footnote to her past" (44), is the first of many on whom Rudi will have a rejuvenating effect: it is "enough in this life just to feel blessed from time to time," she remarks (41). Rudi, Sergei says, seems like "a light intruding upon the shadows to make sense of all our previous gloom" (47). Fittingly the photographs in the couple's album have been gnawed away by silverfish, but through Rudi, Anna returns vicariously to the promise of earlier days. "Her eyes quite honestly sparkled," Sergei notes, "as if she had borrowed them from the boy" (49).

Dancing under Anna's tutelage begins to build Rudi's confidence as well, as he stands up to the jeers of his schoolmates, nearly risks his life to show one of them up at cliff diving, and even strikes back at his father. Amused at Rudi's unfamiliarity with washing his hands, his peasant's pronunciation of newly acquired French words, and his tendency to eat goat cheese like a savage, Anna and Sergei attempt to refine the boy's habits. It is intuition and spirit, not intellect or knowledge, Sergei notes, that Rudi displays in his dancing, qualities that McCann has often attributed to his own writing. Like Rudi's ruffian mannerisms, these are traits that will continue to characterize him. "He was somehow born with dance," Anna tells Sergei; "he was unlettered in it, yet he knew it intimately" (48).

Another character whose life changes through Rudi's inspiration is Anna and Sergei's daughter, Yulia, who lives in Leningrad, where Rudi moves to attend the city's prestigious dance academy. On his arrival he is eager to absorb the city's culture and heads impetuously to the Hermitage to view paintings, while Yulia, with whom he will board, frets over his absence at the train station. Yulia describes Rudi's unapologetic arrival with Promethean overtones as she notes that "a figure finally broke the shadow of the archway" (69). Rudi brings light and warmth to the "grey damp" of Leningrad (68), and Yulia, accustomed to her tedious husband's "policy of gloom," is grudgingly moved by his youth and vitality (66). "So you want to be a dancer?" she asks. "I want to dance better than I already do," he corrects her (70). Rudi dances around Yulia's apartment as if he is "checking the span of his wings" (73) and soon gains entrance into the prestigious Leningrad academy. "He had talked his way in . . . as much as danced," Yulia states, noting, "but they liked his fire and intuition" (74).

While Rudi has an invigorating effect on some, he has a disheartening effect on others, a point made clear by a vignette told in second person. The narrative voice notes, "You see him through the winter and the summer and each time he appears larger to you and you are at a loss to explain what is happening" (80). The passage depicts the effect Rudi has on the more seasoned dancers at the school who are envious of his ability to intuit a move it has taken them three days to master. He mistreats them and taunts them; yet they "cannot shake him" (82). Seeing Rudi anywhere, the passage states, is like stepping into an acid bath, "until he moves away and the acid is gone, you stand alone and you look down and realize how much of yourself has disappeared" (82–83). The dancers resent his success coupled with his perpetual defiance of authority. Following this passage is a letter from his revered academy instructor, Alexander Pushkin, pleading with the director of the school not to expel Rudi for his insubordination, noting he is "clearly prodigious if undisciplined" (83), and offering to allow him to live with him and his wife, Xenia, with whom Rudi quickly begins an affair.

Yet regarding his artistic growth, Rudi is anything but undisciplined. Undertaking a regimen of self-education reminiscent of that engaged in by London's Martin Eden, he packs twenty hours of learning into his day and begrudges four for sleep. He reads Byron, Dostoyevsky, Gogol, Joyce, and Shelley and studies the Dutch masters, all in an effort to be a better dancer. In his notes to himself, interspersed throughout the novel, he quotes Nietzsche: "*Every day I count wasted in which there is no dancing*" (94). And throughout he reveals his Nietzschean sense of overcoming himself and others. "Out-think. Outmaneuver. Out-learn," he writes (94).

Rudi's transformation from his childhood in Ufa is so dramatic that even his mother, who attends his performance in Moscow for Prime Minister Khrushchev, is led to muse: "This is my flesh and blood. . . . This is what I have made" (102). Reprimanded on his twenty-first birthday for bringing champagne on a return flight from Vienna and causing an uproar, Rudi is typically unabashed. Already suspected of homosexuality—which could land him in a work camp for five years—he persuades the pilot to join him in his hotel room that evening. The last passage McCann offers of Rudi before his defection describes his teasing the gay men lurking late on Ekaterina Square, then leaving them because "he was privileged and there were other places for him to go" (114).

McCann juxtaposes this passage depicting Rudi's nascent hedonism with one describing the monastic lifestyle of his future shoemaker, the forty-four-year-old Tom Ashworth. McCann devotes to Tom a six-page sentence, a syntactic liberty he will take again when introducing the sensual Victor Pareci. Tom's and Victor's lives could not be more different; yet they have one thing in common, which McCann's syntax underscores: a passion that gives momentum and continuity to their days. Before the reader learns about Rudi's defection, Tom is preparing forty pair of shoes for his arrival in London. Tom is a perfectionist whose life is as devoted to shoemaking as Rudi's is to dance.

McCann diminishes the sensational effect of Rudi's defection and focuses instead on the emotional impact it has on those left behind, an impact largely revealed through the journal of his sister, Tamara. While Tamara is embittered and Hamet shamed by Rudi's actions, his mother clings to the hope that he will "find himself a nice girl" and come home. She has become at once the mother futilely fishing for her son in McCann's mythical Sloe-Black River and the gutted fish of "Breakfast for Enrique." In her distress she suffers from shingles, which causes Hamet to spread a tomato poultice on her stomach. "The juice made her look red and bloody, as if she had been skinned from the inside out." In the same passage from her journal, Tamara reports her father's bragging that "Rudik was great at gutting the fish with one sweep of the fingers" (124).

Tamara's journal entries reveal her narrow understanding of Rudi's decision to defect, an understanding that is partially the result of the Soviet government's manipulation and omission of the facts it passes on to the family. Securing a job at the elementary school Rudi attended, Tamara recalls the bullying Rudi had endured, seeing it as "punishment in advance" (127) for his defection rather than viewing his defection as salvation for his earlier suffering. That Rudi's defection is a mixed blessing for him, however, quickly becomes evident, and Tamara's entries are frequently marked by contradictions. In one, for example, she describes a raven bashing into her classroom window and dying, an ominous suggestion of Rudi's possible fate. In the next sentence she mentions his life on the beaches of Monte Carlo, where he is rumored to be enjoying an extravagant lifestyle. In the final sentence of the diary entry, a tinge of envy is revealed as Tamara ponders, "Why have I never seen the sea?" (130). Whenever stories of Rudi's good fortune leak their way into the Soviet Union, Tamara assumes Westerners are delusional and laments their inability to know the truth.

While Rudi's absence brings sorrow to his friends and family, it also engenders new beginnings. As the patriotic Hamet softens, he begins an unlikely friendship with the dissident Sergei. And Sergei's daughter, Yulia, inspired by Rudi's daring, leaves her drunken, brutal husband. "Live what you have left" (153), her father tells her, as he celebrates Rudi's defection. On the night before she leaves Yosef, Yulia witnesses a horrific scene that serves as powerful image of the nihilistic ideology Rudi's art and defection aim to defy: some children have made a makeshift soccer field on a former burial ground, using bones for a goalpost and a skull for a ball. In the morning, a soldier, having reinterred the bones, appears through his posture to say: "Our wars are never over" (157). Yulia's act of deliverance in leaving her husband is a small but noble rejoinder to the truth of the soldier's statement.

That Rudi's new life is not free of misgivings becomes clear in the only passage in which he is permitted to explain himself, a response to a bitter letter from Tamara informing him of Hamet's death: "To be away from home is to be away from everything that made me," he explains, adding "It was never my intention to leave, I could have stayed, but if you tread water long enough it is possible you might never learn to swim" (158–59). He assures her his defection was not a political gesture: "Politics is for fat men with cigars. It is not for me. I am a dancer, I live to dance" (159). Expressing his remorse at Hamet's passing, he asks Tamara to tell their mother "that her son dances to improve the world" (162).

Book 2 opens with an epigraph from the Russian poet Osip Mandelstam, a fitting choice, since Mandelstam's own artistic desire to improve the world led to his being exiled and sentenced to five years of hard labor. Unlike Rudi, Mandelstam was unable to elude his captors and died on the way to a labor camp in 1938, the year Rudolf Nureyev was born. Mandelstam's lines, written while in an earlier exile, reveal an indomitable spirit, similar to Nureyev's, within a "body— / . . . Alive to its own span—." A similar resoluteness defines Rudi's defection to the West; he quickly becomes a rich celebrity; yet he reminds himself not to "lose sight of the dance" (174). "Twenty encores," he writes in his journal, "who cares? Remember: Perfection is the duty" (165). Early journal entries indicate his delight at having attracted the attention of such celebrities as Grace Kelly and Marlene Dietrich and at the prospect of Leonard Bernstein and Pablo Picasso attending his performance. But this awestruck name-dropping ceases; and wry recollections of appearing on the Ed Sullivan show, meeting President Kennedy, or drinking with Tennessee Williams reveal his growing indifference to—and annoyance with—celebrity. Yet he is clearly pleased with his fame, as he watches people buy copies of the *New York Times* bearing a photograph of him and thinks, "I am *en l'air* in a million arms" (177)—the closest McCann comes to referencing the anecdote that inspired him to write *Dancer.*

Rudi's simultaneous need for and resentment of attention results in behavior that alternates between cruelty and kindness, a result of his hard-won ascent from poverty and anonymity to riches and fame. He is Darwinian in both his respect for self-reliance in others and in his quickness to bare his teeth at signs of weakness. He has no tolerance for the "paltry existence" of his fawning admirers (171); yet he expects to be treated as royalty. He is childishly spiteful toward his would-be patronesses, slaps a female autograph seeker, and throws coffee in the face of a sniggering waiter. When a jilted lover threatens suicide, Rudi imagines having sex with him a final time before offering him a rope. However, an encounter with a chronically ill child leaves him weeping and annoyed at the photographer who captures his private grief.

By age twenty-three, Rudi is both devil and demigod. He is seemingly invulnerable, revered, and ubiquitous, his face appearing on the cover of *Newsweek* and *Time* during the same week. His duty, he reminds himself with evangelical fervor, "is to disprove those who don't believe" (170). Everything he does, he claims, is "sprayed with my blood" (188). He clearly has a redeeming effect on his new partner, the legendary Margot Fonteyn, who, nearing retirement when she meets Nureyev, will continue to dance into her late fifties. Yet to many Rudi personifies evil. When *Cosmopolitan* magazine names him the world's most beautiful man, someone scribbles devil horns on his photograph and tacks it anonymously on his dressing-room mirror. In his journal Rudi describes a kingfisher tossing its dead prey, an image that suggests creation but also signifies destruction. Furthermore, on stage Rudi is able to transcend earthly limits, to achieve a state "the others call god" (193); yet during intermission he indulges his insatiable sexual appetite. Margot notes that he is as "unperturbed" at being naked before others "as a child getting ready for a bath" (184). His sense of invulnerability that contributes to his ultimate downfall is intimated during a scene in a Jacuzzi. When a woman in the bath admonishes him for entering it with open cuts, he attempts, futilely, to assuage her worries by telling her who he is.

Margo insists that Rudi immerses himself in his excessive dance regime to forget about home, a longing his other excesses can not satisfy. When an investor calls to tell him he has nearly doubled his money on the gold market, Rudi is preoccupied with thoughts of his mother who, he imagines, is darning her old blue smock. A sequence of Rudi's journal entries ends with a line that captures his helplessness, "Tried getting through to Mother but all the lines were down" (214). This sentence is followed by a chapter enumerating the exhaustive list of rare, exotic items Rudi has acquired, including scarves, rugs, books, paintings, and flowers flown in from Hawaii. The chapter seems to be lifted out of Huysmans's decadent classic *Against the Grain*, the protagonist of which surrounds himself with aesthetic excess in an attempt to ward off ennui.

Book 3 opens with an excerpt from "Dancing," a poem by Jim Harrison, which here suggests the pulsing rhythm and inevitable decline of mid-1970s New York City, the setting for this section: "After the passing of irresistible / music you must learn to make / do with a dripping faucet" (219). The first chapter introduces Victor who is rhythm incarnate. As he walks the sidewalks of Manhattan, the "symmetrical roll" of his shoulders shimmers its way down to his toes as if he is "connected by synaptical cogs" (221). Victor, like Rudi, is in "constant motion" (228), and McCann mimics this trait syntactically in his account of a typical day in the life of Victor, which he unravels for thirty-one pages before inserting a period. Like Rudi, Victor is said to break the darkness as he strolls through the "filth and grime" of Manhattan's Lower East Side, "making walking a form of dancing" (221). Victor clearly is Rudi's doppelgänger, a vehicle through whom McCann is able subtly to convey truths about his protagonist. While Victor never so much as attends a ballet, his life is an artistic work in perpetual progress with "no peculiar purpose but the fulfillment of life itself" (248).

Victor, whom McCann based on the flamboyant South American Victor Hugo, the lover of fashion designer Halston and close friend of painter Andy Warhol, personifies the orgiastic nightlife of 1970s Manhattan. Through Victor, McCann told an interviewer, "I wanted to capture the energy of the '70s, and I wanted it to feel like you had gotten a couple of blasts of coke up your nose."[30] Yet Victor also captures the deterioration that succeeded the excess. "People didn't see," continued McCann, "that ultimately . . . all this stuff is going to collapse, and we are going to get this dreadful disease that's going to plough us asunder."[31] But Victor's name suggests the triumphant days. His life has been "a string of lucky strikes" (222), and he keeps one filterless cigarette lit and another "behind his ear for immediate firing" (225). Like Rudi, he is "a seed swelling in its own husk," determined not to "become rooted like the rest" (228).

Rudi and Victor are living myths "cared for and coddled and protected by the mythmakers" (228), who feed off of their energy yet can never claim to know this Olympian pair (229). When they enter a party, they bring the promise of excitement; yet no one can predict whether they will "pull the scaffold out from under the party or be the scaffold itself" (226). They are consummate hedonists, equally comfortable among opulence and squalor; no place is ever "too nice" or "too nasty," as long as it brings pleasure (224). When Victor surprises Rudi with a party, the attendees of which cover every letter of the alphabet from "ambassadors" to "zealots" (236), not to mention Truman Capote, Mick Jagger, and Ted Kennedy, the pair fulfills the expectations of the mythmakers for a period—Rudi smashes six glasses before sitting at the piano and playing Chopin—then sneak off to a gay bathhouse. McCann describes their sensual adventure there in terms of a primal hunt, as the couple moves from body to body. Yet within this hedonism he frames a flashback that reveals "the elemental litter of their hearts" (247): they miss their mothers, a fact their temporal extravagances cannot erase. "Sometimes, Victor, my heart it feels as if it is under house arrest," Rudi says (246). Losing track of Rudi in the baths, Victor continues his escapade, opting for one final dose of "resurrection" amid the meatpacking district, where tractor trailers are teaming with "men in various states of elation and annihilation" (251). The scene concludes with an image of Rudi, silhouetted in the glow of streetlights instead of stage lights, approaching Victor and the others with actoristic "certainty and grace." A thought crosses Victor's mind: "Here comes loneliness applauding itself all the way down the street" (251–52).

Rudi's late-night walk toward further lechery segues into a description of Yulia on an early morning stroll in Leningrad. This juxtaposition emphasizes the contrast between Rudi's dangerous, whirlwind lifestyle and the wholesome, if static lives that continue in his absence from Russia. Yet his inspiration lives on in Yulia who, at fifty, wants to be "the sculptor of something human" (254). She visits the state orphanage and grows attached to a boy named Kolya, whom she spots with a nimbus of sunlight about his head. Her hopes for adopting him are seemingly threatened when a woman at the Ministry of Education learns from her file that she had connections to Rudi, whom the woman denounces but clearly envies. The day Yulia is given custody marks the most joyous occasion of her life. At the orphanage she notices welts on Kolya's body and discovers that he "has been punished for incontinence" (259). This detail is the first of many that connect the boy with Rudi. Incontinence—though lack of sexual control, not the lack of urinary control suffered by Kolya—is the first of three primary sins Dante uses to classify the punished in the *Inferno,* and it is the "sin" that will lead to the welts and suffering that are part of Rudi's future. Yet it is Rudi's passion and imagination, not his sin, that will be the boy's primary inheritance.

McCann follows his account of Yulia with an entry from Andy Warhol's diary, the only nonfictional excerpt in the novel, an entry depicting Rudi as "cheap" and "really mean" (261). But Rudi does not necessarily publicize his acts of kindness and generosity. When Tom Ashworth visits Rudi at his Paris home, Rudi angrily dismisses his twelve high-profile guests for commenting on his own late arrival and then sits drinking and conversing with the meek shoemaker. Later he secretly pays for Tom's wedding to Odile, Rudi's French housekeeper, and moves the couple onto his London estate. Rudi's humanity is further conveyed in his visit to Victor, who has contracted AIDS and is deteriorating quickly; yet the visit serves a further literary purpose, as it becomes clear that Rudi sees his own future in Victor's suffering. Odile, whom he brings along to keep house for Victor, notices that Rudi is "slightly more introspective than usual" (293) and is suffering from a fever. The image of Rudi's specterlike "dance clothes . . . drying on the washing line" foreshadows his passing (294–95), and the image of the men's joint silhouettes further emphasize their shared condition: "They had their arms around each other and their shadows made them look like one person" (295). In Rudi's last glimpse of him, the frail Victor is with gusto blowing smoke into the air, a final suggestion both of his pending dissolution and his unregretting swagger in the face of it.

McCann continues to juxtapose Rudi's life with those of his seemingly inconsequential underlings to demonstrate the beauty and value in the meekest lives. Devastated by Tom's unexpected departure, Odile relinquishes her typical sense of responsibility in exchange for Rudi-inspired recklessness; she ventures to Brighton to join him at a performance or, more likely, to look after him in the absence of her husband. Mistakenly entering Rudi's room as he is getting a massage, she notices the rubber gloves on his masseuse and the welts on Rudi's body, and his decline seems to take her mind off her own loneliness. When she returns, Tom is home, and he tends to a scrape she suffered while trying to prevent homophobic skinheads from destroying posters of Rudi. Moved, Odile feels a kinship with Rudi, recalling a statement he once made while looking at an old photograph of himself in his prime: "Someday this hideous moment will be the sweetest memory" (307).

Book 4 bears out the truth of Rudi's statement, as he returns to the Soviet Union in 1987, his forty-eight-hour visa granting him little more than a fleeting glimpse of the home that looks so dear and familiar to him after twenty-five years. While after a quarter century Tamara is still bitter, noting "there is no soap and the handle of the toilet is broken" (312), she is overjoyed when she sees Rudi, his grin reminding her "of when he was young" (315). She writes, "How was it possible to ever hate him?" (315). After stopping at his father's grave and kneeling to pray in the snow, he visits his sickly mother, but she cannot speak, and he is sure she does not recognize him. Bestowing multiple gifts on Tamara, her husband, and their awestruck daughter—finally dumping a roll of rubles on the table—he leaves their lives, presumably forever. Tamara remarks ironically, "We stood there with all our new possessions" (323).

On a final visit to Yulia, Rudi meets Kolya, now seventeen, and, though he is unimpressed with Rudi, seeing him in his decline, Kolya is clearly carrying Rudi's legacy into the future. His innovative approach to painting resembles Rudi's approach to dance—and McCann's own approach to writing, as *Dancer* illustrates: "He wanted to paint through the traditions in order to find the new" (325). Yulia and Rudi reflect on their lives, looking at one another, McCann notes, like defeated chess players, pleading "Explain to me my loss" (327). But Yulia is no longer resentful toward Rudi for leaving, and she sums up the redeeming effect he has had on everyone he encountered: "Something about him released people from the world, tempted them out" (329). In gratitude, it seems, for inspiring her own liberation, she gives him the china saucer that had survived her parents' exile. Rudi refuses the symbolic item, which represents not only perseverance but a connection to the past, suggesting she give it to Kolya. "Kolya already has it," she remarks (330). As Rudi exits, pirouetting on each landing as he leaves, his life-affirming manner inspires Yulia yet again: "Let this joy extend itself into the morning," she thinks (331).

Rudi's death is treated implicitly in the epilogue, where McCann enumerates items auctioned from his estate, some historically accurate, others invented. The items sell for exorbitant prices, conveying the fact that Rudi increased the value of these items by his mere proximity to them and that many were willing to pay lavishly to feel connected with him. One item, Anna's china saucer, was purchased for $2,750 by Nikolai Mareneov—Kolya—a gesture that indicates not only his gratitude to Rudi but also his financial, personal, and, presumably, artistic independence, a reality made possible only after the totalitarian regime that Rudi defied finally collapsed. Nikolai's name, fittingly, means "victory of the people," and he looks ahead to a figure in McCann's most recent novel, Jaslyn, another orphaned child who comes to represent the possibility of life springing out of loss.

On the final page of Joyce's *A Portrait of the Artist as a Young Man,* Stephen Dedalus prepares to leave Ireland to become a writer, exclaiming "I go to encounter for the millionth time the reality of experience and to forge in the smithy of my soul the uncreated conscience of my race."[32] Joyce, who occasionally signed his letters "James Overman," clearly has the Nietzschean idea of the "transvaluation of values" in mind. That is, Stephen's intent to forge an "uncreated conscience" requires tapping the artist's power to call life-denying moral systems into question and fashion his life and art according to new values. Rudi—whose real-life model was often compared to the mythical Icarus, son of Dedalus—does just this in *Dancer.* And McCann does it too. *Dancer* is a novel about creation, with dance serving as a metaphor for writing, just as in *Let the Great World Spin,* tightrope walking will fill an identical function. McCann commented in 2000 that the time is ripe for a writer to "come along and forge the new international conscience of the race," adding with modesty, "I don't think it will be me."[33] Yet *Dancer* certainly places an iron in that fire. Moving from Russia to France, England, New York City, Venezuela, and back again, and challenging social, political, and moral strongholds, it is a book that, like its central hero and its author, leaps imaginatively across treacherous borders.

## CHAPTER 7

# *Zoli*

In the 14 January 2007 issue of the *Boston Globe,* Gail Caldwell began her review of *Zoli* by pointing to a "sweet incongruity" in the novel's author: "The Irish writer Colum McCann is blessed with the unlikely mix of an adventurer's spirit and an introvert's compassionate eye."[1] Richard Eyre's review in the *Guardian* (London) also highlights the seemingly conflicting forces behind the creation of *Zoli:* "You would have to be wildly reckless . . . to attempt a novel about a singer and poet set among Gypsies in Slovakia after the second world war, and you would have to be as gifted and as skillful as Colum McCann to succeed at it."[2] That McCann's approach to his art blends the Dionysian and the Apollonian is not surprising. Since the publication of "Sisters," with its antithetical pair of siblings, McCann has embraced contradictions in his work, which is precisely what drew him to write about the paradoxical Rudolf Nureyev. And while *Dancer* was an unquestionably ambitious project, it was a slightly less "reckless" ambition than *Zoli,* which led him to spend two months in Eastern and Western Europe visiting Romani/Gypsy camps—not only as a careful observer but also as a casual reveler—despite repeated warnings from friends that he would be robbed and beaten. Neither occurred; instead, McCann returned from his adventure stripped only of his prejudices and began writing his most socially conscious novel, aiming to stir even a little empathy for the perennially persecuted Roma—or, perhaps, trigger Romani writers to tell their own story. *Zoli,* McCann hoped, could serve as "the yeast for the bread that finally comes from the oven."[3]

Published on 31 August 2006 in the United Kingdom and on 9 January 2007 in America, *Zoli* quickly showed signs of living up to McCann's ambitions for it. Like *Dancer, Zoli* seemed to find its place among the best historical treatments of its subject, despite being a work of fiction. Ian Hancock, a leading Romani scholar and political advocate, commented, "I review a great many Roma-themed manuscripts for publishers, but none has ever moved me as profoundly."[4] Santino Spinelli, an Italian-born Rom who teaches Romani culture and language at the University of Trieste, hailed the book as one of the most important contributions to Romani culture in many years.[5] In the fall of 2007 McCann was invited to participate in the Romani Yag Gypsy Festival in Montreal. However, the most gratifying response, he has noted, has been from the large number of Roma who have told him they are no longer hesitant publicly to proclaim their heritage.

Aside from its social impact, *Zoli,* McCann's third international best seller, was greeted by nearly unanimous critical praise. Literary and cultural critic John Leonard began his review in the January 2007 issue of *Harper's,* "Yes, the new year's just beginning, but it's hard to imagine a better novel being published in the months to come than *Zoli.*"[6] Critics celebrated the power of the story and its vivid characters as well as McCann's lyrical handling of both. June Sawyers of the *San Francisco Chronicle* praised McCann's ability to "enter a world few of us know anything about" and called his prose "just plain gorgeous."[7] *Washington Post* reviewer Frances Itani claimed *Zoli* was "beautifully conceived, wonderfully told . . . proof of an indomitable spirit."[8] Eyre, in his *Guardian* review, noted McCann's "pitch perfect control of character and narrative."[9] *New York Times* critic Richard Eder agreed with other reviewers, lauding McCann's "large and driving vision" and the novel's "stunning lyricism and sharp ironic force," although he felt the characters "fall short" of being fully realized.[10] McCann, however, has said that of all his characters, Zoli was the hardest to leave behind, and critics such as Itani, for example, have called her "unforgettable."

As in his other novels—and in his Northern Ireland stories—McCann establishes two conflicting worlds, one vibrant and creative, the other rigid and destructive: in this case the free-spirited Roma and the totalitarian Soviet government. Eyre writes, "McCann takes this self-contained universe, whose politics are 'road and grass,' and confronts it with its polar opposite—a hermetic society at whose frozen heart is the urge to re-engineer and homogenise the soul: postwar communism."[11] In this respect *Zoli* parallels *Dancer.* As Tom Deignan states in the Catholic weekly *America*, "Both novels begin with child protagonists who overcome adversity to become troubled, monumental artists."[12] And Kai Maristed adds in the *Los Angeles Times Book Review* that McCann's "mission" in both *Dancer* and *Zoli* is "to illuminate the phenomenon of artistic creativity" and ask a question that has occupied writers "since Pygmalion fell madly in love with his statue": "What price does the dedicated artist pay?"[13]

The protagonists in *Zoli* and *Dancer* could not lead more divergent lives; yet they are both artists and exiles, and art, whether song or dance, renders suffering more bearable and freedom more visible, the novels suggest. "I was literally looking for a book that would form a peak to my ideas about exile," McCann said.[14] When his wife, Allison, introduced him to Isabel

Fonseca's nonfiction account of Romani life, *Bury Me Standing: The Gypsies and Their Journey,* McCann became fascinated by the story of Bronislawa Wajs, also known as Papusza, the Romani word for *doll.* Papusza was a Polish-born Rom who traveled with a band of families (known as a kumpanija) that made their living as musicians. A singer, she gained fame during the 1950s after being discovered by the Polish poet-critic Jerzy Ficowski, who published her original lyrics. According to Fonseca, Papusza's songs, following in the Gypsy tradition, are often characterized by a yearning to return home; yet there is no Gypsy homeland. "Such yearning is the impetus to travel," Fonseca notes,[15] an idea that has fueled McCann's fiction since "Tresses," his first published story. Papusza's lyrics are often filled with "sons far from home . . . missing their mothers" and stories of "people living as best they can, outside history,"[16] also perennial subjects for McCann. Ficowski was among reformers who supported the "Great Halt," which put an end to the migrant lifestyle of Eastern European Gypsies during the 1950s, and he pointed out that Papusza's "greatest period of poetry writing" occurred "soon after she abandoned the nomadic way of life."[17] Fonseca notes that "Papusza was soon identified among Gypsies as a culprit in the campaign to cancel their traditional way of life."[18] She was tried by her people, found to be *mahrime,* unclean, and exiled for life. McCann had found his ultimate exile—one exiled from a life of exile. Like Nureyev, Papusza had been beaten during her childhood pursuit of her art and then lauded as a hero of her people, only to become "shunned by her own generation and unknown to the next."[19]

McCann decided he had to tell this largely untold story, and he headed once again to the New York Public Library to begin a nearly four-year endeavor, at the beginning of which he knew nothing about the Roma, not even the word *Roma*. Researching for *Zoli* proved challenging, as McCann soon learned that a dearth of scholarship existed regarding this historically nonliterate culture. His empathy quickly deepened, however, as he learned of their enslavement in the eighteenth and nineteenth centuries, their suffering at the hands of the Nazis who exterminated a half million Roma during the Holocaust, and the covert sterilization of Romani women—some of whom he met in his travels—by Slovakian doctors, a practice that persisted at least into the 1990s. "They are the only minority group that we are still allowed to hate," McCann has commented.[20] He believed that the media were largely responsible for the cultural stereotypes—they lie, they cheat, they steal—attached to the Roma and that there was more than one Gypsy story to be told. McCann felt a stronger moral obligation toward Papusza than he did toward Nureyev. "The artist cannot put himself today in the service of those who make history," he later remarked. "You are at the service of those who suffer history."[21] While Papusza lived alone for thirty-four years and eventually died in an insane asylum, McCann did not want Zoli to become "a spectacle of disintegration" but rather to "sing out at the end."[22] As in *Dancer*, he claimed minimal allegiance to so-called facts. "If you can go into the mythical room that has been swept clean by historians and cultural critics, by politicians and journalists," he has stated, "and find a small speck of dust still left there and raise it up into something human and good and valued, then I think you've done your job as a writer in a big way."[23] The indomitable spirit of Papusza was the speck of dust McCann chose to raise up into the story of Marienka Novotna, whose grandfather, having much faith in her future prosperity, teaches her to read and gives her a boy's nickname, Zoli.

While McCann "enjoyed the leap out of gender, the leap out of time, the leap out of cultural background" that *Zoli* allowed him,[24] he still considers *Zoli* an Irish novel. Many critics have pointed up the connection between the plight of Zoli and the plight of the Irish. "It takes an Irishman," writes June Sawyers, "to tell a very powerful story about community, assimilation, and the pain of exile, as well as the joy and anguish of being different."[25] Mark Anthony Jarman points to the "Irish subtext in *Zoli,*" noting that Zoli's people are harpists. The harp, a central symbol in Irish culture, even decorating its coins, has long symbolized pride in Ireland. It serves as a similar symbol in *Zoli,* since, as Jarman notes, Zoli's kumpanija is forced to bury their harps but never allows them to be destroyed. Jarman also calls to mind the Irish tinkers, an ethnically Irish, non-Roma group, also known as "the Travelers," who are often misunderstood, even romanticized, with a disregard for the history of suffering they embody.[26] Yet McCann claims he aimed to neither sentimentalize nor brutalize the Roma. And John Leonard notes the absence of "the Celtic lugubrious" in *Zoli* and in all McCann's fiction, a tendency he attributes to the author's sojourn in Japan.[27] According to Leonard, suffering, like joy, is rendered more powerful by McCann's deft handling of understatement.

McCann begins *Zoli* with three fitting epigraphs. First he quotes the Algerian writer Tahar Djaout: "If you keep quiet, you die. If you speak, you die. So speak and die." Djaout was assassinated in 1993 as a result of his outspoken views on Islamic fundamentalism; he thereby fulfilled his own words, which capture the catch-22 nature of his own and Zoli's situations. The second quote, from the British writer John Berger, points to the limitless "evil and indifference" that have colored so much of the twentieth century and that, as *Zoli* indicates, so frequently have targeted the Roma. Finally, McCann quotes Wendell Berry's poem "Traveling at Home": "To get back before dark is the art of going." McCann frequently portrays day-to-day life as a metaphorical journey, the object of which is to avoid the dark. Ironically, Zoli does all her traveling at night in order to avoid being arrested or killed, but she ultimately finds light, or joy, before her journey ends.

As is each of McCann's novels, *Zoli* is told in a nonlinear fashion from multiple points of view; however the sources of narration are far fewer than in *Dancer* and the jumps between eras far less frequent than in *Songdogs* and *This Side of Brightness*. Three of the seven chapters are related by Zoli, one by the scholar Stephen Swann, and three by a third-person narrator. The third-person accounts take place in 2003 and are located at the beginning, near the middle, and at the end of the novel, giving it a circular motion and serving as reminders, as McCann has noted, of "just how much *hasn't* changed."[28]

In the opening chapter McCann captures the experience of the outsider, a forty-four-year-old, "comfortably fat" Slovakian journalist who crosses into a foreign world, its winding, muddy inroads suggesting the hidden perils that may await, roads McCann himself traveled into the Roma camps in his own attempt to "navigate their secrets."[29] In the final chapter the journalist is given a name, David Smolenak, but his initial anonymity emphasizes his role as one of the faceless "gadže," or non-Roma, with his misinformed, romantic notions of Gypsy life. The detritus covering the "shitscape" foreshadows the neglected lives he will encounter within (3). The first sign of life is "a dog, all bones and scars" (3). The settlement is "marooned on an island in the middle of the river" (4), and the journalist nearly drives into the river as he approaches. His entrance calls to mind that of early European conquerors. After swatting away the pack of children, some naked, and paying off an older boy to guide and protect him, he crosses the rickety bridge into the settlement. While the children cross as surefooted as "a strange line of herons," he totters, sways, and reaches for a handhold that is not there, underscoring his insecurity on this island of "dark-skinned" people (5–6). Amidst the squalor of the camp, he enters a clean, orderly home and is unable to hide his surprise. It quickly becomes evident that, despite his fears and suspicions of the residents, it is he who is the menace. He wins the attention of the chief elder, Boshor, with liquor, money, and cigarettes, and three of the cigarettes peek from their package "like peeping toms" (7), suggesting the voyeuristic nature of his visit. As he becomes less self-conscious, he makes a few glib remarks about Roma tradition, comments that arouse mockery, and when he brings up the name Zoli, he is met with antipathy: "I don't know that name," Boshor responds. "Do you understand me, fat-neck?" (11). The journalist's assumed moral superiority, and that of the race he represents, is bluntly called into question. Yet Boshor's comment simultaneously conveys the questionable sense of justice and the stultifying effects of tradition that allowed the Roma to perpetuate their relentless hatred toward Zoli.

Here the story flashes back nearly seventy years, as Zoli relates to her daughter a narrative revealing the morally conflicted world into which the older woman was born. The device and the speaker's tone calls to mind Louise Erdrich's *Tracks,* as an elder tells the story of her people's joys and struggles to a child living in more modern times. The conflict between the simplicity of the older times and the hardships introduced by the mass culture that promises to improve their lives. It is a theme at the heart of *Tracks* as well as such twentieth-century classics about colonization as Chinua Achebe's *Things Fall Apart,* and also central to *Zoli.* Like Achebe's novel, *Zoli* treats the questions of loyalty that face children who grow up in primitive, patriarchal societies but who are tempted by the modernizing influences of the mainstream world, to the chagrin of their elders. For Zoli the ways of her early childhood will always have the strongest appeal to her, and she spends her life trying to regain a measure of the joy she experienced then, or, as McCann would have it, she tries to go home. Zoli's story fittingly begins with her sitting in back of a horse cart and "staring out at the roads going backwards" (15) after experiencing the first of the many horrible injustices that will color her life. She and her grandfather, Stanislaus, have narrowly escaped being murdered by Hlinka guards, the militia of the Slovakian government, that has forced the rest of Zoli's family onto a frozen lake and lit fires around its perimeter until the Roma fell through, horses and all. Ice becomes a recurring symbol of cracked dreams and transient joy throughout the novel. Zoli recalls a childhood game that involved sliding sheets of ice from blades of grass and trying to keep them whole. She remembers remaining in the fields after the game was over as the sun got higher and "everything began to melt" (21).

Zoli inherits from Stanislaus an attitude of stoicism that becomes her chief means of protection in her precarious world. Stanislaus teaches her that "places were good and most people were good, but the rules they put on the places were vile, and that people became vile with them" (15–16). His skill at building walls for the gadže symbolizes his instinctive need to insulate himself from outsiders; yet he is aware that the rules his own people have enforced for generations can be equally inhibiting.

He thus engenders a sense of curiosity in Zoli and encourages her to read, despite the Roma taboo against it. Stanislaus combines the wisdom his life's journey has taught him—represented by his split boot seams that appear to be mouthing words—with an open-mindedness cultivated by reading. When they begin traveling with a new *kumpanija,* a group of Polish harpists, he comes to blows with another elder after buying a radio and being accused of bringing outside influences into the camp. He insists it his "duty to know" (33). He hides his copy of Marx's *Das Kapital* behind the cover of a catechism to conceal it from the fascists and his own people; yet, Zoli remarks, its pages "confused him as much as they finally confused others" (23). But he does understand Marx's warnings about acquisitiveness and assures Zoli that no one owns the rivers, a statement emphasizing the novel's concern with the sanctity of primal nature: "we were meant for skies not ceilings" (22). He instills in Zoli a sense of self-reliance, resourcefulness, and pride, and she learns to navigate her way between the oppressors among her own people, who slap her when they learn she is attending school, and the white children who drench her with spit in her new classroom. Just as Nureyev counters oppression through dance, Zoli discovers song. And like Nureyev, she begins to release the old art form of her people from its traditional constraints and to rework old themes.

As the Hlinkas become increasingly cruel toward the Roma, Stanislaus, who bears the name of the martyred Polish bishop and saint, is portrayed with Christlike perseverance, a trait best conveyed in a confrontation with a Hlinka guard. When Stanislaus rides into Bratislava with a pocketful of homemade toothbrushes to sell to local prostitutes, he is stopped by the guard, who, he notices, is a fellow Rom that has dyed his hair blond and is clearly a Judas-figure. After he whispers to the soldier "But you are one of us" (50), the man strikes him with the butt of his rifle three times. "On the third time, he rose again," Zoli recalls, unwittingly quoting the Apostles' Creed, "and said Heil Hitler" (50).

Stanislaus is finally martyred after the arrival of the Nazis, whose planes fire on the ambushed Roma caravans. His death, however, results in a rebirth in Zoli, who undergoes a cathartic ritual that marks her independence. Revisiting the lake where her family was drowned, she plunges in and is revitalized through this spiritual reconnection with her origins. She ascends to the shore and sits, her knees raised to her chest in the fetal position, then returns home and burns her grandfather's possessions. "That was the birth of me," she explains; "it always will be" (58).

The end of the war ushers in the hope that Stanislaus had prophesied, but while communism seems to embody the second coming for the Gypsies, it becomes clear that this new savior is actually a false prophet. "I had hope right up until the end," Zoli writes. "It was the old Romani habit of hoping. Perhaps I have never lost it" (60). Through her songs she becomes the unwitting poster child for "the literate proletariat" and the socialist revolution (60), a celebrity and a hero to her people. "It seemed to me that the spring of my life had come," she explains (61). Yet this spring results in a thaw like the one that killed her family, and she relegates the tale of her public years to a few sentences.

The chronicle of that tumultuous rise and fall is, however, detailed by the man ultimately responsible for her banishment, Stephen Swann, an English-born scholar who falls in love with her, or, more accurately, with the idea of her, and only later comes to understand his own shortsightedness. Like McCann,

Swann needs to tell Zoli's story "before it's forgotten or becomes, like everything else, something else" (66). For Swann, the reader discovers, Zoli was a romantic ideal, and, in Western fashion, he was compelled to possess and package her, finally betraying her in a printing mill, "against the hum of the machinery" (66).

Swann, like so many of McCann's exiles, is a fragmented character trying to claim a sense of wholeness, which he thinks he finds in Zoli. His being raised in England by a Slovakian father and an Irish mother contributes to his ethnic confusion. Orphaned in his early teens, a loss that exacerbates his sense of rootlessness, he completes his final two years of school in a Jesuit facility in a Liverpool suburb. "Walking around the edges of rugby fields in a gray V-neck sweater" (68), he is a stark contrast to Zoli. Fascinated with Slovakian culture, he welcomes the invitation from the poet Martin Stránský, loosely based on Ficowski, to translate literary works for Stránský's journal, *Credo*. Swann's role as a translator further underscores his being wedged between cultures. At one point he reflects, "I had for some years considered myself to be Czechoslovakian but, in retrospect, I was too English for that, too Irish to be fully English, and too Slovakian to be in any way Irish. Translation had always got in the way of definition" (91).

When Stránský, who had assisted the Roma during the war, introduces him to Zoli and asks him to record her songs, Swann's displacement is heightened. He admits his discomfort with Zoli's nomadic, outdoor life and notes "the stars are not what I was built for" (86). Yet he is infatuated with Zoli, whose dress adorned "with dozens of tiny mirrors" (85) literally and figuratively reflects his own fragmentation. As he sleeps crammed in a caravan, the knots in the wooden ceiling seem to be judging him "like eyes" (86).

Although they are misguided, Stránský and Swann have good intentions; they hope that publishing Zoli's songs will raise the Gypsies out of the margins. Their effect on Zoli is indeed liberating, as they take her to a bookstore and she incredulously touches the volumes: "It's like not having any walls" (89), she says tellingly. Even Zoli's people are impressed with the celebrity she attains after the publication of her first book. For Stránský and Swann she is the perfect illustration of the effectiveness of socialism. Zoli, however, begins to tire of the clamorous outside world, and, after a reading one day, remarks to Swann, "I want to go home" (96). Swann remarks, "It was, of course, the oldest idea: home. To her it meant silence" (96). Soon her people are wary of her becoming "too gadžo" (99), and their antipathy for outsiders manifests itself one afternoon when they give Swann a beating, cursing him and all his "pale pieces" (101).

Just as Stránský had aimed to "put manners on" Zoli's poetry (88), the government aims to refine the fiercely self-reliant Gypsies in ways that are unwelcome to them. "It was raining hard and we hid from it," Swann recalls, "yet it was our own rain, of our own making, and it promised to bring on a good crop, we were sure of it, so we let it fall" (102). Zoli is outraged when she learns of talk among government officials about "allowing" her people "to halt" and about placing them in public housing to give "them absolute power over their own lives" (106). "How is it," she asks Swann, "that some people always know what is best for others?" (111). Aware that their political hopes are crumbling, Stránský remarks to Swann, "We're drinking off their coffin lids, Swann, you know that?" (113) Swann is too enamored to understand.

"Socialism was like a wine that had turned," McCann has explained regarding the Eastern European political climate of the late 1950s. "And there was worse to come. The bottle would be smashed and the shards used for stabbings."[30] Zoli pleads with bureaucrats to leave her people alone: "Don't try to change us. We are complete," she tells them (118). While Swann's fear for his own safety is more important than any regard for truth, Stránský's outspokenness lands him a death sentence. His integrity intact until the end, he instructs the firing squad: "Come closer, it will be easier for you" (123), a close paraphrase of the words uttered by Erskine Childers, the Irish nationalist, as he faced his own execution in 1922 during the Irish civil war. The echo underscores the universality of the political and social oppression with which *Zoli* is concerned.

In a telling confrontation of forces, troopers converge on Gypsy camps and destroy the intricately crafted wheels of their caravans, some of which are "still perfect after decades" (123), with sledgehammers, saws, drills, knives, blowtorches, and "even bullets when frustration set in" (124). The wheels are burned in huge bonfires, and the state radio touts the event as "generous, decent, Socialist" (124). Zoli begs Swann not to publish her latest poems as her people are growing increasingly suspicious of her ties to the government, but he claims the books are printed. Zoli slaps him and leaves. Suddenly she is "absolutely real" to him, "no longer the Gypsy poet, the ideal Citizen, the new Soviet woman, something exotic to fall in love with" (128). He approaches the printing press, and machinelike himself, he prepares the books for print: "the cogs caught and the rollers spun, and I betrayed her" (128).

According to Fonseca, Papusza begged Jerzy Ficowski to stop the publication of her poems: "If you print these songs I shall be skinned alive . . . my people shall be naked against the elements. But who knows, maybe I will grow another skin, maybe one more beautiful."[31] In the fourth chapter of *Zoli,* the protagonist describes her long walk from Czechoslovakia to Austria during the winter of 1959–60, a journey in which she, too, sheds old skins in hope of growing another. Banished, Zoli finds herself ironically fulfilling the Gypsy stereotype as she is forced into lying and stealing to survive. Zoli's winter journey parallels Treefrog's descent into the tunnel in *This Side of Brightness;* it is painful but ultimately redemptive. Like Treefrog's, her life is reduced to its essential core: she must eat, drink, and stay warm. Zoli's walk calls to mind the naturalistic fiction of Jack London, especially the short story "Love of Life," in which the narrator asks regarding the suffering protagonist, who is forced to eat live chicks in his effort to survive, "Why was he not content to die?"[32] And Zoli is not merely physically battered, she is emotionally and psychologically ruined: "how strange this desire to stay alive, she thinks, how easy, with no integrity nor purity, simply a function of habit" (136). Yet despite her suffering, Zoli's dignity sustains her. She resists the temptation to step in front of a truck and later to plunge off a bridge into the Danube, calling suicide "vacant" and "pathetic," something she associates with the gadže (176).

Zoli, who realizes that she has been betrayed by both whites and Gypsies, admonishes herself for expecting too much from either: "Where happiness was not a possibility, the illusion of it was always more important" (146). Yet her "whiteness" is not the only skin she begins to shed on the road west. As she is forced to violate many of the Romani taboos regarding diet, hygiene, and modesty in order to survive, she gradually relinquishes her allegiance to the antiquated ways of her people. That Zoli is shedding both her modern gadžolike identity as well as her old fashioned Gypsy self is conveyed in the image of her looking backwards during her journey and believing she sees a dead body. She realizes then that she has dropped the overcoat Swann had given her, which, despite her Roma code of modesty, she had draped over her arm. She trudges back to retrieve the coat, which "lies on the roadway in a sprawl, one arm outstretched as if pointing in another direction" (142).

Like many of McCann's characters, Zoli wishes "she might somehow be able to drift back into days that once had been, where there were no poems, just songs . . . before the flashbulbs or the microphones" (143). She wanted her songs "to pierce the difference between stars and ceilings," but her words were "shaped, carved, placed—they had become fact" (143). "I have sold my voice . . . to the arguments of power" (143), she realizes, relishing the silence that now envelopes her.

Zoli's exodus takes on added biblical significance as she encounters an unlikely savior, a deaf-mute whose charity revives her, prompting her to return to Bratislava to purge all traces of her compromised history. Having found her way to a small hut, she stops to rest and decides to extract the aching tooth loosened by a blow from a Gypsy elder at her "trial." The act has ritual symbolism. As the roots are "dragged up from the bottom of her jawbone" (148), she is implicitly absolving herself of the pain brought on by her people. She tosses the tooth with its "clotted and fibrous" roots (148) into a sink. Later the deaf-mute arrives, and she assumes he will shoot her. Instead he leaves her two bread rolls and returns again with his mother and more provisions. Walking away, he smiles at her and opens his palm, in which lies her tooth. In Christlike fashion he has taken her shame and her pain away and given her bread. Feeling "a pulse of strength" (156), she returns to Swann's office, sets fire to her books, and destroys her recordings. After a final furtive visit to the housing blocks where her people are now living, she heads out again, feeling as if "she has just pulled her entire body over a region of barbed wire" (179). Leaving town she is spotted by her childhood friend Conka and her children; the latter spit on her and curse her, but a subtly redemptive act sustains her: Conka does neither. "At least there is that," she thinks. "It is almost enough" (182).

In her unabashed will to live, Zoli begins fulfilling the stereotype of the Gypsy as wild animal as she observes the birds to help locate food, confiscates a fish from an osprey, and eats all but the beak of a dead sparrow, citing "the urgency of hunger" (185). Her self-sufficiency is complemented, however, by a new sense of self-assurance, and she is buoyed by the outlandish hope that she will travel all the way to Paris. Sleeping at a burned out Gypsy camp, she is discovered by two men who are prisoners at a nearby work camp. The older prisoner, recalling seeing her in the newspapers, asks "How have you come to this?" (197). Zoli realizes that his question is also directed at himself, a question so many of McCann's characters try to answer.

As Zoli crosses unknowingly into Hungary, she marvels at the power of boundaries; and the scene that follows underscores the novel's concern with both the irrationality of man's hatred and the unpredictability of fate: "Borders," she remarks, "like hatred, are exaggerated precisely because otherwise they would cease to exist altogether" (198). Hiding from the border patrol, she wonders, "How many dead bodies lie along these imaginary lines?" (199). And hers nearly becomes one of them, but for a whim of nature. A pack of hounds approaches her as searchlights scan the marshland where she is hiding, but she learns the dogs are chasing a herd of deer. She hopes the deer will sweep to the left of her so that she remains unobserved, and they do. As she sees the soldiers in the distance gathered around their kill, its belly split open, and imagines "the guts steaming on the ground," she thinks, "The merest luck . . . has preserved me" (202).

Here McCann returns to the story of the Slovakian journalist, making it clear that things have not changed much regarding either the Roma or the public's sympathy for them. Though he promises to return, the journalist knows he will not. He has no use for these people anymore. After paying off the man who has guarded his car, he is accosted by a man with a teardrop tattooed under his eye. The man shows him a bundle containing a child, no heavier than a loaf of bread, hanging from the ceiling to protect it from rats. The tattooed man pressures the journalist into driving to an automatic teller machine, and a few minutes later, he observes the man sniffing paint thinner that he bought with the money. The journalist speaks the words "paint thinner" into his tape recorder so that he can make use of the fact for his own purposes (214). He realizes, then, that he never learned the name of the tattooed man, a fact that not only reveals his indifference but also suggests that the Roma are all tattooed, branded by stereotypes, many of which they have been forced to fulfill. The journalist wishes he were capable of charity, but instead he utters "no name" into his recorder and drives off, seemingly as indifferent to these people as he is to the "insects smashing against the windscreen" (215).

Another of McCann's prominent themes surfaces tacitly in the following section as it becomes clear that Zoli's suffering has not only engendered a new life for her but made possible the birth of her daughter, Francesca. In his next novel, *Let the Great World Spin,* McCann labels this idea "the ongoing of ourselves." The account of Zoli's life in the West—which she finally has achieved by crossing another border, a lake lined with barbed wire—is delivered in a letter to Francesca, marking the first time she has written in the forty-two years since her banishment. She writes, "I feared that if I tried to give written meaning to my life that I would lose again what I had gained" (221), namely, the mountains, the silence, her husband, and Francesca.

Discovered "half-dead" on her arrival in Austria, Zoli had been placed in a displaced-persons camp, where her friendship with a fellow Rom demonstrates that her physical weakness has not affected her moral conviction. Zoli and the woman, Mozol, are ostracized by other displaced persons. She explains, "we are pulled together by the hatred of those who surround us" (237), a hatred Zoli still cannot comprehend. "They are comfortable only with the whip above their heads, yet so many of us have spent our lives armed with little more dangerous than song. . . . The worst of us has never been amongst the worst of them. They make enemies of us so that they do not have to look at themselves" (237). Being reunited with some of her own people revives Zoli's spirit, as a couple of allegorical anecdotes indicate. First, she recalls a morning when a plague of insects invaded the camp, clinging to the walls until they died. While she was purging her room of them, she notes, one insect "came out of its stiffened pose, and I bore it on a cloth to the open window with the one bit of life still left in it" (241), clearly an analogue for Zoli and Mozol. Later Zoli recalls seeing an ant carrying another ant, which was dead. When she blocked its path with her finger, the ant climbed over, foreshadowing Zoli's coming to Mozol's rescue when her poverty prevents her from traveling to Canada to start a new life with her husband. Zoli exploits the gadže stereotype of the Roma, dressing as a Gypsy is expected to, setting up a makeshift table in town, and telling fortunes to desperate men who pay her well to be told the lies that sustain them. "Some things are more important than the truth," she tells Francesca (246). After putting all her earnings toward Mozol's escape, Zoli walks away from the camp herself one day.

As Zoli moves on toward Italy, she prefers walking to soliciting rides. Sometimes she accepts these rides because a mountain tunnel provides the shortest route, but she fears the dark man-made tunnels. She explains, "It seemed to me that there were two different worlds, that of trees and that of engines: one seemed clear, the other dark" (257). For Zoli the free world is the world of trees, and it is filled with light and silence; the oppressive world is the world of engines, and it is filled with darkness and noise. Referring to an old superstition Zoli tells her daughter, "It is rules not mirrors that steal away our souls" (259). Zoli looks to the natural world to validate her intuitions about reality and recalls riverspiders she observed one night while camping: "They moved quickly across the surface, uncanny, ancient, leaving no circles nor ripples, as if they were part of the water itself" (260). The image is one of connectedness with the natural world, a reality that the engines threaten.

Zoli's misfortunes continue to beget unexpected good fortune, particularly when she is nearly raped and manages to stab her attacker in the eye with a stolen knife. Having hidden in the womblike trunk of a car, she is taken by the car's owner to a priest and told: "There are two things in this part of the world. . . . God and money. You are lucky that you found the first" (264). It is through the priest that Zoli meets Enrico, a gadžo with the heart of a Gypsy, who is above social prejudice. When she inquires "why he had not asked me anything about being a Gypsy," he asks her why she "had never asked him anything about not being one" (268). Enrico, who belongs "to the mountains" (269), guides Zoli across them and endures a beating when it is discovered she is an illegal immigrant. Having come from wealth, Enrico uses his ties to power to secure Zoli a passport, and the two settle into a simple, satisfying rural lifestyle. And when Zoli attempts to cross the Danube to visit her homeland with Enrico, she turns back, realizing she has found her true home. She ends her letter to Francesca with a poem she wrote in 1957, finally able to return to her old life. The poem, actually written by McCann, contains a couplet that seems to capture Zoli's resurrection: "You who were sad now at evening / Will be happy now at dawn" (283).

In the final section, Zoli fulfills her dream of going to Paris, but the visit simply reminds her of the value of her country home and of her conviction that stars will always be preferable to ceilings. She is astounded by the international flavor of the city, where multiple ethnic groups mingle seamlessly; yet she is disturbed by the conditions of the Romani ghettos. She has been invited by Francesca, now a social worker and Romani activist, to a conference on Romani culture, although the word *Romani* has had to be dropped from the title of the conference in order for the group to secure a hotel. Zoli is clearly uncomfortable around all the "white machinery" and other modern conveniences in Francesca's kitchen (295)—she herself never owned a phone or had a lock on her door—but she is proud of her daughter and gratified that she is happy. As she and Francesca sit together in the living room, sunlight surrounding their feet, she wishes she could "freeze" this "perfect moment" and return home (307).

At the conference Zoli feels alienated from the group of esteemed scholars and writers who have gathered at the garish hotel with its recorded bird sounds and claim to comprehend the

Roma experience. She laments that she is missing sunset at her quiet, rural home. When David Smolenak, the Slovakian journalist, introduces himself and is joined by Stephen Swann, Zoli feels as if the windows in the room have all closed, and her breathing sounds like that of "someone drowning" (315), recalling her family's murder. She wishes the crowd would "part like water" (317) so that she could escape. Arriving at Francesca's apartment she lets down her hair and stands naked, "all the ancient codes violated" (321). Clutching a photograph of Enrico to her heart she lies down, thinking, "there are no days more full than those we go back to" (321). When Francesca informs her later that Swann spoke with her apologetically and that he now owns a wine shop in London, she is amused that he is a capitalist; she pictures him returning home at night to read "the books that would make up his mind for him" (324). But later she pities what she considers Swann's existence, his failure, and decides she will go to him, forgive him, and release him (326).

That evening she realizes how "unfinished" her life still is (327), an awareness that is at once disheartening and alive with the possibility of experiencing more joy.[33] The Scottish band that performed at the conference has filled up Francesca's living room, and instead of silencing their late night revelry, she joins it, and prepares to do what she has enjoyed most since childhood: sing. She recalls playing a chladnis in her youth, a sheet of metal sprinkled with grains of sugar that would vibrate when the metal was struck with a bow. She pictures the dancing grains, "settling at the points where there was least sound," just like her people (329). McCann's final description of her is appropriately terse yet revealing: "She smiles," reflecting her having reconciled with both past and present; she "lifts her head," conveying her pride in what she has endured; and "she begins," suggesting the rejuvenating effect the visit with her daughter has had on her (328).

McCann would agree with the critics who discerned recklessness in his desire to delve into the lives of the insular and persecuted Roma. For him this recklessness is a necessary alternative to the complacency that prohibits change. Addressing the graduating class of the School of the Arts, Charleston, South Carolina, in June 2009, he recalled the eighteen-month cross-country bicycle journey he took when he was twenty-one and how it opened him up to the lives of others. He explained that returning from a restroom in a diner along the way, he discovered two twenty-dollar bills tucked in the riding gloves he had left on the counter. "It was another way for somebody to say to me 'Oh, go on! Do the thing that you are doing! Live your life a little bit recklessly for a while.'" He offered the same encouragement to the graduating artists: "Do something in your lives that doesn't necessarily compute on the Richter Scale of success. . . . Go down and help the homeless in Guatemala. . . . Join the Peace Corps. . . . You've got to speak up for the dispossessed, the lost, the broken." "Art," he said, "has the ability to restore, at least for a while, the life which has been devalued by others."[34]

CHAPTER 8

# *Let the Great World Spin*

On 26 February 2008 Colum McCann joined Chimamanda Adichie, Michael Cunningham, Edwidge Danticat, Ha Jin, Toni Morrison, and other ethnically diverse contemporary novelists to celebrate the fiftieth anniversary of the publication of Chinua Achebe's novel *Things Fall Apart* at Town Hall in New York City. After reading William Butler Yeats's poem "The Second Coming," from which Achebe drew the title for his novel, McCann stated, "The best literature is connected. We are word-linked. What gives off the deepest sparks is that democracy of storytelling."[1] These three separate but related points are at the heart of the novel he was working on at the time, *Let the Great World Spin,* which synthesizes the dichotomies that have pervaded his fiction: exile and return, cynicism and hope, despair and possibility, self-absorption and empathy, fear and faith, horror and beauty, loss and redemption, oppression and self-realization, ignorance and enlightenment, cruelty and compassion.

*Let the Great World Spin* is connected to a wealth of "the best literature" that precedes it. One critic referred to the novel as "a North American pastiche" containing allusions to the work of Leonard Cohen, F. Scott Fitzgerald, Denis Johnson, Toni Morrison, Michael Ondaatje, as well as to American movies.[2] McCann's seventh book, which revolves around a day in the life of a colorful assortment of New Yorkers in the summer of 1974, is actually more of an international pastiche, as the author also draws on the work of Achebe himself, John Berger, T. S. Eliot,

Jack Kerouac, José Martí, Friedrich Nietzsche, William Shakespeare, Alfred, Lord Tennyson, and Walt Whitman, to name only a few sources. Moreover, critics have noted the novel's affinity with James Joyce's *Ulysses,* not merely because of its thickly textured, allusive style but also because it takes place primarily on one day, captures the character of a major city, merges multiple perspectives, and frequently makes use of stream-of-consciousness narration.

The idea that "we are word-linked" suggests that literature has the power to cross generational, political, and cultural boundaries to bring people together. McCann tells a story set in New York City in 1974 but draws clear parallels to any city in the present time. In the novel's prologue thousands of strangers converge in a reverent hush to observe an act of shocking beauty, a man a quarter of a mile above preparing to walk between the towers of the World Trade Center. He is suspended on a barely visible wire—the novel's multilayered central motif—which in Matteo Pericoli's drawing on the dust jacket of the first American edition is strung across the entire city, an apt illustration of McCann's theme of the unifying power of beauty. Many reviewers described being similarly mesmerized by McCann's verbal rendering of the incident; they consistently referred to *Let the Great World Spin* as a high-wire act in itself. A reviewer for the *USA Today* remarked that after the "stunning five-page set piece" describing the moment before the walker steps out, "out goes McCann on his own literary tightrope."[3] And a reviewer for the *Observer* in London added, "And it is always thrilling to follow him."[4]

McCann's fifth novel also illustrates his claim that storytelling is a form of democracy. Quoting Achebe, he elaborated: "If you don't like someone's story, tell your own."[5] Like McCann's two preceding novels, *Dancer* and *Zoli, Let the Great World Spin* is concerned with the validity of so-called facts that have been manipulated for social or political ends. "I think that if someone looks back in fifty years at what writers are doing today," McCann told an interviewer in 2009, "they will see that we're taking these real people and creating fiction around them. The facts have been so stolen from us and abused." He continued, "There's a difference between a factual truth and a textual truth. And I think that fiction is more honest than most nonfiction because of its interest in what Faulkner described as 'the human heart in conflict with itself.'"[6] Within the pages of *Let the Great World Spin* a motley array of characters—as diverse as a thirty-eight-year-old Bronx hooker and grandmother of two, the Irish monk who looks after her, and the judge from Park Avenue who sentences her—is each granted the opportunity to tell his or her story. In addition to being a pastiche of literary predecessors, the novel stitches together the stories from the points of view of eleven characters (twelve, if one includes the city itself, from whose collective perspective the prologue is delivered), causing critics to refer to it alternately as a mosaic, a panorama, a symphony, a tapestry, a polyphonic novel, and a sprawling epic.

*Let the Great World Spin* is founded on the idea of connectedness. Both aesthetically and thematically it is marked by a preoccupation with unity. It transcends literary boundaries and hopes to expand the consciousness of its readers. McCann praised Achebe for writing a "radical social novel," a description that applies equally as well to *Let the Great World Spin* and *Zoli*. Achebe, he noted, allowed readers to "rip the cloth and open up the window. That's what Chinua Achebe did. He opened up the windows of his room, his own room, his own story. And he created in that space an everywhere."[7] Here

McCann is paraphrasing another of his literary influences, the Irish fiction writer John McGahern, who believed that "the local is the universal with the walls removed."[8] McCann makes use of this trope in the concluding passage of *Zoli,* as the protagonist's feelings of loneliness and alienation subside and "the room feels as if it is opening, one window, then another, then the walls themselves."[9] *Let the Great World Spin* also concludes with the cathartic image of a character's world opening up, as she parts the curtains in a dark room and lifts "the window frame minutely."[10] *Let the Great World Spin* is filled with darkness, as are *Zoli* and *Things Fall Apart;* yet each novel conveys the idea that the most potentially horrifying darkness has its origin within men's minds, which are filled with ignorance, prejudice, self-centeredness. As one of the prostitutes laments in McCann's novel, "If you think of the world without people it's about the most perfect thing there ever is. It's all balanced" (230). Other dark forces—namely time and circumstance—also threaten to topple McCann's characters; yet as *Let the Great World Spin* conveys, the world finds mysterious ways of correcting the balance. McCann stated in his Achebe tribute, "Things fall apart, things come together."[11] This statement expresses the central theme of his 2009 novel.

Maintaining or restoring balance has always been a concern of McCann's work. In the title story of his first collection, *Fishing the Sloe-Black River,* a group of mothers casts fishing lines into a black, drifting river, an image of their desperate need to reconnect with their vanished sons. In *Let the Great World Spin* the tightrope artist and his accomplices propel a fishing line across the dark, abysmal void above Manhattan and then string less and less tenuous cords over it until the wire can support the weight of a man. Not only do these images, which bookend

McCann's body of work to date, mirror the thematic cord he has spun through his fiction over the course of fifteen years, they convey the very human need to bridge the emptiness that threatens to render life meaningless. Just as the mothers are made whole by their children, the tightrope walker is made whole by his art. The delicate yet dauntless lines launched by McCann's tightrope walker, and by McCann himself, are analogous to the filament that the isolated spider on "a little promontory" launches "out of itself" in Walt Whitman's "A Noiseless Patient Spider," an act the poet compares to his soul's own desperate need "to connect" amid the "measureless oceans of space." Whitman describes the soul's process: "Ceaselessly musing . . . / Till the bridge you will need be form'd, till the ductile anchor hold / Till the gossamer thread you fling catch somewhere, O my soul."[12] Whitman's verse and McCann's poetic novel are in themselves metaphors for the artist's attempt—as Robert Frost defined it—to provide, at least, "a momentary stay against confusion."[13] Lawrence Ferlinghetti also portrays the artist as tightrope walker in his 1957 existential poem "Constantly Risking Absurdity."

*Let the Great World Spin* is an existential novel, an allegorical reconsideration of the fathomless horror that the twin towers came to represent after the 11 September 2001 terrorist attack on them. Yet McCann alludes to this event only once in the book, as he is more interested in capturing "that moment of grace, of creation rather than destruction, of how to get across from one side to the other."[14] McCann has remarked, "we must fight against the absolute of despair. . . . Isn't this what all the great fiction is about? . . . It becomes a stay against meaninglessness and despair."[15] His words call to mind the French existentialist Albert Camus's boulder-pushing Sisyphus whose knowledge of the absurdity of his plight allows him to defy despair and find joy in his toil. Camus described "The Myth of Sisyphus" as "a lucid invitation to live and create in the very midst of the desert,"[16] precisely the invitation the tightrope walker seems to be offering in *Let the Great World Spin,* as he laughs "into the teeth of the wind" (158).

Gloria, one of the novel's many bereaved mothers, remarks, "It had never occurred to me before but everything in New York is built upon another thing, nothing is entirely by itself, each thing as strange as the last, and connected" (306). Ultimately, the novel illustrates, this connectedness ignores socioeconomic boundaries. Despite the surface differences in the life of Gloria, an African American woman living in the Bronx projects, and of Claire, a white woman living in a penthouse on Park Avenue, both lives are inherently valuable, and the pains each character suffers and the cure each ultimately hopes for render them deeply kindred. John Corrigan, the Irish monk, acknowledges the existential angst that few are immune to. Regarding the local prostitutes he remarks, "It's about fear. You know? They're all throbbing with fear. We all are" (29). And Tillie, one of the black prostitutes, who like the Park Avenue mother and the Bronx mother, has lost a child, claims, "It's no less love if you're a hooker, it's no less love at all" (213). At one point, another down-and-out character, Lara, a would-be artist raised in affluence and currently high on cocaine on a sidewalk, is tossed a quarter. "*E pluribus unum,*" she reflects with irony (125). The phrase, the Latin original of the title of McCann's early story "From Many, One," captures the author's concern with the essential human unity that underlies cultural diversity, an idea that New York City epitomizes. Moreover, it is a paraphrase of what the British Romantic poet Samuel Taylor Coleridge called the "oldest" and "safest" definition of beauty, which comes from the Greek philosopher Pythagoras: "the reduction of many to one."[17] Certainly both interpretations, social and aesthetic, are present in *Let the Great World Spin.* Its title, taken from Tennyson's poem "Locksley Hall," suggests the necessity of accepting the abiding laws that govern the universe and its inhabitants, which, although they effect great, often destructive change, also beget life and beauty. Tennyson writes, "Forward, forward, let us range, / Let the great world spin forever down the ringing grooves of change."[18]

McCann knew he needed to distill meaning from the horror of the 11 September bombings, which his father-in-law narrowly escaped, but was not sure how he would approach the subject. In an e-mail a few months after the tragedy, he wrote:

> Life is crazed here in the city. Everyone still raw and sad, but recovering. Allison's father was in the WTC but managed to get out of the building with ninety seconds to spare. He was knocked off his feet by the blast as he ran away. He awoke, surprised to find that he was alive. He walked to our apartment. My four-year-old daughter, Isabella, ran down the corridor to greet him and jumped into his arms. Suddenly, though, she recoiled and ran away. We asked her later what had happened (since she dearly loves her grandfather). She said that she saw the debris on his suit and clothes and then smelled smoke from his shirt—so that she thought he was burning from the inside out. How beautiful and awful. Stories like this all over town. . . . But I do wonder how art and artists are ever going to deal with all of this—it's not that it's special, or different, since it has happened in varying (and worse) degrees in other parts of the world, but the simple enormity of it has made a level

> ground of meaning. . . . So that the eight-year-old child's drawing is as powerful as the Poet Laureate's rendering.[19]

It was Paul Auster's 1982 essay about Philippe Petit's "On the High Wire" that caused McCann to realize that the image of Petit traversing the void was the image with which he needed to begin.

McCann has stated that *Let the Great World Spin* was the easiest of his seven books to write, primarily because it did not require him to transplant himself into a subway tunnel or European city nor did it require endless hours at the New York Public Library. Yet the book did require research. McCann patrolled the streets with New York City police officers, such as Edward Conlon, author of the 2004 memoir *Blue Blood.* He consulted doctors, computer technicians, lawyers and judges, among others, and—in addition to Petit's books—he studied rap sheets and crime literature and listened to oral histories of 1970s prostitutes.

Even before the novel's release on 30 June 2009, reviewers began validating the extraordinary publicity that began with an excerpt being printed in the *Paris Review* in Fall 2008 and culminated with *O: The Oprah Magazine* listing it as the first pick among twenty-five "irresistible" books of summer. As these two diverse benchmarks suggest, *Let the Great World Spin* was bridging the gap between the literary and the popular novel. The *Seattle Times,* for example, described the novel as "Dizzyingly satisfying to read and difficult to put down."[20] *Esquire* called it "the first great 9/11 novel" and described it as "a novel about beginnings rather than endings . . . a birth certificate chiseled on a tombstone."[21] The *Washington Post,* however, while praising McCann's ability to craft "penetrating phrases," claimed his theme was "stale" and criticized aspects of plot and style as well.[22] Jonathan Mahler's review in the *New York Times* reflected the zeal with which most reviewers greeted the book: "Colum McCann has repurposed Petit's daring act as the leitmotif for 'Let the Great World Spin,' one of the most electric, profound novels I have read in years." Mahler compared McCann's use of multiple voices to "a great pitcher in his prime . . . constantly changing speeds" and praised the deft linking of stories and the "surprising and deeply affecting conclusion."[23] On the book's late summer British release, reviewers wholeheartedly echoed Mahler's comments. The *Observer* (London) noted that Petit's walk "has waited thirty-five years for its full poetic drama to be inhabited in the sinew and cadence of McCann's sentences."[24] In late August *Let the Great World Spin* became McCann's first *New York Times* best seller, and in November the novel received the National Book Award for fiction.

The novel opens with a dedication to McCann's wife, Allison, and three of his literary mentors and friends, John Berger, Frank McCourt, and Jim Harrison. The epigraph that follows is taken from Aleksander Hemon's 2008 novel *The Lazarus Project:* "All the lives we could live, all the people we will never know, never will be, they are everywhere. That is what the world is."[25] Hemon's words, which occur in the mind of a poor character who catches a glimpse of a rich woman through the window of her home before she pulls the curtain, introduces the motif of connectedness pervading the novel, which is about self-realization as much as communion with others. *Let the Great World Spin* peers behind anonymous curtains to reveal the various and valuable lives they conceal. McCann told an interviewer in 2009, "Part of the beauty of fiction is that we come alive in a body that we don't own."[26] And in a discussion with Hemon six years earlier McCann noted the importance of recognizing "those things that Faulkner talked about—courage and honor and hope and pride and compassion and pity and sacrifice . . . found in the small gesture, or the small life." He pointed out further that the stories taking place in "the small anonymous corners" are not merely "individual stories, but stories relating to our larger nature, to the human condition. That each story has grand importance."[27]

Reading Paul Auster's essay, "High on the Wire," McCann recognized the allure of a tightrope walker's performance for the "smaller" lives below. Having observed Philippe Petit in Paris in 1971 as he walked between the towers of Notre-Dame Cathedral, "a dot of life against the sky," Auster comments that unlike a stuntman, who caters to his audience's "almost sadistic anticipation of disaster, the good high-wire walker strives to make his audience forget the dangers, to lure it away from thoughts of death by the beauty he does on the wire itself. Working under the greatest possible constraints, on a stage no more than an inch across, the high-wire walker's job is to create a sensation of limitless freedom."[28] While Auster is referring to the tightrope walker's own "dangers," "thoughts of death," and "limitless freedom," McCann's tightrope walker inspires this same feeling of possibility and transcendence in his observers as well as in the novel's readers. Auster continues: "Juggler, dancer, acrobat, he performs in the sky what other men are content to perform on the ground. The desire is at once far-fetched and perfectly natural, and the appeal of it, finally, is its utter uselessness. No art, it seems to me, so clearly emphasizes the deep aesthetic impulse inside us all. Each time we see a man on the wire, a part of us is up there with him."[29] Those who observe McCann's tightrope walker just after sunrise share "a reverence for the man's irreverence" (6); he is "a dark toy against a cloudy sky" (3). McCann again uses an overtly Nietzschean symbol to convey the idea of transcendence. In *Thus Spoke Zarathustra,* Nietzsche's paean to self-creation, the author compares man to a tightrope strung between two towers: "beast and overman."[30] It is the task of the metaphorical tightrope walker to transgress this middle state, to become "a new beginning, a game, a first movement, a self-propelled wheel, a sacred 'Yes.' For the game of creation, my brothers, a sacred 'Yes' is needed," Nietzsche writes.[31]

If the mass of lifted, awestruck faces is not enough to suggest this is a novel about 9/11, McCann introduces one of many ironic suggestions of the future, comparing the far tower to "a wounded thing waiting to be reached" (7). McCann also connects the art of the tightrope walker with the art of the writer in this passage, comparing him to "a pencil mark" (7), a metafictional motif that reappears at the end of the novel when Jaslyn "turns the pencil around to safety" (349), as it dangles from the edge of Claire's table, and McCann's performance nears completion. He continues in the prologue, "The man above them was a word they seemed to know, though they had not heard it before" (7). This idea, too, recurs, as other characters allude to an elusive "word" that seems to describe a type of primal freedom they only know very deeply within, perhaps the freedom to release the unfettered expression of "the deep aesthetic impulse inside all of us" that Auster describes.

One of those who observes the walker that Wednesday morning is the novel's pivotal character, John Corrigan, a thirty-one-year-old monk who grew up in Dublin and is stationed in the Bronx. McCann based Corrigan on the poet and radical Jesuit priest Daniel Berrigan, known for his social and political activism, particularly during the Vietnam War. After receiving "the most extraordinary and generous letter" from Berrigan regarding *This Side of Brightness,* McCann says, "I got to know him and read his poems, and I fell in love with the ideas of Berrigan, his ideas on liberation theology, his activism, his radical Christ."[32] Liberation theology calls on Christians actively to assist the oppressed, a call Corrigan answers with Christlike alacrity as he leaves his door unlocked so that local prostitutes can use his bathroom and provides recreational activities for the residents of a nearby nursing home. His story is narrated by his brother, Ciaran, who follows him to America after the Dublin bombings of spring 1974. Like the siblings in McCann's story "Sisters," the brothers have always been polar opposites. Ciaran is a cynic who sees the world as vicious and claims that the edict "Love thy neighbor as thyself" is "rubbish" (40). Corrigan is an optimist who also recognizes that the world is vicious but who wants "quite simply, for the world to be a better place" so that "someday the meek might actually want it" (20). Furthermore Corrigan's energy and purposefulness has always been in direct contrast to Ciaran's complacency and aimlessness, ever since Corrigan "took control of the top bunk" from his older brother during childhood (13) and sneaked out into the cold night to offer his blanket to a homeless man.

Like Sheona in "Sisters" Ciaran seeks out his younger, more grounded sibling as a way of connecting with less complicated times. "Family," he states, "is like water—it has a memory of what it once filled, always trying to get back to the original stream" (57). A reviewer for *Booklist* aptly referred to *Let the Great World Spin* as a "wise and elegiac novel of origins and consequences."[33] As Ciaran's impatience with his brother's ceaseless altruism begins to change to respect, he remarks, "He was at the origin of things and I now had a meaning for my brother—he was a crack of light under the door, and yet the door was shut to him" (67). Corrigan is the incarnation of the "original grace" that the novel's characters are desperately seeking. He is the "radical Christ" that McCann found in the works of Berrigan, the name McCann had originally given him before changing it to Corrigan, which not only suggests *origin* but underscores his being "at the core" of things, an expression used by several characters. Most important, *Cor* is the Latin word for *heart;* thus his nickname, Corr, emphasizes his innate compassion, and his initials, J.C., further align him with Christ.

As Joseph Lennon points out, Corrigan's first name, John, "suggests an evangelical dimension," yet he always uses his surname.[34] This choice underscores his role not as a messenger of the gospel but as the incarnation of it. He tells his brother that he lives as he does to put "flesh on my words" (30). Few people even know he belongs to a religious order. Christ, Corrigan points out to his brother "went where He was supposed to go. He stayed where he was needed. . . . He never rejected the world" (20). Ciaran explains, "What Corrigan wanted was a fully believable God, one you could find in the grime of the everyday" (20). While much of the imagery and diction used in describing Corrigan brings out his Christlike presence, he remains, nonetheless, a flesh-and-blood savior. Ciaran recalls seeing him as a child, "isolated on a sandbar, tangled in light," and after being summoned three times he "returned waist-high through the water" (27).

While Corrigan may not have attempted to walk on the water, he is certainly an analogue for the demigod tightrope walker. Ciaran recalls the child John Corrigan "balanced on top of the seawall, arms held wide" (12), an image that conjures both Christ and the walker. Furthermore, Corrigan is said to have "sparked people alive" (18), and like the tightrope walker, his "presence sustained people, made them happy, drew out their improbable yearnings" (14). It is clear that he is walking his own tightrope. He explains to his brother, with ominous 9/11 overtones and echoes of Eliot's *The Waste Land,* that like everyone else he is "throbbing with fear. . . . Bits of it floating in the air," he says. "It's like dust" (29). His next words could apply easily to high-wire walking: "If we stopped to take account of it, we'd just fall into despair. But we can't stop. We've got to keep going" (30), although, he admits, he is not sure why. Corrigan soon reveals that the strong faith with which he has managed to keep fear at bay is wavering. Yet his internal moral crisis raises the same question "Sisters" seems to ask: At what point does a life of self-denial begin to impoverish the soul it intends to nurture?

Ciaran believes that those Corrigan helps are "taking the life out of him" (39). And it is clear that his discovering genuine love with another human being has been a vitalizing, if tormenting new experience for him. Corrigan's relationship with Adelita, a nurse at the retirement home, begins with her massaging his arms. Corrigan suffers from a blood disease that takes on symbolic meaning, and he goes to Adelita with the seemingly innocent intent of having her "move the blood around a little" (53). He confesses to Ciaran that when he first kissed her, he "wanted nothing but the here and now, and nowhere else. On earth as it is in heaven" (54). When she touched him, he claims "it was like she put her hands down deep in the earth (51)" or, perhaps, the "core" of his being, the heart that he had told his brother had been yearning to be reached.

Corrigan is essentially martyred, pierced in the heart by his steering wheel after helping the teenage prostitute Jazzlyn avoid a prison sentence so that she could remain with her children. But ironically Jazzlyn is killed instantly when Corrigan loses control of the van. His constant spiritual dilemma is captured in the image of his foot resting on both the accelerator and the brake, which causes the engine to roar. On his deathbed he is consoled, not by a priest but by having seen "something beautiful" (72), the tightrope walker. Corrigan's dying inspires a kind of awakening in Ciaran, who utters to himself: "Teach me who I might be. Teach me what I can become" (72). As with the falling of the twin towers, the fall of, what McCann calls, two "small and ordinary towers,"[35] Corrigan and Jazzlyn, engenders new beginnings for many unsuspecting others.

Claire Soderberg, another pivotal character in the novel, walks a tightrope of grief and self-consciousness in her Park Avenue penthouse as she prepares to host a group of mothers who, like her, have lost sons in Vietnam. She is married to a respected representative of the establishment, Judge Soderberg; yet the death of her son, Joshua, causes her most genuine loyalty to surface. She wishes she had told her son the truth that "the world is run by brutal men and the surest proof is their armies" (84), but Joshua quickly understood the vanity behind war: "Hate your enemy, know nothing of him" (102). As she awaits the other grieving mothers, she is embarrassed by her display of wealth, imagining how she might downplay the luxuriousness of her apartment in order to more fully bond with the other women: "The walls between us are quite thin. One cry and they all come tumbling down" (78). Her remark, of course, is meant to convey the truth she learns through Joshua's death, and it spawns her lifelong friendship with Gloria, an African American who has lost all three of her sons. When the women tell Claire about the tightrope walker's stunt, she is appalled by what appears to her as a disregard for the value of life. Although she is described as tottering at first, she gains her footing, steps out to join the women like stepping onto a wire, and eventually stops shaking, recognizing she is not alone: "We hurt, and have one another for the healing" (114).

Another character who undergoes an awakening is twenty-eight-year-old Lara Liveman, a passenger in the car that first strikes Corrigan's van. Like Claire, Lara and her husband long for "the gone days" (76), which they attempt to recapture in the absurd practice of dressing in the style of the jazz age. "At our core," she says, "even we knew we were not being original" (120). In an attempt to escape the dissipation of their drug-crazed lives, they move to a cabin in upstate New York, but Lara realizes her life has become fragmented. Hearing about President Nixon's resignation in a local diner the day after the wreck, she laments that things have gone badly in the country since Robert Kennedy's assassin "pulled the malevolent trigger" (131). Her thoughts recall the elusive word, *freedom,* which the tightrope walker embodies: "Freedom was a word that everyone mentioned but none of us knew" (131). Her own release begins when she goes first to the hospital to check on John Corrigan and then to Jazzlyn's funeral. The preacher's words seem spoken to her: "Life must pass through difficulty in order to achieve any modicum of beauty" (145). She confesses her role in the accident to Ciaran, and the two share a drink and an unacknowledged emotional bond. She decides she must "walk out into a clean elsewhere" (153), but first, like Corrigan, she must overcome her "fear of love" (156).

Book 1 closes with a vignette from the tightrope walker's perspective; as he practices in the Rocky Mountains and then performs his walk between the twin towers, the novel's concern with connectedness becomes increasingly encompassing. It is clear that the tightrope walker feels a reverence for the beauty he observes in the natural world, and he has sacrificed six years and repeatedly risked his life to be part of that beauty, to live up to it with his own act of creation. The vignette recalls the work of the American Transcendentalists as the walker relishes his solitude and delights in watching a red-tailed hawk return to her nest to drop "red hunks of flesh" into the mouths of her three squawking chicks, "with the sort of ease that there was no vocabulary for" (157), a reference to the ineffable beauty of nature's laws at work. "It was moments like this that kept his training on track," McCann writes (157). Like Thoreau, who recalled a sparrow alighting on his shoulder while he was hoeing and felt "more distinguished by that circumstance than I should have been by any epaulet I could have worn,"[36] the walker is ecstatic when the elk begin staying to watch him practice. When on a whim one morning he jumps off the wire and becomes trapped in the snow, he realizes that he could die and that it is "his business to live"(159). It is a reminder he seems to have needed, and his rise back up to the wire is depicted in the imagery of a resurrection. Like Thoreau, the walker abides by the credo "live deliberately,"[37] and, as a result, he sees in everything "purpose, signal, meaning" (162). Like Claire he realizes he must laugh in the face of death. Finally on the wire above the city, he begins "carrying his life from one side to the other" (164), and, McCann notes, "The core reason for it all was beauty" (164).

Book 2 begins with the stories of two lonely, neglected, young men whose otherwise banal existence is given meaning through the act of creation. Like so many of the characters in the novel, they have found what they feel is a new frontier, and, like the walker, they are made new. The first young man, a fourteen-year-old named Fernando, ventures deep into the subway tunnels to photograph the work of street artists, criminals who, like the walker, risk their lives for their art. The photographer's persistence is rewarded when he follows the police officers he thought were following him and snaps the iconic photograph—the walker on the cable between the twin towers and an airplane overhead—that appears on page 237 of the novel. The photograph, actually taken by *New York Post* photographer Vic Deluca, looks eerily ahead to 2001 and visually captures McCann's theme of the bold beauty of creation in the face of potential destruction.

The other forlorn character introduced in book 2 is a computer hacker named Sam who, with his coworkers at a California technology institute, has routed a call to a pay phone outside the twin towers, an act that allows him to be part of the Manhattan audience. His attention is itself rerouted when he begins talking to a young woman who is watching the walker. When the woman finally hangs up, Sam tries desperately to contact her again (later, the tightrope walker hears a pay phone ringing while he is escorted to a police car). Sam is a "brand-new guy" after making a connection with this woman on the other end of the country (196), whom, as the novel's epigraph suggests, he "will never know." Yet the contact fills him with a sense of the world's vastness and possibility, which he also feels while writing computer code: "You hit the frontier. You can go anywhere. It's about being connected" (197).

Of all the characters in the novel, Tillie Henderson best illustrates what McCann called in his Achebe speech "the democracy of storytelling." A prostitute since the age of fifteen, Tillie, who is serving a prison sentence, delivers a nearly forty-page monologue in the form of a daily journal that renders her one of the most sympathetic characters in the novel, despite the "facts" on her rap sheet. One of Tillie's most endearing traits is her candor. She is unashamed of her career and claims that she "never wanted no square job" (199). Hooking is the only life she's known, since her mother was also a prostitute, which explains her deep fatalism. She says of one of her former lovers/pimps, "if he loves you more, he beats you more too. That's just the way it is" (203). Corrigan had once told Tillie that there are at least a thousand reasons to live, but in her closing statement it is clear she will make good on her promise to hang herself. Like Claire and the women in her support group, Tillie is devastated by the loss of her child, Jazzlyn. Tillie's life has been a string of catch-22s. She "worked the stroll" to keep Jazzlyn off the stroll. She then kept Jazzlyn on the stroll to keep her away from drugs. Now she will take her life so that the only things she has left to live for, her two granddaughters, will not end up on the stroll as well. Tillie is one the few characters in McCann's fiction who gives up her search for "home," concluding "They're ain't no such thing as getting home. That's the law of living far as I can see" (236). Yet her death and that of her daughter prove redeeming, ironically, for Tillie's granddaughters and their adopted mother, Gloria, whose situation illustrates the idea McCann refers to later in the novel as finding "in others the ongoing of ourselves" (349). It is at the end of Tillie's chapter that McCann places the photograph of the airplane approaching the tower above the tightrope walker; the novelist thereby underscores the deaths of Jazzlyn and Tillie, symbolized in the towers, and the rebirth of the others, symbolized in the walker.

Book 2 concludes with a passage conveying the peace the tightrope walker finds a quarter mile above the chaotic city as he imagines death must be like this moment, a simple easing away from "the noise of the world" (242). The physically heightened perspective of the walker mirrors the clarity and depth of his perception, and this technique is often used by existentialist writers such as Camus and Sartre to emphasize a character's detachment from the myopic masses. But soon the walker is forced by police to rejoin the noisy crowd below, and as they prepare to take him to his arraignment, a journalist asks him "Why?" "The towers were there," he thinks. "That was enough" (243), words—echoed on the final page by Tillie's granddaughter Jaslyn—suggesting the Emersonian edict, "Beauty is its own excuse for being."[38]

Book 3 introduces Judge Soderberg, a prostitute himself in many ways, who is entrusted with the fates of Tillie, Jazzlyn, and the tightrope walker. Though Soderberg has the appearance of living a privileged life, his dreams have not panned out. While the walker is "entirely himself" on the wire (239), the judge, in his elevated seat, is a persona, and, like Tillie, "he was caught, he was just a part of the system, . . . a part of the Parts" (256). Regardless of his personal feelings, he must uphold appearances. While he recognizes that the tightrope walker is guilty of public endangerment and criminal trespass, he is thrilled by the audacity of his act, especially as it takes him away from the tedium of his own daily performance. Soderberg cannot "afford" to indulge his personal feelings, such as his grief for his lost son for whom he cries "in the bath of all places, but only when the water is running" (263). He would like to agree with Claire that the war is horrible but must believe that it is proper. Yet he knows his son through his early death was "a custodian of the truth" (263). It is his easygoing friend Harry, a restaurant owner who, believing the American dream "was composed of a good lunch and a deep red wine" (261), brings out the best in him and unwittingly persuades him that the tightrope walker is more of a hero than a criminal. Soderberg fines him a penny for each story of the tower, which in reality was the fine imposed on George

Willig, a man who scaled the South Tower in 1977. He also sentences the walker to a children's performance, a nod to 9/11, since Philippe Petit was invited to do the same thing after the towers fell. Yet Soderberg is not easy on Tillie, because nothing is to be gained from this act of leniency. In fact, he seems to add two months to her sentence simply because she treats him with familiarity in front of all the reporters for whom he is performing.

The story of the Guatemalan nurse, Adelita, follows that of Judge Soderberg. Though his first name, Solomon, suggests wisdom, he appears foolish in comparison to Adelita, a genuine civil servant whose name, meaning "winged," conveys her angelic nature. Like the tightrope walker who knows he will later find solace in recalling his privileged moments above the city, Adelita comforts herself by remembering a day one week before Corrigan's death. Her reminiscence recalls the stasis glorified in Keats's "Ode on a Grecian Urn," as she preserves the image of Corrigan in a fixed present, which, in Keats's words "shalt remain, in midst of other woe."[39] "There is, at least, always this" (275), she begins, recalling that morning in the present tense. Adelita had realized that Corrigan's needs for divine and human sexual love were not mutually exclusive. She remembers his looking up at the ceiling where the neighbor's could be heard awakening, imagining him thinking "up there, . . . God, but first my neighbors" (276), a reference to his very earthbound Christian worldview. Perhaps the most significant reference in Adelita's story is to the "mirilla," or peepholes, on every door in her house, peepholes that either narrow or broaden the view of the room they look into and that symbolize the idea that "depending on what side you happen to be on" (278), one's future may appear tiny or vast. She recalls wishing they had a garden, an allusion to an Edenic world where neither Corrigan's sense of guilt nor anyone's pain would exist, a place to "find our own space" (281). She pictures a vast area where buildings appear to be blades of grass and stone flowers below their feet, certainly a reference to the liberating perspective enjoyed, momentarily, by the tightrope walker, an association reinforced earlier in the section when Corrigan refers to himself jokingly as "an acrobat" (276). But once again, a character cannot find the word to describe the magical, resuscitating feeling she has experienced, in this case through love: "Try to describe the taste of a peach" (279).

Of all the characters trying to maintain or regain a sense of wholeness, no one's life has been torn asunder like Gloria's; yet she is the most valiant and ultimately resilient character in the novel. The grandchild of slaves, she grew up during the Great Depression as "things were falling apart" (285). She lost two brothers to World War II and all three of her sons to Vietnam. Two husbands left her, and she's been mugged at least eight times since moving to New York City. For the sake of convenience, she allows everyone to hold a stereotype of her as "churchy" (290); yet she says that she has not "seen God since those early days when I left Missouri" (289). Gloria left home for Syracuse, New York, after receiving a college scholarship; she was on the verge of a promising new life, but somehow that life evaded her. She let "the years slip by, like folk do" (289). Gloria's is certainly a story of "origins and consequences." She says, "I ached for the backroads of my hometown in Missouri" (303) where her parents waited in vain for her return; yet she allowed herself to be led into situations that shackled her. Like Judge Soderberg she suffers from ennui; she is a victim of what Sartre calls "bad faith," the tendency to deceive oneself about the dead-end nature of one's present circumstances. She explains, "Sometimes we just walk into something that is not for us at all. We pretend it is. We think we can shrug it off like a coat, but it's not a coat at all, it's more like another skin" (305).

Gloria admits she has found it difficult to develop her own "skin" after growing so accustomed to the love and security of home. Her parents, having grown up in even greater hardship than Gloria's, demonstrated a tenacity that Gloria has lacked. Her mother had kept the exchange slip from her own mother's sale into slavery "to remind her of where she came from"(286), but she eventually sold it to a museum and bought a sewing machine in her effort to prove "a colored woman could get herself a better place in the world" (287). On the afternoon on 7 August, Gloria also seems to realize that "if you start forgetting you're already lost" (299). Intent on traveling "all the way home" from Claire's apartment on her own after the morning meeting of the support group (301), Gloria embarks on a painful two-hour walk, only to take a return cab to Claire, a choice with unforeseen life-changing consequences. The walk is described much like that of the tightrope walker, as Gloria places "one foot in front of the other," attempting to "shuck the loneliness," calling to mind the motive Claire had given for the tightrope walker's own solitary walk: "He was up there out of a sort of loneliness" (112). When Gloria arrives, Claire runs a bath for her, a bath that foreshadows the catharsis both undergo as they connect with a genuineness absent in the morning's meeting. Their joy is dampened somewhat when Solomon arrives home to boast of having sentenced the tightrope walker. As Solomon ignores Gloria, Claire looks down to the floor, "like she could see all the way through to the molten iron, the core of everything" (318). Aside from its 9/11 associations, what Claire "sees" is what Gloria has felt all her life. Like the nameless hero of Ellison's *Invisible Man,* her skin color renders her a nobody. As Solomon absentmindedly unbuttons his shirt to prepare for a shower, Gloria notes, "It was like he was opening a door at his chest and trying to push me out" (317). Yet Claire is able to break through his self-absorption and tell him who Gloria is. He seems genuinely humbled by his mistake and offers her his condolences, saying, "I miss my boy too sometimes" (319). Gloria sees through his persona, noting, "It's hard to be just one person. The key is in the door and it can always be opened" (319). Though Judge Solomon Soderberg remains wrapped up in his own boredom, fear, and helplessness, McCann leaves him on a redemptive note. As Gloria exits she hears Solomon's "bath still running," and the reader can infer that he is crying.

Gloria's decision to return to Claire's apartment leads not only to a rejuvenating lifelong friendship with Claire but, serendipitously, to her discovery of Jazzlyn's orphaned daughters who are being taken away by social workers as she returns to the projects that night. A "deep-down feeling that must've come from long ago" (285) arises in her, and she makes a deliberate choice. Having always avoided Jazzlyn and her family, Gloria approaches the children, Janice and Jazzlyn (later Jaslyn), and when asked if she knows them, she responds, "Yes." "That's what I finally said, as good a lie as any: 'Yes,'" she explains (322), echoing the affirmative conclusion of Molly Bloom's soliloquy in *Ulysses,* "Yes."[40]

Recalling the move to her eleventh-floor apartment in the Bronx, Gloria notes: "Sometimes you've got to go up to a very high floor to see what the past has done to the present" (306). Accordingly, the novel's final chapter, "Roaring Seaward, and I Go," which takes its title from the final line of "Locksley Hall," offers the reader a historical vantage point by jumping ahead more than three decades to October 2006, a nod to an influential and thematically related literary work, Barack Obama's *The Audacity of Hope*, which was published that month. The ascent of Jaslyn, Tillie's granddaughter and Jazzlyn's daughter, from the ashes of three generations of prostitution parallels the breaking down of many social barriers, a process that gained momentum in the early 1970s and culminated in 2008 with the election of the first African American United States president, an event McCann has referred to as "a moment of enormous metaphorical significance."[41] McCann provides suggestions of this parallel, when Jaslyn, having arrived in New York to visit her "Aunt Claire," as she came to know her, is confronted by some of Claire's blood relatives, in what seems to be a celebration of their forthcoming inheritance, since Claire is dying. Among the guests invited to the house are a number of local realtors. Jaslyn, uninterested in any financial gain, can feel she is not welcome, and she offers a wave that she recalls as being somewhat "Presidential" (336). She has been working with the victims of Hurricanes Rita and Katrina and trying to help them put the remaining fragments of their lives in order. "Weren't you working for the Democrats or something?" an arrogant young male relative of Claire's asks as the others giggle (336). McCann's description conjures president-elect Obama facing the cynics: "They are facing her, all of them, watching, as if she has, at last, made it to the stage" (336).

While McCann's novel hints at the tragic parallels between 1974 and the aftermath of 9/11—the Vietnam War and the wars in Iraq and Afghanistan, diminished trust in Presidents Richard Nixon (who resigned the day after Petit's walk) and George W. Bush, questions of faith and values during both eras—this final chapter is a tribute to all the boundaries that have tumbled because of the Corrigans of the world, the selfless optimists. Early in the novel Ciaran Corrigan captures the nature of his brother's character: "He consoled himself with the fact that, in the real world, when he looked closely into the darkness he might find the presence of a light, damaged and bruised, but a little light all the same. . . . Out of that came some sort of triumph that went beyond theological proof, a cause for optimism against all the evidence" (20).

Jaslyn, like McCann, finds this "presence of light" in the now-famous photograph of the airplane hovering above the tightrope walker between the towers, which she keeps framed in her suitcase when she travels, moved by the fact that this act of beauty occurred on the day of her mother's death. She knows that in this moment, at least, "the plane passes, the tightrope walker gets to the other end of the wire. Things don't fall apart" (325) She wonders "what sort of ontological glue" holds the walker that high in the air (325). Her thoughts echo Claire's question to Gloria a few pages earlier, as the couple drives towards the Bronx: "All these people. Did you ever wonder what keeps us going?" (320) McCann's novel, like the photograph, reticently provides an answer: in spite of the world's destructiveness, the creative force, the need for beauty, is ultimately indomitable. Jaslyn considers the "enduring moment" captured in the photograph: "man alone against scale, still capable of myth in the face of all other evidence."(325–26).

When Paul Auster observed Philippe Petit, he "sensed intuitively that his motives were not those of other men. . . . he wanted, simply, to do what he was capable of doing."[42] The same can be said of Corrigan and Jaslyn, as well as of Pino, the Italian Jaslyn meets in the airport, whose status as a member of Doctors without Borders, conveys McCann's delight with the increasingly international character of the world. McCann has referred to Corrigan as "the original 'international bastard.' He is comfortable everywhere. He doesn't gaze home. His home is in others. He can return there anytime he wants. Corrigan is the man of elsewhere."[43] In 2008 McCann provided an essay, "An Imagined Elsewhere," for Matteo Pericoli's *World Unfurled,* a ten-foot foldout replica of Pericoli's mural that spans nearly four hundred feet along the walls of John F. Kennedy Airport. The mural contains 415 buildings from seventy countries lined up as if on one stretch of landscape. McCann remarks regarding Pericoli's drawing, "There is surely an understated political intent in play: the buildings are placed beside each other almost as if they could—and should—learn from each other." He continues, "This ability to cross through periods of time, and to create a believable international landscape, and then to invite us to inhabit it—and maybe even reinhabit it—is something not many artists, let alone politicians, have ever contemplated."[44] It is within this transgenerational, transnational landscape that McCann, international mongrel of letters, works—most evidently in this novel that is as much about New York City in 1974 as it is about any imagined elsewhere.

In the final pages of the novel, Jaslyn recalls the drive she took to visit the projects where she was born. Stalled in traffic she observes a modern centaur—apparently half-man, half-machine—rising from the sunroof of a limousine, eventually straddling the roof, and conjuring the image of a radical street preacher. He is pointing to a coyote wandering amid the traffic, heading for the city (346). The image hearkens back to McCann's first novel, *Songdogs,* which has at its symbolic center the Navajo myth that coyotes, songdogs, were the progenitors of creation, singing the universe into existence. The authorities in

*Let the Great World Spin* shoot the coyote, an act that symbolizes modern man's tendency to kill his most life-affirming instincts.

This scene is followed, however, by Jaslyn's stepping off a metaphorical "ledge" (348) to lie down with Claire, an unimaginable scenario decades earlier. Though Claire's response is ambiguous, she seems to recognize her visitor, since she moves her fingers "up and down as if playing a piano" (348), an image that perhaps recalls lost son, Joshua, a pianist. Jaslyn recognizes beauty and a sense of immortality in human connectedness: "We stumble on," she thinks, "bring a little noise into the silence, find in others the ongoing of ourselves. It is almost enough" (349). She imagines biting into an apricot, the ineffable sensation of participating in beauty, of breaking through "the skin of it" to reach the core, "the sweetness" (349). She finds a privileged peace in the silence: "The world spins. We stumble on." Like the walker she finds satisfaction in beauty, regardless of, perhaps because of, its transience: "It is enough."

In a 25 September 2001 article in the *Irish Times* titled "Are All the Bad Planes Gone, Dad?"—a reference to a question McCann's four-year-old daughter asked him the night after the 11 September attacks—McCann writes that on that day New York City became "a commonwealth of despair" where a "chilling connective tissue" pervaded everything. He writes, "This is an American story. An Afghani story. An Irish story. An Australian story. . . . If there is any triumph to come from this it will be that the grief-stricken will all be acknowledged and that race, color, and creed will all be irrelevant." McCann expresses pride in the fact that "the borders of consciousness have been noticeably dissolved, that a collective anguish has not been limited by any hint of nationality."[45] It is these "borders of consciousness" that McCann aims to dissolve in his fiction so that the souls of all his exiled characters, and readers, can take a step toward the place they can earnestly call "home." In *Let the Great World Spin,* Ciaran Corrigan pays more than one million dollars to repurchase the childhood home he sold years earlier, learning, quite literally, the moral of Mary Lavin's *The Second-Best Children in the World*—McCann's childhood favorite: the value of one's home increases dearly the further and longer one travels away from it.

# Notes

## Chapter 1. Understanding Colum McCann

1. "Take Five with Colum McCann," Philadelphia Free Library Blog, 12 March 2007. Online at http://libwww.library.phila.gov/blog/index.cfm?srch=3&postid=417 (accessed 3 March 2010).

2. Mary Lavin, *The Second-Best Children in the World* (Boston: Houghton Mifflin, 1972), 36.

3. "The Power of Story," *Irish Echo*, 24 January 2007, 29.

4. Anna Metcalfe, "Small Talk: Colum McCann," *Financial Times*, 29 August 2009. Online at http://www.ft.com/cms/s/2/7ea126ca-9362–11de-b146–00144feabdc0.html (accessed 2 March 2010).

5. Unpublished interview with John Cusatis, 12 March 2008.

6. Travis Mahmout, "About Colum McCann." Online at http://www.colummccann.com/about.htm (accessed 3 March 2010).

7. Ibid.

8. Unpublished interview with Cusatis, 12 March 2008.

9. Dan Cryer, "The Burning Season," *Long Island Newsday*, 19 November 1995, 32.

10. Ibid.

11. Joseph Lennon, "Colum McCann," in *Dictionary of Literary Biography 267: Twenty-First-Century British and Irish Novelists*, ed. Michael R. Molino (Detroit: Bruccoli Clark Layman / Gale, 2003), 184.

12. Unpublished interview with Cusatis, 12 March 2008.

13. Dermot Bolger, *The Vintage Book of Contemporary Irish Fiction* (New York: Vintage, 1994), xxvii.

14. McCann chronicled his journey in "Ten Days to Killarney," *Irish Times* (Dublin), 14 July 1994, 13.

15. Unpublished interview with Cusatis, 12 March 2008.

16. Joyce Carol Oates, "An Endangered Species," *New York Review of Books,* 29 June 2000. Online at http://www.nybooks.com/articles/37 (accessed 3 March 2010).

17. McCourt, "Amazon Exclusive: Frank McCourt on *Let the Great World Spin.*" Online at http://www.amazon.com/Let-Great-World-Spin-Novel/dp/1400063736/ref=amb_link_84507931_4?pf_rd_m=ATVPDKIKX0DER&pf_rd_s=center-2&pf_rd_r=0S3SH2WM6WT3HMDYYT3G&pf_rd_t=101&pf_rd_p=479351351&pf_rd_i=390919011 (accessed 10 March 2010).

18. Motoko Rich, "J. J. Abrams Wants to 'Let the Great World Spin,'' *New York Times,* 11 December 2009. Online at http://artsbeat.blogs.nytimes.com/2009/12/11/jj-abrams-wants-to-let-the-great-world-spin/?scp=1&sq=%22J.%20J.%20Abrams%20Wants%20to%20'Let%20the%20Great%20World%20Spin'%22&st=cse (accessed 3 March 2010).

19. Basu, "Walking a Tightrope," 29 January 2010.

20. Luke Clancy, "Writer and Wanderer," *Irish Times,* 21 June 1994, 9.

21. Carolyn T. Hughes, "The Adventurist," *Poets & Writers* 35 (January–February 2007): 54.

22. Thomas E. Macklin, "Universal Truths," *World of Hibernia* 6 (Summer 2000): 156.

23. McCann, "An Imagined Elsewhere: The City of Cities," in *World Unfurled,* by Matteo Pericoli (San Francisco: Chronicle Books, 2008).

24. McCann, "Ben Kiely: Let Us Hear Him," in *The Collected Stories of Benedict Kiely* (London: Methuen, 2001), ix.

25. Joseph Lennon, "An Interview with Fiction Writer Colum McCann," *Poets & Writers* (online only), 14 March 2003. Online at http://www.pw.org/content/interview_fiction_writer_colum_mccann (accessed 2 March 2010).

26. Mahmout, "About Colum McCann."

27. Unpublished interview with Cusatis, 27 December 2007.

28. Peter McDermott, "The Wanderer," *Irish Echo Online,* 7 February 2007. Online at http://www.irishecho.com/search/searchstory.cfm?id=18291&issueid=509 (accessed 2 March 2010).

29. Ibid.

30. Unpublished interview with Cusatis, 29 April 2008.

31. McCann, "Tresses," in *The Hennessy Book of Irish Fiction,* ed. Ciaran Carty and Dermot Bolger (Dublin: New Island Books, 1995), 60–69.

32. "Take Five with Colum McCann," 12 March 2008.

33. Ben Forkner, "The Irish Short Story (1980–2000): Ireland Anthologized," *Etudes Anglaises* 54, no. 2 (2001):151–66.

34. Robert Birnbaum, "Birnbaum v. Colum McCann," *Morning News,* 3 May 2007. Online at http://www.themorningnews.org/archives/birnbaum_v/colum_mccann.php (accessed 4 March 2010); also online at http://www.colummccann.com/interviews.htm (accessed 18 May 2010).

35. Unpublished interview with Cusatis, 27 December 2007.

36. Ibid.

37. Katie Bolick, "Some Strange Vessel," *Atlantic Online,* 16 July 1998. Online at http://www.theatlantic.com/unbound/factfict/ff9807.htm (accessed 2 March 2010).

38. Unpublished interview with students at the School of the Arts, Charleston, S.C., 29 August 2008.

39. Lennon, "The First Man to Whistle," forthcoming in *This Side of Brightness: Essays on the Fiction of Colum McCann,* ed. Susan Cahill and Eóin Flannery (Bern: Peter Lang, 2011).

40. Dave Weich, "There Goes Colum McCann," 3 January 2007. Online at http://www.powells.com/authors/mccann.html (accessed 4 March 2010); also online at http://www.colummccann.com/interviews.htm (accessed 18 May 2010).

41. McCann, "Conversation with Aleksander (Sasha) Hemon." Online at http://www.colummccann.com/interviews/hemon.htm (accessed 4 March 2010).

42. McCann, "Ben Kiely: Let Us Hear Him," ix.

43. Ibid, xii.

44. Unpublished interview with Cusatis, 29 April 2008.

45. Ibid.

46. Eamonn Wall, "Winds Blowing from a Million Directions: Colum McCann's *Songdogs*," in *New Perspectives on the Irish Diaspora*, ed. Charles Fanning (Carbondale: Southern Illinois University Press, 2000), 282.

47. Ibid.

48. Ibid.

49. Ibid.

50. Robert Birnbaum, "Colum Interviewed by Robert Birnbaum," 2003. Online at http://www.colummccann.com/interviews/birnbaum.htm (accessed 4 March 2010).

51. Unpublished interview with Cusatis, 27 December 2007.

52. Unpublished interview with Cusatis, 17 June 2008.

53. Ibid.

54. "*Everything in This Country Must* Interview." Online at http://www.colummccann.com/interviews/everything.htm (accessed 4 March 2010).

55. Birnbaum, "Colum Interviewed by Robert Birnbaum," 2003. Dostoyevsky's discussion of consciousness as an illness occurs at the outset of *Notes from the Underground.*

56. Michael Hayes, "*Zoli* Interview." Online at http://www.colummccann.com/interviews/hayes.htm (accessed 4 March 2010).

57. Farah Miller, "A Conversation with Colum McCann," on the Web site of *O: The Oprah Magazine,* July 2009. Online at http://www.oprah.com/omagazine/Colum-McCann-Interview-About-Let-the-Great-World-Spin/2 (accessed 2 March 2010).

58. Metcalfe, "Small Talk," 29 August 2009.

59. McCann, "Identity–Being Irish," *Irish Times,* 21 October 2000, 62.

60. Dermot Bolger, *Ireland in Exile: Irish Writers Abroad* (Dublin: New Island, 1993), 9.

61. "*Everything in This Country Must* Interview."

62. McDermott, "The Wanderer," 7 February 2007.

Chapter 2. *Fishing the Sloe-Black River*

1. Carol Illig Lake, "Between Myth and History: Irish Author Fishes a Fascinating River of Despair," *Austin American-Statesman,* 10 November 1996, E6.

2. Christopher Tilghman, review of *Fishing the Sloe-Black River, Los Angeles Times,* 13 April 1997, 6.

3. In the first American edition, the original British publication date was erroneously printed as 1993, an error which has been perpetuated in bibliographies and other references regarding McCann's work.

4. Nick Hornby, "Short and Sweet," *Sunday Times* (London), 25 July 1993, 12.

5. James Saynor, "Books: (Short Stories): Squelching," *Observer* (London), 1 August 1993, 53.

6. Matt Holland, "All the Words in the World," *Times* (London), 26 August 1993, 34.

7. Philip MacCann, "Dangerous Places and Lunatic Times," *Guardian* (London), 17 May 1994, 10.

8. Christina Konig, "Celtic Tales of Our Day," *Times* (London), 23 May 1994, 31.

9. Victoria White and Mary Morrissy, "The Ills of Ireland Home and Away," *Irish Times,* 28 May 1994, 8.

10. Robert Taylor, "McCann Excels at Depicting Irish," *Boston Globe,* 4 December 1996, F4.

11. Review of *Fishing the Sloe-Black River, Publishers Weekly,* 23 September 1996, 55.

12. David W. Madden, "Lives on the Fringe: Irish Writer Tells Tales of Odd Heroes," *San Francisco Chronicle,* 2 December 1996, E3.

13. Ambrose Clancy, "Pieces of an Irish Past," *Washington Post,* 15 December 1996, X6.

14. Tilghman, review of *Fishing the Sloe-Black River,* 6.
15. Unpublished interview with Cusatis, 17 October 2008.
16. Unpublished interview with Cusatis, 10 January 2008.
17. McCann, *Fishing the Sloe-Black River: Stories* (New York: Metropolitan Books, 1996), 1. Further references to this book are noted parenthetically in the text.
18. McCann, "About Men, About Women," 25.
19. Ibid.
20. Ibid.
21. *The Penguin Book of Irish Fiction,* ed. Colm Tóibín (New York: Viking, 1999), xxiii.
22. Philip Larkin, *Collected Poems* (New York: Farrar, Straus & Giroux, 2003), 129.
23. Patrick Kavanagh, *Selected Poems* (New York: Penguin, 1996), 84.
24. William Butler Yeats, *Reveries over Childhood and Youth* (New York: Macmillan, 1916), 131.
25. Bolger, *Ireland in Exile,* 9.
26. Eamonn Wall, *From the Sin-é Café to the Black Hills: Notes on the New Irish* (Madison: University of Wisconsin Press, 1999), 6.
27. McCann, "A Conversation with Colum McCann and Frank McCourt," in *Zoli* (New York: Random House, 2007), 342.
28. James Joyce, *A Portrait of the Artist as a Young Man* (New York: Penguin, 2003), 263.
29. McCann's increasing concern for the Irish landscape is conveyed in two essays, "Ten Days to Killarney" (1994) and "Wild Irish Roads" (2007).
30. *Publishers Weekly,* 23 September 1996, 55.
31. *The Penguin Book of Irish Fiction,* ed. Tóibín, xxi.
32. Unpublished interview with Cusatis, 28 December 2007.
33. Bonnie Smothers, "*Fishing the Sloe-Black River,*" *Booklist,* 1 October 1996, 321.
34. White and Morrissy, "The Ills of Ireland Home and Away," 8.
35. Peter Berresford Ellis, *Celtic Myths and Legends* (New York: Carroll & Graf, 2002), 61.

36. Stephen V. Camelio, "An Interview with Colum McCann," *Nua: Studies in Contemporary Irish Writing* 3, no. 1–2 (2002): 94–95.

37. Yeats, *The Collected Poems of W. B. Yeats: Revised Second Edition,* ed. Richard Finneran (New York: Scribner Paperback Poetry, 1996), 131.

38. *The Anchor Book of New Irish Writing,* ed. John Somer and John J. Daly (New York: Anchor, 2000), xv11.

39. Taylor, "McCann Excels at Depicting Irish," F4.

Chapter 3. *Songdogs*

1. Wall, "Winds Blowing from a Million Directions," 281.

2. McCann, *Songdogs: A Novel* (New York: Metropolitan Books, 1995), 72. Further references to this book are noted parenthetically in the text.

3. Mary Morrissy, "The Dogs of Creation," *Irish Times,* 20 June 1995, 12.

4. Tim Adams, "Lives Constructed from Snapshots," *Observer* (London), 9 July 1995, 15.

5. Scott Veale, "Troubled Waters," *New York Times Book Review,* 5 November 1995, 24.

6. Ian Parker, "No Place Like Home," *Independent* (London), 16 July 1995, 37.

7. Robert Cremins, "Parents' Past Is Son's Quest in Irish Novel," *Houston Chronicle,* 4 February 1996, 27.

8. Review of *Songdogs, Publishers Weekly,* 7 August 1995, 441.

9. Veale, "Troubled Waters," 24.

10. Hermione Lee, "Seven Days," *New Yorker,* 6 November 1995, 174–75.

11. Camelio, "An Interview with Colum McCann," 94–95.

12. Lennon, "An Interview with Fiction Writer Colum McCann," 14 March 2003.

13. The vignette that opens *Songdogs* was originally a poem McCann wrote while living in Texas.

14. Lee, "Seven Days," 175.

15. Morrissy, "The Dogs of Creation," 12.

16. *The Penguin Book of Irish Fiction,* ed. Tóibín, xxi.

17. Wall, *New Perspectives,* 285.

18. Ibid.

19. Lee, "Seven Days," 175.

Chapter 4. *This Side of Brightness*

1. Review of *This Side of Brightness, Publishers Weekly,* 5 January 1998, 57.

2. McCann, *This Side of Brightness: A Novel* (New York: Metropolitan Books, 1998), 183. Further references to this book are noted parenthetically in the text.

3. Unpublished interview with Cusatis, 5 June 2009. McCann sets the tunnel explosion in 1916, rather than 1905, aligning it with the Easter Rising, an event that led to the war for Irish independence and the eventual establishment of the Republic of Ireland.

4. "*This Side of Brightness* Interview." Online at http://www.colummccann.com/interviews/brightness.htm (accessed 5 March 2010).

5. Richard Eder, "Extremes: *This Side of Brightness,*" *Los Angeles Times,* 22 March 1998, 2.

6. Bonnie Smothers, review of *This Side of Brightness, Booklist,* 1 March 1998, 1096.

7. Sylvia Brownrigg, "Wednesday's Book: *This Side of Brightness* by Colum McCann," *Independent* (London), 21 January 1998, 4.

8. Gail Caldwell, "The Light in the Darkness: Colum McCann's Sweeping Novel of Men, Work, Danger and the Deep Tunnels of the Heart," *Boston Globe,* 22 March 1998, G1. The comparison with Doctorow is particularly apt. Like McCann, Doctorow views fiction writing as an uncharted journey of discovery and merges historical figures with fictional ones in an effort to challenge the "facts" handed down by historians and journalists. The 1905 East River tunnel explosion figures into Doctorow's 1975 novel, *Ragtime.*

9. David Willis McCullough, "Tunnel Vision," *New York Times Book Review,* 5 April 1998, 8.

10. John Burnside, "A World of Love, Death, Prejudice, and Hard Labour," *Herald* (Glasgow), 12 September 1999.

11. Ambrose Clancy, "Manhattan Transfer," *Washington Post,* 19 April 1998, X10.

12. Camelio, "An Interview with Colum McCann," 94.

13. "*This Side of Brightness* Interview."

14. Ibid. William Styron, a white southerner, had to answer to this question decades after the success of *The Confessions of Nat Turner* (1967), his fictional first-person narrative about the imprisoned African American slave awaiting execution for his role in a massive rebellion.

15. Smothers, review of *This Side of Brightness,* 1096.

16. "*This Side of Brightness* Interview."

17. Ibid.

18. Unpublished interview with Cusatis, 5 June 2009. The troubled subterranean protagonists of *Invisible Man* and *This Side of Brightness* are clearly influenced by Dostoyevsky's narrator in *Notes from the Underground,* a novel to which both Ellison and McCann have frequently alluded.

19. Unpublished interview with students at the School of the Arts, Charleston, S.C., 11 April 2008.

20. Friedrich Nietzsche, *Thus Spoke Zarathustra,* trans. Walter Kaufman (New York: Penguin, 1978), 195.

21. During his American bicycle journey, McCann met on the West Coast a Canadian bicyclist who revealed to him that he was heading to Mexico to commit suicide because he had touched his daughter inappropriately. Months later McCann received a letter from the man saying he had returned home and reconciled with his family. This story was the impetus for Treefrog's action.

22. Henry David Thoreau, *Walden* (New York: Harper & Row, 1965), 67.

23. Alfred, Lord Tennyson, *Selected Poems,* ed. Aiden Day (New York: Penguin, 1991) 213.

24. William Shakespeare, *Hamlet, The Riverside Shakespeare* (Boston: Houghton Mifflin, 1974), 4.4.1172.

25. Ibid., 3.2.1162.
26. Ibid., 2.2.1159.

Chapter 5. *Everything in This Country Must*

1. Tom Deignan, "The CRAIC: Notes from the New Irish," *Irish Voice,* 21 March 2000, 31.
2. Charles Taylor, "Cheerless in Ireland," *New York Times Book Review,* 19 March 2000, 15.
3. Deignan, "The CRAIC," 31.
4. Camelio, "An Interview with Colum McCann," 94.
5. McCann, "Sounds of Silence," *New York Times,* 8 May 2007.
6. Deignan, "The CRAIC," 31.
7. Gail Caldwell, "Balancing Death and Beauty in His Novella and Stories, Colum McCann Echoes the Lyrical Melancholy of the Classic Irish Masters," *Boston Globe,* 12 March 2000, C1.
8. Taylor, "Cheerless in Ireland," 15.
9. Oates, "An Endangered Species," 24 June 2000.
10. John Kenny, "Slim Book, Substantial Issues," *Irish Times,* 29 April 2000, 70
11. Maggie O'Farrell, "No Balaclavas or Colleens," *Independent* (London), 18 June 2000.
12. Michael Pakenham, "Northern Ireland's Agonies Defy Everything Except Art," *Baltimore Sun,* 26 March 2000, G12.
13. Ibid.
14. McCann, *Everything in This Country Must* (New York: Metropolitan, 2000), 3. Further references to this book are noted parenthetically in the text.
15. Mackin, "Universal Truths," Summer 2000.
16. McCann, *Fishing the Sloe-Black River,* 159.
17. Unpublished interview with Cusatis, 5 June 2009.
18. "*Everything in This Country Must* Interview."
19. Ibid.
20. Ibid.
21. Ibid.

22. McCann, "Wood," *New Yorker,* 29 November 1999, 112.

23. "*Everything in This Country Must* Interview."

24. Declin Meade, "Colum McCann," 2001. Online at http://www.stingingfly.org/issue9/mccann.html (accessed 2 March 2010).

25. Unpublished interview with Cusatis, 5 June 2009.

26. Ibid.

27. "*Everything in This Country Must* Interview."

28. Susan Salter Reynolds, review of *Everything in this Country Must, Los Angeles Times Book Review,* 5 March 2000, 11.

29. J. D. Salinger, *The Catcher in the Rye* (New York: Little, Brown, 1951), 244.

Chapter 6. *Dancer*

1. Bolick, "Some Strange Vessel," 16 August 1998.

2. Unpublished interview with Cusatis, 6 July 2009.

3. Bolick, "Some Strange Vessel," 16 August 1998.

4. Laura McCaffrey, "*Zoli* Interview." Online at http://www.colummccann.com/interviews/zoli.htm (accessed 7 March 2010).

5. Nicola McAllister, "A Star Is Born Under a Shower of Knickers and Broken Glass," *Sunday Independent* (London), 12 January 2003, 15.

6. Lennon, "An Interview with Fiction Writer Colum McCann," 14 March 2003.

7. Unpublished interview with Cusatis, 6 July 2009.

8. Hubert Saal, "Nureyev: Tartar of the Dance," *Newsweek,* 19 April 1965, 91.

9. Unpublished interview with Cusatis, 6 July 2009.

10. Ibid.

11. Ibid.

12. Ibid.

13. Ibid.

14. Rudolf Nureyev Foundation official Web site. Online at http://www.nureyev.org/rudolf-nureyev-news-informations/dancer-colum-mc-cann-book-nureyev (accessed 7 March 2010).

15. Meade, "Colum McCann," 2003. Online at http://www.stingingfly.org/issue9/mccann.html (accessed 7 March 2010).

16. Unpublished interview with Cusatis, 6 July 2009.

17. Ibid.

18. Ibid.

19. Adam Dunn, "Dancer from the Dance," *Publishers Weekly,* 13 January 2003, 36.

20. Eve Patten, "Dancing in the Dark," *Irish Times,* 1 January 2003. Online at http://www.irishtimes.com/newspaper/weekend/2003/0104/1040226952313.html (accessed 7 March 2010).

21. Peter Kurth, "A Story with Legs," *New York Times Book Review,* 19 January 2003, 14.

22. Dan Cryer, "A Fascinating Novel on the Life of Rudolf Nureyev," *Chicago Tribune,* 12 January 2003.

23. Sarah Coleman, "A Brilliant Leap of Imagination," *San Francisco Chronicle Book Reviews,* 12 January 2003, 2.

24. Laura Miller, "Dancer from the Dance," *New Yorker,* 20 January 2003. Online at http://www.newyorker.com/archive/2003/01/20/030120crbo_books?currentPage=all (accessed 7 March 2010).

25. Patten, "Dancing in the Dark."

26. Unpublished interview with Cusatis, 24 March 2009.

27. McCann, *Dancer* (New York: Metropolitan, 2003) 2. Further references to this book are noted parenthetically in the text.

28. Nietzsche, *Thus Spoke Zarathustra,* 41.

29. Ibid., 26–27.

30. Birnbaum, "Colum Interviewed by Robert Birnbaum," 2003.

31. Ibid.

32. Joyce, *A Portrait of the Artist as a Young Man,* 276.

33. Philip Marchand, "Writers without Borders," *Toronto Star,* 5 October 2000, D1.

## Chapter 7. *Zoli*

1. Gail Caldwell, "Gypsy Serenade," *Boston Globe,* 14 January 2007. Online at http://www.boston.com/ae/books/articles/2007/01/14/gypsy_serenade/ (accessed 8 March 2010).

2. Richard Eyre, "Romany Roads," *Guardian* (London), 30 September 2006, 16.

3. Michael Hayes, "*Zoli* Interview."

4. Hughes, "The Adventurist," January–February 2007.

5. John Leonard, "New Books," *Harpers,* January 2007, 81.

6. Unpublished interview with Cusatis, 13 June 2009. McCann and Spinelli shared the stage at Festivaletteratura in Mantua, Italy, on 6 September 2007.

7. June Sawyers, "In a Gypsy Poet's Life, Borders Are Painful," *San Francisco Chronicle,* 7 January 2007, M2.

8. Frances Itani, "A Gypsy Melody," *Washington Post Book World,* 28 January 2007, 6.

9. Eyre, "Romany Roads," 16.

10. Richard Eder, "Ultimate Exile: A Gypsy Poet Expelled by Her People," *New York Times,* 8 January 2007. Online at http://www.nytimes.com/2007/01/08/books/08eder.html (accessed 8 March 2010).

11. Eyre, "Romany Roads," 16.

12. Tom Deignan, "Gypsy Poet, Exiled," *America,* 2 July 2007. Online at http://www.americamagazine.org/content/article.cfm?article_id=10037 (accessed 8 March 2010).

13. Kai Maristed, "Inspired by Actual Events," *Los Angeles Times Book Review,* 4 February 2007, 10.

14. Hayes, "*Zoli* Interview."

15. Isabel Fonseca, *Bury Me Standing* (New York: Vintage, 1995), 5.

16. Ibid.

17. Ibid., 7.

18. Ibid., 8.

19. Ibid., 9.

20. Unpublished interview with Cusatis, 27 December 2009.

21. McCann, "The Artists of the Future," unpublished commencement address, North Charleston Performing Arts Center, North Charleston, S.C., 6 June 2009.

22. Weich, "There Goes Colum McCann," 3 January 2007.

23. Ibid.

24. Ibid. *Zoli* follows in the tradition of Willa Cather's *Death Comes fro the Archbishop*. Both Cather and McCann "leap" boundaries of gender, time, and culture in their respective works, while reimagining history.

25. Sawyers, "In a Gypsy Poet's Life," M2.

26. Mark Anthony Jarman, "On the Romany Road," *Globe and Mail* (Canada), 24 March 2007, D14.

27. Leonard, "New Books," 81.

28. Weich, "There Goes Colum McCann," 3 January 2007. The Roma continue to be the victims of horrific hate crimes in Eastern Europe. On 27 August 2009 a crowd of sixty thousand jeered pop singer Madonna, accompanied onstage by Romani performers, when she criticized the prejudice directed toward the Roma.

29. McCann, *Zoli* (New York: Random House, 2007), 8. Further references to this book are noted parenthetically in the text.

30. Unpublished interview with Cusatis, 1 July 2009.

31. Fonseca, *Bury Me Standing,* 9.

32. Jack London, *The Call of the Wild and Selected Stories* (New York: Signet, 1960), 168.

33. In his 3 May 2007 interview with Robert Birnbaum, McCann quotes the writer John Berger: "If I'd known as a child what the life of an adult would have been, I would never have believed it. I never could have believed it would be so unfinished."

34. McCann, "The Artists of the Future," 6 June 2009.

### Chapter 8. *Let the Great World Spin*

1. McCann, "Things Come Together," *PEN America* no. 9 (2008): 39. An audio recording of McCann's speech can be heard at the Web site of the Pen American Center. Online at http://www.pen.org/viewmedia.php/prmMID/2594/prmID/1064 (accessed 9 March 2010).

2. Mark Anthony Jarman, "Country on a Wire," *Globe and Mail* (Canada), 10 July 2009. Online at http://www.theglobeandmail.com/

books/let-the-great-world-spin-by-colum-mccann/article1213903/ (accessed 9 March 2010).

3. Bob Minzesheimer, "'The Great World' Walks a Tightrope: Setting, History and Characters in Fine Balance," *USA Today,* 2 July 2009, D5.

4. Tim Adams, "*Let the Great World Spin* by Colum McCann," *Observer* (London), 30 August 2009, 19.

5. McCann, "Things Come Together," 40.

6. Kevin Rabalais, "A Moment of Grace," *Australian,* 31 July 2009. Online at http://www.theaustralian.news.com.au/story/0,25197,25848049–5001986,00.html (accessed 31 July 2009).

7. McCann, "Things Come Together," 40.

8. John McGahern, "Readings & Conversations: John McGahern with Hermione Lee," 7 April 2004. Lannan Foundation Web site. Online at http://www.lannan.org/docs/john-mcgahern-040407–trans-read.pdf (accessed 12 May 2010 ).

9. McCann, *Zoli,* 328.

10. McCann, *Let the Great World Spin* (New York: Random House, 2009), 349. Further references to this book are noted parenthetically in the text.

11. McCann, "Things Come Together," 39.

12. Walt Whitman, *The Complete Poems,* ed. Francis Murphy (New York: Penguin, 1996), 463.

13. Robert Frost, "The Figure a Poem Makes," *Collected Poems, Prose & Plays* (New York: Library of America, 1995), 776.

14. Rabalais, "A Moment of Grace," 31 July 2009.

15. Lennon, "The First Man to Whistle," forthcoming in *This Side of Brightness,* ed. Susan Cahill and Eóin Flannery.

16. Camus, preface to *The Myth of Sisyphus and Other Essays,* trans. Justin O'Brien (New York: Vintage, 1955).

17. Coleridge, *Biographia Literaria,* ed. John Shawcross (London: Oxford, 1907), 238.

18. Alfred, Lord Tennyson, *Selected Poems,* 104.

19. McCann, e-mail to John Cusatis, 8 January 2002.

20. Moira Macdonald, "*Let the Great World Spin:* Mesmerized by a Man on a Tightrope," *Seattle Times,* 12 July 2009. Online at http://seattletimes.nwsource.com/html/books/2009449094_br12mccann.html (accessed 9 March 2010).

21. Tom Junod, "*Let the Great World Spin:* The First Great 9/11 Novel," *Esquire,* August 2009, 27. Other prominent novels inspired by the tragedy include *Extremely Loud and Incredibly Close* (2005) by Jonathan Safran Foer; *The Good Life* (2006) by Jay McInerney; *The Emperor's Children* (2006) by Claire Messud; *Terrorist* (2006) by John Updike; *Falling Man* (2007) by Don DeLillo; and *Netherland* (2008) by Joseph O'Neill.

22. Mike Peed, "Walking the Tightrope of Big City Life," *Washington Post,* 15 July 2009, C4.

23. Jonathan Mahler, "The Soul of the City," *New York Times,* 2 August 2009, 9.

24. Adams, "*Let the Great World Spin* by Colum McCann," 19.

25. Hemon's original quotation reads: "All the lives I could live, all the people I will never know, never will be, they are everywhere. That is all that the world is."

26. Adam Dunn, "Interview with Colum McCann," *San Francisco Chronicle,* 3 July 2009, F7.

27. McCann, "Conversation with Aleksander (Sasha) Hemon."

28. Paul Auster, *Collected Prose* (New York: Picador, 2005), 437–38.

29. Ibid., 438.

30. Nietzsche, *Thus Spoke Zarathustra,* 14.

31. Ibid., 27.

32. Lennon, "An Interview with Fiction Writer Colum McCann," 14 March 2003.

33. Donna Seaman, review of *Let the Great World Spin, Booklist,* 1 May 2009, 61.

34. Lennon, "An Interview with Fiction Writer Colum McCann," 14 March 2003. On a similar note, McCann certainly intends for

John Corrigan—and the tightrope walker—to call to mind John 1:14, "And the Word was made flesh, and dwelt among us."

35. "*Let the Great World Spin* Q&A." Online at http://www.colummccann.com/interviews/LTGWSinterview.htm (accessed 9 March 2010).

36. Thoreau, *Walden,* 205.

37. Ibid., 67.

38. Ralph Waldo Emerson, "The Rhodora," in *Selected Writings of Ralph Waldo Emerson,* ed. William H. Gilman (New York: Signet, 1965), 489.

39. John Keats, *The Complete Poems,* ed. John Barnard (New York: Penguin, 1988), 345.

40. Joyce, *Ulysses* (New York: Vintage International, 1990), 783.

41. McCann, "Thank You, Obama. At Last I'm Proud to Be an American," *Daily Mail* (London), 7 November 2008, 12.

42. Auster, *Collected Prose,* 439.

43. Lennon, "An Interview with Fiction Writer Colum McCann," 14 March 2003.

44. McCann, "An Imagined Elsewhere: The City of Cities."

45. McCann, "Are All the Bad Planes Gone, Dad?" *Irish Voice,* 25 September 2001, 29–30.

# Bibliography

Works by Colum McCann

*Books*

*Fishing the Sloe-Black River: Stories.* London: Phoenix House, 1994; New York: Metropolitan Books, 1996.

*Songdogs: A Novel.* London: Phoenix House, 1995; New York: Metropolitan Books, 1995.

*This Side of Brightness: A Novel.* London: Phoenix House, 1998; New York: Metropolitan Books, 1998.

*Everything in This Country Must: A Novella and Two Stories.* New York: Metropolitan Books, 2000; London: Phoenix House, 2000.

*Dancer.* New York: Metropolitan Books, 2003; London: Weidenfeld & Nicolson, 2003.

*Zoli.* London: Weidenfeld & Nicolson, 2006; New York: Random House, 2007.

*Let the Great World Spin.* New York: Random House, 2009; London: Bloomsbury, 2009.

*Uncollected Short Stories*

"Tresses." In *The Hennessy Book of Irish Fiction,* edited by Ciaran Carty and Dermot Bolger. Dublin: New Island Books, 1995, 60–69.

"As Kingfishers Catch Fire." *Story* 45 (Spring 1997): 30–37. Republished in *The Pushcart Book of Short Stories: The Best Short Stories from a Quarter-Century of the Pushcart Prize,* edited by Bill Henderson. Wainscott, N.Y.: Pushcart Press, 2002.

"Sumac." *Story* 47 (Spring 1999): 104–6.

"As If There Were Trees." *Story* 47 (Autumn 1999): 125–28. Republished in *New Dubliners,* edited by Oona Frawley. Dublin: New Island Books, 2005.

"Whirligig." *Portal,* 3 August 2000, 3–5, 14.

"All That Rises, All That Falls." *Esquire,* December 2003, 174–75.

"What Is It Called, Your Country behind the Mountain?" In *The Best New Irish Short Stories of 2005,* edited by David Marcus. New York: Carroll & Graf, 2005, 257–58.

*Selected Nonfiction*

"Ten Days to Killarney." *Irish Times* (Dublin), 14 July 1994, 13.

"About Men, About Women." *Observer* (London), 30 October 1994, 25.

"Feeling Like the First Man to Whistle." *Irish Times* (Dublin), 25 August 1997, 9.

"The Mole People." *Irish Times* (Dublin), 27 September 1997, 60.

"Through the Grey Diamonds." In *Playing the Field: Irish Writers on Sport,* edited by George O'Brien. Dublin: New Island Books, 2000, 62–73.

"Identity—Being Irish." *Irish Times* (Dublin), 21 October 2000, city edition, weekend, 22.

"Ben Kiely: Let Us Hear Him." In *The Collected Stories of Benedict Kiely.* London: Methuen, 2001, i–xvii.

"Are All the Bad Planes Gone, Dad?" *Irish Voice,* 25 September 2001, 29–30.

"The Real Life of Anna V." *New York Times,* 24 February 2002, 70.

Foreword to *My Discovery of America,* by Vladimir Mayakovsky, translated by Neil Cornwell. London: Modern Voices, 2005, vii–x.

"Tragic Tales and Sounds of Silence: What I Love about New York." *Financial Times* (London), 25 November 2006, 17.

"No Place Like Home." *New York Times,* 31 December 2006, sec. 14, 9.

"Wild Irish Roads." *Los Angeles Times,* 17 March 2007, A23.

"Sounds of Silence." *New York Times,* 8 May 2007.

"An Imagined Elsewhere: The City of Cities." In *World Unfurled,* by Matteo Pericoli. San Francisco: Chronicle Books, 2008.

"Things Come Together." *PEN America* no. 9 (2008): 39–40.

"Thank You, Obama. At Last I'm Proud to Be an American." *Daily Mail* (London), 7 November 2008, 12.

"But Always Meeting Ourselves." *New York Times,* 16 June 2009, A21.

Introduction to *Norman Mailer, Moonfire: The Epic Journey of Apollo 11,* by Norman Mailer. Cologne: Taschen, 2009, 12–19.

"Looking for the Rozziner." *Granta 109: Work* (Winter 2010): 81.

Works about Colum McCann

*Web Site*

McCann's official website. Online at http://www.colummccann.com (accessed 2 March 2010). An essential resource, including biography; transcripts of interviews with Robert Birnbaum (2003, 2007) and others, and conversations with Aleksander Hemon (2003) and Michael Ondaatje (2008); audio interviews; tour dates; and links to articles by McCann.

*Selected Interviews and Profiles*

Bantick, Christopher. "A Voice That Was Other than Irish." *Canberra Times* (Australia), 10 May 1998, A18. McCann discusses *This Side of Brightness,* making his home in New York City, and the future of Irish writing.

Basu, Chitralekha. "Walking a Tightrope." *China Daily,* 29 January 2010. Online at http://www.chinadaily.com.ch/life/2010-01/29/content_9396618.htm (accessed 13 May 2010). McCann discusses *Let the Great World Spin* and having his work translated into Chinese.

Bolick, Katie. "Some Strange Vessel." *Atlantic Online,* 16 July 1998. Online at http://www.theatlantic.com/unbound/factfict/ff9807.htm (accessed 2 March 2010). An important early interview in which McCann elaborates on responses to previous interviewers.

Camelio, Stephen V. "An Interview with Colum McCann." *Nua: Studies in Contemporary Irish Writing* 3, no.1–2 (2002): 89–100.

A thorough interview in which McCann discusses poets, the social novel, and career details.

Clancy, Luke. "Writer and Wanderer." *Irish Times*, 21 June 1994, 9. McCann discusses his writing career, his penchant for travel, and the outdoors.

Cryer, Dan. "The Burning Season." *Long Island Newsday*, 19 November 1995, 32. Contains substantial biographical details as well as discussion of *Songdogs*.

Deignan, Tom. "The CRAIC: Notes from the New Irish." *Irish Voice*, 21 March 2000, 31. McCann and fellow Irish transplant Eamonn Wall talk about modern Ireland and the new Irish writing.

Donnely, Pat. "Empathizing with 'the Other.'" *Gazette* (Montreal), 20 October 2007. Online at http://www.canada.com/montreal gazette/news/books.story.html?id=48e838bee37d-4d98-a756 -7963d1000508d (accessed 13 May 2010). McCann discusses the plight of the Roma and his novel *Zoli*.

Dunn, Adam. "Dancer from the Dance." *Publishers Weekly*, 13 January 2003, 36. McCann discusses *Dancer* and the advantages that fiction has over nonfiction.

———. "Interview with Colum McCann." *San Francisco Chronicle*, 3 July 2009, F7. McCann discusses his attempt in *Let the Great World Spin* to come to terms with the 11 September 2001 terrorist attacks.

Fisher, Mark. "People Who Live Down Below." *Herald* (Glasgow), 29 July 1999. McCann discusses New York's subway dwellers and *This Side of Brightness*.

Hughes, Carolyn T. "The Adventurist." *Poets & Writers* 35 (January–February 2007): 48–54. Thoroughly chronicles McCann's career, devoting most attention to *Zoli*.

Lennon, Joseph. "An Interview with Fiction Writer Colum McCann." *Poets & Writers* (online only), 14 March 2003. Online at http://www.pw.org/content/interview_fiction_writer _colum_mccann (accessed 2 March 2010). McCann discusses writing *Dancer* and reflects briefly on *Songdogs*.

Levasseur, Jennifer, and Kevin Rabalais. "Interview with Colum McCann." *Glimmer Train* 69 (Winter 2009): 56–73. A detailed interview in which McCann discusses researching and writing his fiction.

Mackin, Thomas E. "Universal Truths." *World of Hibernia* 6 (Summer 2000): 156. McCann discusses *Everything in This Country Must* and his identity as an Irish New Yorker.

Marchand, Philip. "Writers Without Borders." *Toronto Star,* 5 October 2000, D1. McCann, Aleksander Hemon, Ha Jin, and Lawrence Norfolk talk about "literary exile."

McDermott, Peter. "The Wanderer." *Irish Echo Online,* 7 February 2007. Online at http://www.irishecho.com/search/searchstory.cfm?id=18291&issueid=509 (accessed 2 March 2010). McCann discusses being a novelist, writing *Zoli,* his Dublin upbringing, and his travels.

Meade, Declin. "Colum McCann." Online at http://www.stingingfly.org/issue9/mccann.html (accessed 2 March 2010). Includes two detailed interviews previously published in the Irish journal *Stinging Fly* in 2001 and 2003. The first focuses primarily on *Everything in This Country Must* and the second on *Dancer.*

Metcalfe, Anna. "Small Talk: Colum McCann." *Financial Times,* 29 August 2009. Online at http://www.ft.com/cms/s/2/7ea126ca-9362–11de-b146–00144feabdc0.html (accessed 2 March 2010). McCann responds to ten questions about his reading, writing, and other personal interests.

Miller, Farah. "A Conversation with Colum McCann." Posted on the Web site of *O: The Oprah Magazine,* July 2009. Online at http://www.oprah.com/omagazine/Colum-McCann-Interview-About-Let-the-Great-World-Spin/2 (accessed 2 March 2010). McCann discusses sources for and characters in his 2009 novel.

"The Power of Story." *Irish Echo,* 24 January 2007, 29. McCann responds to eleven questions regarding his opinions on writers, writing, and Ireland.

Rabalais, Kevin. "A Moment of Grace." *Australian,* 31 July 2009. Online at http://www.theaustralian.com.au/news/a-moment-of

-grace/story-0–1225755958661 (accessed 31 July 2009). McCann discusses *Let the Great World Spin,* and Rabalais provides helpful insights into McCann's work.

Rich, Motoko. "Significant (Little) Moments Pulled from Obscurity." *New York Times,* 27 November 2009, C1. Thorough profile published after McCann won the National Book Award.

"Take Five with Colum McCann." Philadelphia Free Library Blog, 12 March 2007. Online at http://libwww.library.phila.gov/blog/index.cfm?srch=3&postid=417 (accessed 3 March 2010). McCann responds to five questions primarily regarding his reading preferences.

*Selected Criticism*

Brown, James F. "Things Not Meant to Heal: Irish National Allegory in Doyle, McCabe, and McCann." *Nua: Studies in Contemporary Irish Writing* 1, no.1 (1997): 31–51. Treats McCann's *Songdogs,* along with Roddy Doyle's *Paddy Clarke Ha Ha Ha* and Patrick McCabe's *Butcher Boy,* as "national allegory," all three bearing the stamp of Ireland's past and present struggles.

Cahill, Susan. "Corporeal Architecture: Body and City in Colum McCann's *This Side of Brightness.*" *Etudes Irlandaises* 32 (Spring 2007): 43–58. Analyses the symbolic connections between McCann's descriptions of the human body and those of the urban landscape, particularly the subway tunnels.

Flannery, Eóin. "Terrorised Youths: Colum McCann's *Everything in This Country Must* and the Northern Irish Troubles." In *Essays on Modern Irish Literature,* edited by John Strachan and Alison Younger Sunderland, U.K.: University of Sunderland Press, 2007, 169–83. Discusses McCann's use of the short story "to illuminate basic truths" in the context of the Troubles.

Gabinsky, Andrzej. "Challenging History: Past Reconstruction in Colum McCann's *Songdogs.*" *Estudios Irlandeses* no. 2 (2007): 44–56. Discusses McCann's use of photographic images and a nonlinear plotline as a means of reconciling the protagonist, Conor Lyons, with his past.

Healy, John F. "Dancing Cranes and Frozen Birds: The Fleeting Resurrections of Colum McCann." *New Hibernia Review / Iris Eireannach Nua: A Quarterly Record of Irish Studies* 4 (Autumn 2000): 107–18. A helpful analysis of the nature of redemption in McCann's fiction.

Ingersol, Earl G. *Waiting for the End: Gender and Ending in the Contemporary Novel.* Madison, N.J.: Fairleigh Dickinson University Press, 2007, 63–74. Ingersoll discusses *This Side of Brightness* as "a classic example" of what he calls "the masculine narrative paradigm."

Lennon, Joseph. "Colum McCann." In *Dictionary of Literary Biography 267: Twenty-First-Century British and Irish Novelists,* edited by Michael R. Molino. Detroit: Bruccoli Clark Layman / Gale, 2003, 181–91. Provides biographical details and critical insight regarding McCann's first four books.

Mari, Catherine. "Tell-Tale Ellipsis in Colum McCann's *Everything in This Country Must.*" *Journal of the Short Story in English* 40 (Spring 2003): 47–56. Examines the importance of "what's left unsaid" in the three stories included in McCann's fourth book.

Slack, John S. "Telling Shots: Photography in/as/and Literature in Colum McCann's *Songdogs.*" *Nua: Studies in Contemporary Irish Writing* 4, no.1–2 (2003): 77–85. Analyzes McCann's use of photography as means of and metaphor for storytelling in *Songdogs.*

Storey, Michael. *Representing the Troubles in Irish Fiction.* Washington, D.C.: Catholic University Press, 2004, 216–17. Storey briefly analyzes "Everything in This Country Must" as a commentary on the sectarian conflict in Northern Ireland.

Wall, Eamonn. "Winds Blowing from a Million Directions: Colum McCann's *Songdogs.*" *New Perspectives on the Irish Diaspora,* edited by Charles Fanning. Carbondale: Southern Illinois University Press, 2000, 281–88. Views *Songdogs* as giving voice to the Irish diaspora.

# Index